Narrative Psychiatry and Family Collaborations

Narrative Psychiatry and Family Collaborations is about helping families with complex psychiatric problems by seeing and meeting the families and the family members, as the best versions of themselves, before we see and address the diagnoses.

This book draws on ten years of clinical research and contains stories about helping people, who are heavily burdened with psychiatric illnesses, to find ways to live a life as close as possible to their dreams. The chapters are organized according to ideas, values, and techniques. The book describes family-oriented practices, narrative collaborative practices, narrative psychiatric practices, and narrative agency practices. It also talks about wonderfulness interviewing, mattering practices, public note taking on paper charts, therapeutic letter writing, diagnoses as externalized problems, narrative medicine, and family community meetings. Each chapter includes case studies that illustrate the theory, ethics, and practice, told by Nina Jørring in collaboration with the families and colleagues.

The book will be of interest to child and adolescent psychiatrists and all other mental health professionals working with children and families.

Nina Tejs Jørring, MD, founded The Family Therapy unit to combine Narrative Therapy and Child and Adolescent Psychiatry. Her vision is that child and adolescent psychiatry becomes more family-focused offering co-created treatments. When a child suffers from psychiatric problems, the whole family suffers, therefore the family deserves to receive help together.

June Alexander founded The Diary Healer to connect with people who have experienced an eating disorder, trauma or other mental health challenge, to inspire them through the use of the narrative, to live a full and meaningful life. June mentored Nina's writing from the very beginning of the book.

David Epston along with Michael White, are the inventors of Narrative Therapy. David has a long history of teaching all over the world, has published widely, and founded the Journal of Contemporary Narrative Therapy. David has been Nina's mentor for more than two decades.

Narrative Psychiatry and Family Collaborations

Nina Tejs Jørring with
June Alexander and David Epston

LONDON AND NEW YORK

Cover image: © Illustrations by Martin Lasthein

First published 2022
by Routledge
4 Park Square, Milton Park, Abingdon, Oxon OX14 4RN

and by Routledge
605 Third Avenue, New York, NY 10158

Routledge is an imprint of the Taylor & Francis Group, an informa business

© 2022 Nina Tejs Jørring with June Alexander and David Epston

The right of Nina Tejs Jørring with June Alexander and David Epston to be
identified as authors of this work has been asserted in accordance with
sections 77 and 78 of the Copyright, Designs and Patents Act 1988.

All rights reserved. No part of this book may be reprinted or reproduced or
utilized in any form or by any electronic, mechanical, or other means, now
known or hereafter invented, including photocopying and recording, or in
any information storage or retrieval system, without permission in writing
from the publishers.

Trademark notice: Product or corporate names may be trademarks or
registered trademarks, and are used only for identification and explanation
without intent to infringe.

British Library Cataloguing-in-Publication Data
A catalogue record for this book is available from the British Library

Library of Congress Cataloguing-in-Publication Data
A catalogue record has been requested for this book

ISBN: 978-0-367-77486-8 (hbk)
ISBN: 978-0-367-77484-4 (pbk)
ISBN: 978-1-003-17162-1 (ebk)

DOI: 10.4324/9781003171621

Typeset in Bembo
by MPS Limited, Dehradun

Contents

Foreword		vii
Acknowledgements		xvii
	Introduction	1
1	A narrative family psychiatrist	12
2	Collaborative family therapy	25
3	I am not the problem! We are the heroes!	37
4	Mattering is at the heart of the matter	50
5	Not untidy scribbles but a beautiful illustration of my life	62
6	The helping map as a guiding light	77
7	Therapeutic letter writing	90
8	Telling stories that make sense and inspire	103
9	Naming? How might a diagnosis be best for me?	116
10	Me, the medicine, and my diagnosis	128
11	Developing and co-creating shared wisdom	141
12	Empowering the entire family	154

vi *Contents*

13 Family community meetings that matter   166

14 Weaving the collaborative spirit through all our practices   177

15 A continuously curious learning team   189

16 The art of true helping; dare to care   202

    Afterword   214
    Addendum   222
    Index   227

Foreword

David Epston

I have been perplexed and fretting as to how to introduce this book. The options were many. I must have spent a fortnight in a daze before deciding how to proceed. I would tell some exemplary tales that Nina's book has brought to mind. A kind of reminiscence for the future; a genealogy hopefully relevant to what follows; an elderly man telling stories to the next generation.

The philosopher, Thomas Kuhn, in *Structure of Scientific Revolutions* (1967) bequeathed to the English Language the term "paradigm shift". Kuhn convincingly argues that essential to any such paradigm was what he referred to as a "puzzle". By that he meant, "a special category of problems that serve to test the ingenuity or skill in solution" (Kuhn, 1970, p. 35). I have been asking myself if I could articulate what our puzzle was that tested our ingenuity.

I think what troubled us most in the early 1980s was the presumptuous arrogance of professional representations and descriptions of "the others". Those "others" were people who came seeking our service. We knew them well and liked them a lot. To us, they possessed a great deal of rich character rather than being "characterless". We immediately grasped the significance of the anthropologist Garfinkel's term "ritual of degradation" (Garfinkel, 1956) to describe social events such as the psychiatric assessment. I invented the term "regrading" (Epston, 1989, pp. 111–119) to reference our intention to seek counter practices that would restore their honour and dignity and, more specifically, to capture their "moral character". We were aware how undignifying and dishonouring such pathologizing discourses were to those who suffered. Let me put this another way: how do professionals like ourselves come to know those who seek our help and by the same token, how do they come to know us?

Several of the abovementioned tales have haunted me most of my work life. They have been the most friendly and benign of ghosts. I am reminded of the Apache Nick Thompson telling the anthropologist Keith Basson about such stories:

"So, someone stalks you and tells you a story.... It doesn't matter if other people are around- you are going to know he's aiming the story at you. Suddenly it hits you. It's like an arrow they say. It goes in deep and starts working on your mind" (Basso, 1966, p. 35).

viii *Foreword*

These are some of the stories inscribed in my memory. (Three more stories appear in the Afterward.) My hope, dear reader, is that these stories, together with those told by Nina, might do something of the sort for you.

Tale One

I will describe an uncanny incident that happened nine years ago. But the story really begins in August 1984, when Michael White visited me in Auckland. From 1981 onwards, Michael and I had collaborated on an outline of what was to become Narrative Therapy.

Michael agreed to act as guest teacher in a series of classes I was giving to trainees in Psychiatry at the University of Auckland School of Medicine. I suspected that my colleagues and their students would be interested in Michael's evolving practice with those who suffered "psychotic experience" (White, 1995).

As well, I was curious how Michael would be received by Auckland Psychiatry. Although it was only a two-hour lecture, he presented videotapes of his practice with his customary eloquence as well as theorizing it as he went along, similar to what Argyris and Schon (Argyris, 1974) referred to as "theory in practice". The blend of the two strands of his presentation drew considerable interest and Professor Bob Large, in closing the session, praised Michael for his respectfulness.

Afterwards, we walked to catch our homeward bound bus. Michael fell silent on leaving the Medical School as if he were spellbound. Clearly, he was deep in thought. I was wondering why. Was he disappointed with his presentation? Had he felt injured by an innocent remark of a student? Or had something bothered him that I had overlooked?

When Michael did break his silence, I was so aware of that very moment that decades later I can return to the exact physical spot, approximately six paces from the streetlights. He turned to me, pulling himself free of his reverie, and shared his private reflections on the comments about respectfulness. I committed his comments to memory.

"It is not only a matter of us being 'respectful'. It is more a matter of our clients experiencing our respect for them", Michael said.

I cannot recall if we spoke further about this at the time. I think we both fell silent, navigating the rush hour pedestrian traffic. But I have had cause over the years to repeatedly return to and reconsider Michael's statement: how can our clients feel our respect for them?

I believe this is at the heart of many of the practices that distinguish narrative therapy practice.

That night I had an evening meeting with a family and their ten-year-old daughter, Lee-Marie, a follow up to our only other meeting a month before. Michael, given his vast experience with young women and their families who had suffered from anorexia nervosa, willingly agreed to join us when explained that Lee-Marie had gone from our first meeting, after three years of starvation, and immediately re-commenced eating. Her parents had been overjoyed by this dramatic turn of events as her hospitalization had been scheduled for the very next day.

Twenty-nine years later, on April 5, 2013, I am attending an event at Te Noko Kotahitanga "marae" on the grounds of UNITEC Institute of Technology. This translates as "the house of the respectful heart". A marae is a sacred communal meeting place that serves both religious and social purposes in Polynesian societies.

I am invited to participate in an annual ritual in the Undergraduate Bachelor of Social Practice degree programme. Prior to their first field placement, all 100-plus second-year students spend two days and a night on the "marae" ritually preparing themselves individually and collectively for their future. I am invited to do a live interview in a specific format to begin:

> Why are you so proud of the Problem from the Past that you overcame, somehow or other?

My questions will be simultaneously shown on an overhead screen. After the interview, I will explain my practice and answer queries. This is something I look forward to, to demonstrate a "respectful practice" that I hope might live up to Michael's concerns expressed 29 years previously – to have another person experience our respect for them. In this instance, the person will be a classmate of the assembled students. This tradition is well known to the students and a list of candidates has been submitted by colleagues at UNITEC on my arrival.

I have a lot on my mind. This very day is the fifth anniversary of Michael's death in 2008. As I cycle there, I remind myself how Michael affected the people he met. Especially, I remember Michael joining me in 1984 at the final interview with Lee-Marie and her family. Lee-Marie's parents had thought highly of him.

Over lunch before today's interview, a woman approaches, somewhat reticent, and inquires, "Do you live in Balmoral?"

"Yes!" I reply, curiously.

"I met you there 29 years ago when I was 10!" she says.

I stare at her but she, of course, is no longer that ten-year-old girl and is unrecognizable. "What is your name?"

"Lee-Marie".

Before she can continue, I interrupt and propose her surname. She is stunned and we both fall silent momentarily.

Lee-Marie adds, "My parents send their regards to you and want you to know they saved your and Michael's letters".

I am further flummoxed when she says, "It is because of meeting you and Michael that I am here doing this degree!"

With time short and the afternoon "interview" about to begin, I explain the prospect of such an interview and ask, "Are you willing to participate in this interview? Unlike any of your classmates, I was a witness 29 years ago to you overcoming a considerable Problem". Lee-Marie willingly consents.

x *Foreword*

I introduce Lee-Marie to her 100-plus classmates and explain how we met 29 years before and how she had overcome what would have been regarded as an impossible Problem to overcome in a single session. I add, "You are going to find out how that meeting with Lee-Marie also changed the course of my life!"

Here is an edited transcription of my interview with Lee-Marie:

David: Why are you proud of the Problem from the Past that you overcame somehow or other?

L-M: I feel I have a life now. I am proud of that. And I have a family. And I am studying for this degree.

David: Is your presence here a testimony to you as a ten-year-old girl and your mother and father and the family you come from?

L-M: Definitely!

David: If you could acknowledge your ten-year-old self for overcoming a Problem that could have taken your life away from you before you had hardly lived it, what would you acknowledge your ten-year-old self for?

L-M: Just to be thankful to that ten-year-old for overcoming it so that she went on to lead the life I have led so far.

David: Is there anything special that you appreciate her for now that you have 29 years to look back on her life?

L-M: Definitely my children. They are the biggest things. And, of course, meeting my partner.

David: You may not be aware that the Problem you overcame as a ten years old would have been regarded at that time as almost impossible to overcome. What was so remarkable about you, and the family you come from, that you did so in merely 60 minutes?

L-M: I think having strong parents and them not putting me in hospital. Their will to keep me going was a big one and also the help from your therapy. It all happened when we met. It came about from that.

David: Can you trace the "will" you speak of, in relation to your mother and father, to your grandparents in any way?

L-M: I can because it was my grandfather who noticed and pushed it (D: I recalled that he had contacted me and made the appointment for his granddaughter). He kept telling my family that that something wasn't right. He was very strong about not giving up. That was huge! And he phoned you.

David: Do you know any stories from your paternal family that show how they don't give up when the going gets tough?

L-M: There were bad financial times and my family kept on going. Nothing gets them down and they overcome their challenges. They think of other ways. I've seen it. They can be very strong in that way.

Foreword xi

David: What are your recollections, all those 29 years ago, of meeting me in Balmoral?

L-M: I remember your house (smiling). I remember the exercises you gave me. I remember my older brothers moaning about having to come along. Yah, our whole family. I remember it.

David: Do you remember the questions I asked you?

L-M: You asked a lot about my nana (grandmother). My nana was a giver, and she would always give a lot. And we touched on the Problem – Anorexia. Yah, and we externalized it (she Lee-Marie had learned this term in her undergraduate studies). And we touched on how if I managed to eat my lunch or not, I should do certain things.

You gave me exercises. I had to have a plate and if I couldn't eat the food, I had to scrape it in the rubbish bin and pretend that it was Anorexia that was making me do it. And I was beating it. So, it wasn't beating me! (grinning and we both laugh). I just thought (acting as if she is scraping the remains of a dinner into a rubbish bin) that I was dealing with it, "Anorexia, you are not beating me; I am beating you". Otherwise, dad was sitting next to me, forcing me to eat and I was vomiting.

David: Under those circumstances of forced feeding, did you feel that you had failed your family?

L-M: I did. I felt like I let them down and that I couldn't fight it, Anorexia. But this way, with the plate, I could see it. When the Problem now occurred, I knew, "Oh no, here it comes again! (pushing her hands outwards against something invisible) I've got to try and fight it!"

David: You say, "I could now see it". Before that, was the Problem invisible to you?

L-M: I was known as the little girl with Anorexia. So, I was just like that. That was how I lived. Before I saw you, I had Anorexia for three years. Yah! I remember our meeting and we all sat there (indicates with her hands the seating arrangements of her, her parents and two brothers). And Mum mentioned babies and you said that when I was older that Anorexia would forbid me from having children. Then we dug deeper into this likelihood and I think that was a turning point.

David: Really?

L-M: Yes! I loved little kids!

David: When you look into the eyes of your daughters, does that justify the choice you made 29 years ago to take your life back from Anorexia?

L-M: It does! I haven't thought about it so deeply before. When I came into university today, I realized I might not have been alive today and would not have my precious children. It makes it real special that I overcame IT (Anorexia)!

xii *Foreword*

David:	When you started eating after our first meeting, what came next?
L-M:	Hard times! It was very hard but now I had the skills and knowledge. It was a long process. I still have a little bit (of Anorexia) (raising her voice), but I know that it will never get to that stage (referring to when seven years old to ten years old) again. I know how to stop it.
David:	What contribution do you figure your mum and dad made over those hard times?
L-M:	They were always looking out when times were rough. They knew when Anorexia was about and, they comforted me.
David:	How do you see all these things are linked with your decision to do a Social Work degree?
L-M:	Just by me overcoming it – the Anorexia. It made me stronger because I knew I could make a difference in people's lives if I could make such a difference in my own.
David:	You started practicing (social work) on your own life at age….
L-M:	(interrupting and finishing my question) 10!
David:	Say, in several years you attend the graduation ceremony and walk from the stage with your degree, who will you speak to first?
L-M:	Myself (laughing). I'll say to myself, "You've done it!" I'll be happy, doing what I have wanted to do after so many years.
David:	Do you have any questions about our meetings and how this led me to develop anti-anorexia and *Biting the Hand that Starves You: Inspiring Resistance to Anorexia/Bulimia* (Maisel, 2004)?
L-M:	How did your work go?
David:	It went downhill after you. No one else walked out after only one session and freed their lives life in due course of Anorexia.
L-M:	At the time I would eat only a pea but that night after our meeting I went out and ate some chicken. I took that stand. It was amazing!
David:	That meeting led me to embark on 20 years of this work. And it all began in such a modest way. It is wonderful to meet you again on this very day.
L-M:	Same for me. I wanted to see you and thank you.
David:	I wanted to thank you.
L-M:	Yeah, but if you didn't do it, I wouldn't be here (alive) today!
David:	I wouldn't be here either (laughter) even though for me it wasn't a matter of my life or death when we met 29 years ago.

Later, Lee-Marie's parents forwarded the letters that Michael and I had separately written to them 29 years before. The letters had been carefully preserved. Here is a short excerpt from my letter:

> *This, of course, does not mean there may not be an odd hiccup in the future; that is to be expected. But I have supreme confidence in you both to deal with anything*

that comes your way. Your daughter is fortunate to have such wonderful parents and it comes as no surprise to me that she, herself, is aware of this.

I am honoured to have known you and to see your family tackle such a problem that can cost many young women all or part of their lives.

Yours respectfully, David.

This led me to many considerations regarding Michael's conclusion on respectfulness. The sociologist, Richard Sennett writes:

> Respect is an expressive performance. That is, treating others with respect doesn't just happen, even with the best will in the world; to convey respect means finding the words and gestures which make it felt and convincing. These expressive acts, when they occur, reveal something about how character takes form: character as the aspect of self capable of moving others (Sennett, 2003).

Tale Two

On previous flights travelling from Detroit to Boston, time passed quickly. I am used to 12-hour flights from Auckland to Los Angeles and the same duration for my repatriation. This winter's day in 1994 was different. The first sign that all was not well was the continual delaying of the flight and then learning that there was a blizzard along the eastern seaboard of the United States. Boston was at the heart of it. Hours later, we boarded the airplane to be told take-off would be delayed until Boston airport had designated a snow-cleared runway. I found that sitting for hours in an airplane on the ground was different to hours in the air. Some passengers get claustrophobic fears. After an hour or so, the knuckles of the woman seated next to me started turning white from holding her hand rests so tightly. She was also over-breathing. I rushed to her rescue by engaging her in a conversation to distract her and myself to our circumstances. We eventually landed in Boston Airport eight hours later than the scheduled arrival time.

I worried about arriving late as my sponsor was expecting 100-plus attendees at my two-day workshop scheduled to start at 9 am the next day. Arriving at my colleague's home at 10 pm, I felt relieved, presuming that now all would be well. However, almost immediately the "bad" of my flight turned to "worse". My colleague asked me to call Linda, a training group member, who had arranged for a family to join me in a live interview the next day.

"It's a psychiatric emergency!" she warned. Trying to be nice, I inquired about this arrangement about which I knew nothing. My colleague produced a hard copy of an email explicitly requesting she arrange a live interview early on the first day of the workshop. I pleaded that this would be impossible. "I am wreck! A psychiatric emergency! I am not up to it!" She sympathetically suggested I phone Linda promptly.

xiv *Foreword*

Before making the call, I retired to the toilet feeling nauseous and gave myself a moment to consider my predicament. Almost immediately I had a flash of inspiration. I phoned Linda asking her not to tell me about the Problem until she heard my proposal. Why? Because if I heard the Problem, I would have felt the urgent requirement to respond to it the next morning. My proposal was that, given my stressful flight, I considered myself only "50 per cent of a therapist". I requested she submits the following proposal to the family: that since two days are scheduled for the workshop and I am 50 per cent of a therapist, are they willing to attend two days instead of one? That way, by the end of the two days they will have experienced 100 per cent of a therapist. Fortunately, the family appreciated my situation and agreed to my proposal.

My relief was short-lived because now I had to figure out to complete an hour-long interview without knowing the Problem. How could I make this interview highly pertinent to a family experiencing a "psychiatric emergency" as well as 100-plus attendees who were expecting to witness a live interview?

In such circumstances, necessity is the mother of invention! Fortuitously, I awoke the next morning with a resolution to my dilemma. I would get to know the family members "against" the Problem rather than "with" the Problem. Essentially, I chose an inquiry that by implication would ask them what they collectively had to bring to bear to the psychiatric emergency. What histories could be shared that could likely be at odds with the pathologizing histories that would be commonplace in an interview such as this? I formulated my question like this:

"Suzie (aged 13), can I get to know you outside the Problem so we all get to know what you have going for you that you can put against the Problem that is besetting you? And tomorrow we will find out everything there is about the Problem? Today I will ask you about your talents, abilities, your moral character, and generally what people think is wonderful about you".

Attempting to meet the exigencies of the family's situation in the best way, I had no idea how this proposal would turn out. I was upturning or reversing the conventional order of the 200-plus year convention of the assessment interview, which usually has two stages: "What is the Problem?" and "What do we do about it?".

I was asking "What have you got to put against the Problem?" before "What is the Problem?" to follow. I had no idea that this would achieve anything more than surviving the day. However, my personal circumstances had serendipitously forced me to do something new. In retrospect, I think of it as an unforeseen natural experiment. But there was more to come that made this an extremely unusual experiment.

On meeting mother, stepfather, and Suzie, we re-negotiated what must have seemed an unusual arrangement, but the family wholeheartedly consented for me to proceed. I embarked on an hour-long interview, which had been ethically cleared, to reveal what the family had to put against the Problem. Essentially this was to be the family's side of the "match up" with the unknown Problem. That is, the Problem was unknown to me;

the family knew it well. But now they had the right to go first, and the Problem came second. I was determined to lavish every possible means to represent this family as a worthy adversary for the psychiatric emergency they were facing. Due to this strange first meeting, the family was no longer "demoralized" but rather "remoralized" (Frank, 2004).

Might this family see themselves differently through such an interview format? My major concern right then was just getting through this hour-long interview and giving myself another day to recover my wits. To my delight, this meeting turned out entirely different from my forebodings. Serendipitously, I had chanced upon the means I had been seeking to get to know people as "respectworthy" (Hilde Lindeman Nelson in private correspondence, 2006.) rather than pathologically. Each member of this family was able to impress themselves upon me in ways that would have been impossible through a conventional interview format. I came away thinking how fortunate and honoured I was to know each of them. Solidarity had been engendered between us rather than splintering them into individual parts according to the individualizing bias of clinical interviews.

In some ways, this hour-long interview was like what the legendary Harvard sociologist, Sara Lightfoot Lawrence refers to as "the art and science of portraiture" (Lawrence-Lightfoot, 1997). This is how she describes it:

I wanted to create a narrative that bridged the realm between science and art, merging the systematic and careful description of good ethnography with the evocative resonance of fine literature. I wanted the written pieces to convey the authority, wisdom, and the perspectives of the subject but I wanted them to feel it somehow managed to reveal their essence. I wanted them to experience the portrait as both familiar and exotic so that they would be introduced to a perspective they would not have considered before. And finally, I wanted them to feel seen, fully attended to, recognized, appreciated, respected, and scrutinized. I wanted them to feel both the discovery and the generosity of the process as well as the penetrating and careful investigation.

I summed up what I believed to be the first half of the interview, "Well, we now know what you have individually and collectively to put against this Problem that is besetting you. But tomorrow I will learn all there is to know about the Problem".

I looked forward to this second half of the meeting. Whatever the Problem was, I felt it shrinking as the family's dignity and honour increased. However, my anticipation was interrupted later that first day when Jane, the mother, called to say the family had to cancel the Sunday meeting as an uncle had died.

Many attendees were concerned about what had transpired and there was considerable debate. Given the contentious nature of these interviews – the one they had attended and the one the family had cancelled – it was fortunate that Linda had scheduled an appointment for the family at 7 pm the following Monday. Remember the interview had occurred at 10 am on Saturday. What happened? The psychiatric emergency was 13-year-old Suzie's conviction when she awoke on school days for the past two months that she was unable to

xvi *Foreword*

see and thereby unable to attend school. Over this period, several consultations with ophthalmologists had yielded nil diagnoses. Suzie's diagnosis was a "conversion disorder".

On Monday, however, Suzie awoke and without further ado went to school. Her mother was satisfied with this outcome. The emergency was over. I suspect if the second half of the interview had taken place first, I would have been unable to grant anywhere near such an effect. The hour-long interview regarding what was wonderful about each family member, or each person's moral character, had produced a result beyond my expectations.

My association has been long and happy with Nina. We first met when she was studying at the Dulwich Centre (Adelaide, Australia) with Michael White, myself, and associates in 2004–2005. I soon came to appreciate Nina's moral stamina and her determination to bring to Child Psychiatry in Denmark some of, if not more than, the concerns and conundrums that my tales allude to. She and the teams she has surrounded herself with over the years have been undaunted in their quest. They have achieved through sheer perseverance, rigorous and deliberate practice, and sparks of genius, the participation and collaboration of all concerned – professionals and clients/patients, no matter what their age or status.

I have consulted often via email and made visits to Copenhagen to meet with Nina and her team in 2014 and 2015. As you can see in Chapter 11, I have also engaged in agency co-research with the team's consulting clients and consider those times among my most rewarding experiences. There was much to learn from such consultations, as with the inaugural meeting that I came to refer to as agency co-research, in Boston in 1995 (see Tale Four in Afterword).

I commend this book to you.

References

Argyris, C., & Schon, D. A. (1974). *Theory in practice: Increasing professional effectiveness.* Jossey-Bass.

Basso, K. H. (1966). Wisdom sits in places: Landscape and language among the Western Apache. University of New Mexico Press.

Epston, D. (1989). *Collected papers.* Adelaide: Dulwich Centre Publications.

Garfinkel, H. (1956). Conditions of successful degradation ceremonies. *American Journal of Sociology, 61*(5), 420–424. Retrieved from http://www.jstor.org/stable/2773484

Kuhn, T. S. (1970). *The structure of scientific revolutions* (2nd ed.). Chicago: University of Chicago Press.

Lawrence-Lightfoot, S., & Davis, J. H. (1997). *The art and science of portraiture.* Jossey-Bass.

Maisel, R., Epston, D., & Borden, A. (2004). *Biting the hand that starves you: Inspiring resistance to Anorexia/Bulimia.* New York, NY: W.W. Norton & Co.

Sennett, R. (2003). *Respect in a World of Inequality.* New York, NY: W.W. Norton.

White, M. (1995). Psychotic Experience and discourse. In *Re-authoring lives: Interviews & essays* (pp. 112–154). Adelaide: Dulwich Centre Publications.

Acknowledgements

I want to thank all my different families.

My husband Ulrik and our three sons Adam, Christian and David have patiently listened to my ramblings, which began when the boys were only a few years old (they are now past 30 years old). I am grateful to them and my daughters-in-law Menaka, Anne and Linnea for their patient listening about ethical and political issues, narrative ethics and techniques, child and adolescent psychiatry at large, and now this book. They have supported me beyond anything I could have imagined.

If I could, I would name all the people I have met in the worldwide narrative community and in psychiatry, both patients, their families, and my colleagues. They have all influenced who I am and what I do today. I owe colleagues who have worked in the Family Therapy Team my gratitude for going along with my ideas, arguing with me, disputing, and helping me to co-create our collaborative family therapy for "our families" burdened with complex psychiatric problems.

I especially want to thank those families who have participated in the writing of this book. I want to thank Valiant's family, The Braveheart family, Charlotte's family, Iris and Karen's family, Laura's family, Lielle's family, Andy and Mandy's family, Katja and Filippa and her little sister Isabella, Agnes, Isac's family and Suzan. Thank you, dear team-members, my family, friends, trainees, and colleagues, who have helped me and read the manuscript: Kirsten, Janni, Camilla, Signe, Marianne, Mia, Hanne, Yamuna, Ida, Kirsten, Clara, Linnea, Gabriele, Charlotte, Elisabeth, Astrid, and Ulrik. Your thoughtful comments have been a huge support in creating the book. I am truly grateful, and your participation has been one of my greatest joys.

A special thanks to my illustrator Martin Lasthein for his attentive curiosity and creative talent. His illustrations perfectly convey the joy I experience when working collaboratively with our families.

Our team couldn't have created and implemented our collaborative therapy, while carrying on the daily load of clinical work, without financial support from the Danish philanthropic fund TrygFonden.[1] This fund has supported our ideas and our research project on two occasions. Its donations have made both the project and this book possible.

xviii *Acknowledgements*

David Epston and William Madsen have been immensely supportive in many ways, despite their shared initial reluctance to the word "manual". Thank you for your never-ending support and trust in the ideas, the team, and in me. Without you, none of this would have happened.

William Madsen's book *Collaborating with Multi-Stressed Families* (Madsen, 2007) became a fundamental source of inspiration. William Madsen visited and helped us work with juxtaposing discourses, co-creation, and mattering. His suggestions were especially helpful in finding ways to both acknowledge and talk about people's symptoms and problems while focusing on the preferred outcomes from a non-pathologizing stance.

David Epston has been my mentor for almost 20 years and became our team's mentor. David initiated the transformation of our notetaking in the medical records into therapeutic letter writing. His workshops with us became crucial in developing our "constantly-curiously-learning-team-culture". He interviewed us about our dreams, values, and intentions. He also interviewed some of our patients to help us see how our practices were perceived and experienced. This co-research was hugely influential on our work.

David "found" June Alexander for me, who was enthusiastically on board with the idea from the very beginning helping me with all aspects of the writing project. I am grateful for all the discussions we have had and the support and belief from Routledge in our book concept.

Nina Tejs Jørring

Note

1 TrygFonden is a philanthropic fund. "Tryg" translates in English to "Safe". They formulate their vision this way: We work for a society where fewer people get mentally ill, where more people are able to live a good life with their illness, and where there is tolerance for people affected by mental illness.

Introduction

When one person is struggling with a psychiatric illness, their family struggles too. Therefore, the whole family deserves help together.

I do not believe in individual therapy for children. Imagine a child saying, "Hey Mum, I have learned these new things about myself, and I will act differently from now on. Therefore, I expect you to change your behaviour accordingly". That situation would be impossible for a child. I believe parents are in a better position to change the way family members interact with each other and their problems.

This book grew out of the work of the Family Therapy Team established in 2010 in the Child and Adolescent Mental Health Services of the Capital Region in Denmark. Our purpose was to develop a treatment based on narrative family therapy to help families struggling with complex psychiatric problems so severe that regular treatment, both in the hospital and in the community, had been inadequate. This book is based on the knowledge we created during the unit's first decade.

This book provides guidance in helping people who are heavily burdened with psychiatric illnesses. The aim is to help these patients, in collaboration with their families, to find ways to live a life as close as possible to their dreams.

We call our treatment Collaborative Family Therapy (CFT). It is based in a child and adolescent mental health setting with these visions (Jørring & Jacobsen, 2014):

1. Combining narrative therapy and the bio-psycho-social model used in the health care sector to address psychiatric problems.
2. Taking a family approach, not an individualistic approach.
3. Creating a team culture consistent with narrative ethics.
4. Honouring and using the knowledge and wisdom of people who seek help in psychiatry.

This book contains more than my voice. Families with experience of CFT also participate. Their opinions were sought in deciding the content and they were invited to read the drafts. E-mails, descriptions, and comments from family members validate and enrich the stories.

DOI: 10.4324/9781003171621-1

2 *Introduction*

A psychiatry of two minds

When I began training in psychiatry in the 1990s, the stigma and taboos of psychiatry were paramount. There was a lot of secrecy and disrespect for psychiatric patients in society (Lieberman & Ogi, 2015; Strong & Sesma-Vazquez, 2015). My first psychotherapy training was in psychodynamic therapy. I have worked with many wonderful psychodynamic therapists, but some of those therapists I trained with then expressed a worldview of being smarter, more worthy, and have more wisdom than their patients. We were to be "the gods", who helped the fragile patients. This approach was alluring with its self-glorifying practices. We spoke about the "cases" at the conferences, and I learned that we "knew better". This attitude didn't fit with the values of mutual respect and collaboration I found in other therapeutic literature (Byng-Hall, 1998; Denborough, 2019; Duncan et al., 2009; Freeman et al., 1997; Maisel et al., 2004; White & Epston, 1990).

Changes in hospital administration practice in the 1980s and 1990s introducing New Public Management (Pedersen & Löfgren, 2012) and Lean Hospital Management (Pedersen & Huniche, 2011; Usman, 2020) led to the administration viewing our service more as a production facility. These developments served to extend the gap between me and those I wanted to help.

The public mental health services are also driven by many values that I hold in high regard, i.e., that we cannot squander our few and precious financial resources and that we must be accountable to those we serve.

My medical training, especially in child and adolescent psychiatry (Rutter & Stevenson, 2008; Thapar et al., 2017), provides tools to read and understand medical science and medical models. I learned how to use those models as facts and metaphors for imagining how a brain might work, and what might happen if we do this or that. The medical training helped me to become organized, systematic, and find patterns in big complex cases and situations. I have used this knowledge to set up a team that can work clinically within a mental health service, create new treatments, implement a manual and do effectiveness studies (Ejbye-Ernst & Jørring, 2017, Ejbye-Ernst et al., 2015; Jørring & Gjessing Jensen, 2018; Jørring & Jacobsen, 2014; Jørring & Juul, 2013, 2018).

I use social constructionist theories (Madsen, 2006; Morgan, 2002) when reflecting on how the different sciences affect my relationships with patients, their families, colleagues, and psychiatry. The narrative practices of externalizing and examining discourses have helped me to stay true to my values.

The way health professionals and society view mental health problems and psychiatric illnesses has a profound effect on how we treat the illnesses and the patients (Luhrmann, 2001). Discussions of soma and psyche and questions of whether a problem has a biological/neurological, psychological, or a social cause will continue because we long to find simple answers to our problems. But psychiatric problems stem from complexities of problems (Engel, 2012). All the causes are influential factors at the same time, and we must address them simultaneously. We can use the bio-psycho-social model to help us

Introduction 3

understand psychiatric problems (Borrell-Carrió et al., 2004), and we have to embrace the fact that psychiatry is a messy and wonderfully fascinating endeavour.

However, using the bio–psycho–social model to understand the illness is not enough. The next problem is how to address the illness. Is the illness located within a single person's mind, or is it a relational problem? An older colleague said, *"Psychiatric illnesses are communicative illnesses, they are trying to tell somebody something, and we must listen!"* I like this way of describing and understanding these problems. The person has a relationship with these problems, and the problems are trying to communicate. When we adopt this perspective, it makes no sense to treat only one person, without involving those the messages are intended for, which most often are family members.

My hope is that we can expand our understandings and approaches to psychiatry so that we help the families as well as the person with the psychiatric illness or mental health problems. The whole family is struggling, not only one person. Treating the child or youth alone, telling them to go home after a session loaded with the responsibility to change the communication with their dear ones and their shared problems, makes no sense.

I believe a more beneficial outcome for families can be achieved by merging the bio–psycho–social model with social constructionist theory. Social constructionist theory explains how language, ideas, metaphors, and the understandings we give to different words determine how we live, i.e., how we experience ourselves as ill or not, as patients or not (Besley, 2010; Braiden et al., 2010; Brinkmann, 2020; Gergen & Davis, 1985).

I trained as a child and adolescent psychiatrist and a narrative family therapist at the same time. This joint study had a profound effect on my future work aspirations. I imagined working in a mental health service that adhered to the ethics of caring and helping that I was taught in medical school and also adhered to the ethical values of narrative therapy. These values embrace collaboration with my patients, based on respect, curiosity, trust, and hope and consider patient and family wisdom as being of equal value to my medical knowledge.

I wanted to find ways to practice within the mental health services based on both the values of medical science and the values of narrative therapy.

About language, words, and naming

Textbooks use academic language that is concise and to the point. This language tries to avoid misunderstandings by using specific words that are clearly defined and known to those within that field. This makes reading easy for those with an academic education but can make comprehension difficult for others.

I learned my narrative therapy theory in English and have struggled to translate it into Danish. Many narrative therapy words were as foreign to "the lay person" as many words in the medical language, and this created a chasm

4   *Introduction*

between me and my medical colleagues when I used psychological and philosophical words from narrative therapy. In the same way, medical "lingo" can create an abyss between doctors and patients.

We all ascribe personal and professional meaning to words, especially the names we give to each other, our actions, intentions, hopes, and dreams. Terms such as "patient", "client", "psychiatry" "treatment", and "mental health services" may have different meanings to different people depending on our contexts.

When words convey a certain kind of power or meaning that we, or those we are in a dialogue with, are opposed to, we can try to change our wording (Meuter et al., 2015). Sometimes this helps. But when I write one thing that somebody likes, there's a chance somebody else feels the opposite. In my experience, this is not always due to different values and beliefs, but due to different cultural practices, contexts and ways of using our words and language. That's where communication theory is helpful, as it provides tools for communicating about the language we speak and the meaning we create (Bruner, 1993; Ejbye-Ernst & Jørring, 2017; Ejbye-Ernst et al., 2015; Epston, 1998, 2014; Epston et al. 2012; Malinen & Anderson, 2004; Pearce, 1989; Phillips, 2011). I apologise in advance that I might step on some of your values unintentionally and hope that you will keep this in mind while reading this book.

I mostly use the first names of people and families in this book, but also refer to patients, treatments, and illnesses. I use "conversations" instead of "therapy sessions" because "conversation" is the word I use when meeting with my patients. This is one way to address the hierarchical effects of using certain words.

The families I meet have initially sought help in a hospital. One of the children is the ascribed patient, and I am the doctor. Many people like the word "patient" because it literally reminds us that a lot of patience is required to be a patient. Some people like the word client because it removes some societal blame experienced for being in a specific predicament. Many people dislike the word "patient" and also the word "client" because they experience these words as placing people in positions of lesser worth. My hope with this book is to describe practices that help people step into positions of being a patient with dignity and respect, knowing they are worthy of and entitled to receive proper treatment and help. Practices that encourage the patient to participate in the co-designing and co-decisions of their treatment, in collaboration with their health professionals (Frank, 2018).

Accordingly, this book is written in a mix of mostly doctorial, psychological, and lay-person "languages". I use different "languages" when speaking with families, trainees or colleagues in many different contexts. Mostly, however, I use externalizing language, based on narrative theory and poststructuralism (Thomas, 2002). My hope is for this book to be a living example of the principles put forward. For example, narrative therapists do not write, "I am depressed", but rather, "I am struggling with depression" or, "I am attacked by anxiety" (Morgan, 2000; White, 2006, 2007; White and Epston, 1990).

Throughout, I try to avoid specific words known only to one group of people. When specific narrative or medical words are used, references are provided for further reading.

When we experience how the language constructs our experiences, taking care and being gentle becomes imperative in using our words. David Epston and William Madsen have taught that the use of many words, and especially extraordinary words that are seldom used, adds to the significance of what is said, making our conversations powerful therapeutical tools for empowering those we seek to help. Therefore, this book contains more descriptive words than some classic textbooks.

I also want to emphasize that my therapy transcriptions in this book are not original. Many stories are built from memory, and many have been "through a check-up" with the families concerned to ensure they are as true to their memory as possible. The purpose is not to present traditional research findings but teaching, so the conversations are not "word by word". They are abbreviated and paraphrased to present sentences that carry a teaching message. I draw attention to this as there has been criticism of this type of autoethnographic practice of writing (Ellis et al., 2010).

Bringing a guide or a manual to life

I teach trainees in child and adolescent psychiatry. When I began using our guide (also known as a manual) on CFT in my teachings, I received positive reviews, but also many complaints and demands. The trainees liked the structure and clear guidelines but wanted more examples on how to do it. They said, *"It lacks those stories you tell us. We learn from those stories and carry them with us"*. That feedback inspired me to start writing stories, and the idea to write this book was born.

The manual *Collaborative Family Therapy with Psychiatric Multi-stressed Families* (Jørring & Juul, 2013, 2018) has become a guide for use in non-research environments. Accordingly, this book contains some stories that I tell my younger colleagues, and that they then carry with them. The stories illustrate how helpful it has been for my personal and professional development, to invite families to collaborate and to give advice about what is helpful for them.

Several stories include comments from the families. I want you to experience the same humbling effect as I have experienced, when these families share their stories, ideas, and wisdom about what constitutes good treatments. I hope you also get a sense of what it is like to be on the receiving side of mental health services.

The stories show how the letter-writing has been crucial for our development in our team as therapists and health professionals, and how this approach has improved our skills in asking good questions.

The chapters also describe how our team works between sessions. These practices are important in sustaining us in our daily practices as mental health workers.

Most of all, I hope the stories convey the immense joy we experience when working with families, rather than individuals.

I expect most readers will have prior knowledge about psychiatry, medicine, diagnoses, narrative therapy, and family therapy. Accordingly, this book is neither a textbook on psychiatry nor narrative therapy. This book draws on ideas based on the empowerment and recovery movement, action research, shared decision making, and on different types of psychotherapy, including psychodynamic, cognitive-behavioural therapy, and milieu therapy. The exemplary stories illustrate how to collaborate with families, based on the understanding that one single truth on the meaning of a good life does not exist. Rather, life is multi-storied (Madigan, 2019, pp. 27–62).

If you feel inspired to use these ideas in your own work, our guide can be downloaded for free (Jørring & Juul, 2013, 2018).

Multi-storied clinical work and research

When the Family Therapy Team was established in 2009, I wanted to write a manual and undertake efficacy studies. While some colleagues on my team were reluctant to embark on such a project, others liked the idea of a guide. A guide or a manual would help them know what was expected of them, would provide clear guidelines, and a checklist to help when an impasse occurred on whether to do this or that.

Other colleagues, who were narratively trained, were appalled. The word "manual" had a whole other meaning for them. They felt physically restrained. They believed that a manual would leave no room for creating individualised conversations based on what the family needed. They were concerned that each family would become a number, where the research became more important than the individual family (Ejbye-Ernst & Jørring, 2017, p. 49).

We had to address the different stories that informed the different perceptions of research and manuals, and we found ways to embrace both of these worlds. This work helped us co-create a team founded on our shared values; we co-created a multi-storied team with multi-storied treatments (Jørring & Jacobsen, 2014).

To do so, we had to explore the different interpretations of the word "manual", our stories, training and values. We found the word "cookbook" served as a metaphor to describe the purpose for our manual. Since we all liked to cook and bake, we had the shared experience and knowledge of following a new recipe closely at first, when unfamiliar with the recipe, then later when confident and familiar with the principles, starting to improvise with knowledge based on the results of our experience. Our ultimate aim was to continuously improve the outcome. In this way, the word "cookbook" resonated for us in creating and using our treatment manual.

My vision for this book

This book is about helping families with complex psychiatric problems by seeing and meeting the families and the family members, as the best versions of themselves, before we see and address the diagnoses.

I want to inspire you to become the best version of your professional self. During the writing process, I've imagined that I am telling stories to younger colleagues and trainees who work with families struggling with mental health problems. The narrative approach to teaching has inspired me for many years, especially the concept of exemplary tales (Carlson et al., 2016; Carlson, 2017; Epston, 2018, 2016; Ingamells, 2016a, 2016b). I hope my stories can become such tales and be applied in this way.

How to read this book

The book's chapters are organized according to ideas, values and techniques. The initial focus is on family-oriented practices. The book then weaves through narrative collaborative practices, narrative psychiatric practices, and narrative agency practices.

You will become acquainted with some of my families through the stories. Some stories are stand alone. Other stories are woven into several chapters, as they illustrate different aspects of our work.

You can read the book from start to end and get the stories in chronological order. Or you can read the different chapters according to your interest.

About the authors

Nina Tejs Jørring, MD, simultaneously trained to become a child and adolescent psychiatrist in Copenhagen, Denmark and a narrative family therapist at Dulwich Centre, Australia. She is a senior consultant and certified specialist and supervisor in narrative family psychotherapy at the Child and Adolescent Mental Health Services in the Capital Region of Denmark.

Nina first immersed herself in working with families affected by anorexia nervosa before she began helping families with complex psychiatric problems. This led to the establishment of The Family Therapy Team in 2009, the first unit to combine Narrative Therapy and Child and Adolescent Psychiatry. The team conducted implementation and efficacy studies, and through her research and work Nina has written articles both in her native language and in English, and demonstrated, how this approach truly empowers families being treated at the Child and Adolescent Mental Health Services.

Narrative Psychiatry and Family Collaborations grew out of the team's innovative treatments and research, the families' appraisal of the help they received, her teaching experiences, her joy of collaborating with families struggling with psychiatric problems, and a deep desire to help create a better world for families in general.

8   *Introduction*

Nina's vision is that child and adolescent psychiatry becomes a family psychiatry offering co-created treatments. This vision is based on the understanding that when a child suffers from psychiatric problems, the whole family suffers, therefore the family deserves to receive help together.

As a writer of blogs and articles, she aims to reduce stigma and encourage medical services to build teams and organizations with leadership that honours the ethical principles of respect, curiosity, trust, and hope. Nina is active on several committee boards and serves as vice chairman of the Danish Society for Child and Adolescent Psychiatry. She was awarded the child and adolescent trainees' award for advancing teaching environment in Denmark in 2018 describing Nina's unique teaching and supervisory approach as "innovative, enthusiastic, and inspiring teaching with exemplary tales and engaging metaphors".

Nina lives with her husband Ulrik, whom she has built a life since they were 20 years old. Together they share a love of travelling, including a year sailing the Pacific. They have three grown sons and have recently become grandparents.

Contact Nina on e-mail through ninatejs@hotmail.com or through her website: ninatejsjorring.com or ninatejsjorring.dk.

David Epston, along with Michael White (1950–2008), was one of the originators of Narrative Therapy. Both were social worker/family therapists. Together, they co-authored, Narrative Means to Therapeutic Ends (1990) and Experience, Contradiction, Narrative and Imagination (1992). Altogether he has co-authored/authored 11 books, most notably Freeman et al. (1997), *Playful Approaches to Serious Problems: Narrative Therapy with Children and their Families*; Marsden, Epston and Markham (2016), *Narrative Therapy in Wonderland: Connecting with Children's Imaginative Know-how*, and Maisel et al. (2004), *Biting the Hand that Starves You: Inspiring Resistance to Anorexia/Bulimia*. David, a New Zealander, has archived many of his publications at www. narrativeapproaches.com and is founding editor of the Journal of Contemporary Narrative Therapy.

June Alexander PhD is the founder of the online platform, The Diary Healer, which provides inspiration and hope through the use of the narrative and connects with people who live with a mental health challenge.

June has written nine books about eating disorders. Prior to writing books, which include her memoir, *A Girl Called Tim*, June had a long career in print journalism. She combines her writing expertise with the life experience of recovering from long term anorexia nervosa, trauma and other comorbidities, to advocate for a greater understanding of mental health challenges. Her contribution to the eating disorder field was recognized at the 2016 Academy for Eating Disorders International Conference in San Francisco where she was awarded the Meehan/Hartley Award for Public Service and Advocacy.

In 2017, June graduated as a Doctor of Philosophy (Creative Writing). Her research focused on using extracts from unsolicited diaries to create a book about the usefulness of journaling in recovering from an eating disorder.

June is a co-chair of the National Eating Disorder Collaboration (NEDC) Steering Committee Evidence of Experience Group in Australia and is an advisory panel member for Families Empowered and Supporting Treatment of Eating Disorders (FEAST).

Today June is a writing mentor – helping people to self-heal and find purpose in their life through story-telling. She lives with her dog Maisie and two cats by the sea, and enjoys visits from her main inspirations, her four children and five grandchildren.

Contact June on e-mail through june@junealexander.com or through her websites: www.thediaryhealer.com and www.lifestoriesmentor.com.au

References

Besley, A. C. T. (2010). Foucault and the turn to narrative therapy. *British Journal of Guidance and Couselling, 30*(2), 125–143. doi:10.1080/03069880220128010

Borrell-Carrió, F., Suchman, A. L., & Epstein, R. M. (2004). The biopsychosocial model 25 years later: Principles, practice, and scientific inquiry. *Annals of Family Medicine, 6*(6), 576–582. doi:10.1370/afm.245

Braiden, H., Bothwell, J., & Duffy, J. (2010). Parents' experience of the diagnostic process for autistic spectrum disorders. *Child Care in Practice, 16*(4), 377–389. doi:10.1080/135 75279.2010.498415

Brinkmann, S. (2020). *Diagnostic cultures. A cultural approach to the pathologization of modern life.* London: Routledge.

Bruner, J. (1993). *Acts of meaning*. Harvard University Press.

Byng-Hall, J. (1998). *Rewriting family scripts: Improvisation and systems change*. The Guilford Press.

Carlson, T. S., Corturillo, E. M., & Freedman, J. (2016). There's always a puppy (and Sometimes a Bunny): A story about a story about a story. *Journal of Systemic Therapies, 35*(3), 73–82. doi:10.1521/jsyt.2016.35.3.73

Carlson, T. S. E. A. (2017). Learning narrative therapy backwards: Exemplary tales as an alternative pedagogy for learning practice. *Journal of Systemic Therapies, 36*(1), 94–107.

Denborough, D. (2019). *Family therapy: Exploring the field's past, present and possible futures.* Adelaide: Dulwich Centre Publications.

Duncan, B. L., Miller, S. D., Wampole, B. E., & Hubble, M. A. (2009). *The heart and soul of change: Delivering what works in therapy.* Washington, DC: American Psychological Association.

Ejbye-Ernst, D., & Jørring, N. T. (2017). Doing it collaboratively! Addressing the Dilemmas of designing quantitative effect studies on narrative family therapy in a local clinical context. *Journal of Systemic Therapies, 36*(1), 48–66. doi:10.1521/jsyt.2017.36.1.48

Ejbye-Ernst, D., Jørring, N. T., & Jacobsen, C. B. (2015). Klientperspektiver på anvendelsen af spørgeskemaer i opstartsfasen af et psykoterapeutisk behandlingsforløb. *Fokus på familien, 43*(2), 109–125. doi: 10.18261/ISSN0807-7487-2015-02.

Ellis, C., Adams, T., & Bochner, A. (2010). Autoethnography: An overview. *Forum: Qualitative Social Research, 12*(1). doi:10.17169/fqs-12.1.1589

Engel, G. L. (2012). The need for a new medical model: A challenge for biomedicine. *Psychodynamic Psychiatry, 40*(3), 377–396.

10 *Introduction*

Epston, D. (1998). Expanding the conversation. In *Catching up with David Epston. A collection of narrative practice-based papers* (pp. 95–110). Adelaide: Dulwich Centre Publications.

Epston, D. (2014). Ethnography, co-research and insider knowledges. *Australian and New Zealand Journal of Family Therapy, 35*(1), 105–109. doi:10.1002/anzf.1048

Epston, D. (2018). In pursuit of goodness: Dignity and moral character in narrative therapy. *Journal of Narrative Family Therapy, 3,* 2–26.

Epston, D., & Carlson, T. S. (2016). Introduction to special series for "The Corner": Exemplary tales: Virtual apprenticeships. *Journal of Systemic Therapies, 35*(2), 54–55. doi:10.1521/jsyt.2016.35.2.54

Epston, D., Stillman, J. R., & Erbes, C. R. (2012). Speaking two languages: A conversation between narrative therapy and scientific practices. *Journal of Systemic Therapies, 31*(1), 74–88. doi:10.1521/jsyt.2012.31.1.74

Frank, A. W. (2018). What is narrative therapy and how can it help health humanities? *Journal of Medical Humanities, 39*(4), 553–563. doi:10.1007/s10912-018-9507-3

Freeman, J., Epston, D., & Lobovits, D. (1997). *Playful Approaches to Serious Problems.* New York & London: W. W. Norton.

Gergen, K. J., & Davis, K. M. (1985). *The social construction of the person.* New York: Springer – Verlag, New York, Inc.

Ingamells, K. M. (2016a). Learning how to counter-story in narrative therapy (with david Epston and Wilbut the warrior). *Journal of Systemic Therapies, 35*(4), 58–71.

Ingamells, K. M. (2016b). Wilbur the worrier becomes wilbur the warrior: A teaching story for narrative family therapists. *Journal of Systemic Therapies, 35*(4), 43–57. doi:10.1521/jsyt.2016.35.4.43

Jørring, N. T., & Gjessing Jensen, K. (2018). Treatment efficacy of narrative family therapy for children and adolescents with diverse psychiatric symptomatology. *Scand J Child Adolesc Psychiatr Psychol, 6*(2), 107–114. doi:10.21307/sjcapp-2018-012

Jørring, N. T., & Jacobsen, C. B. (2014). Narrative therapy in CAMHS: Creating multistoried treatments. *Journal of Systemic Therapies, 33*(1), 89–101. doi:10.1521/jsyt.2014.33.1.89

Jørring, N. T., & Juul, J. (2013). Collaborative family therapy with psychiatric multistressed families. Retrieved June 8th 2021 from https://www.researchgate.net/publication/336512754_English_manual_rev_October_2013

Jørring, N. T., & Juul, J. (2018). Manual for Samarbejdende familieterapi. Retrieved June 8th 2021 from https://www.researchgate.net/publication/329269185_Manual_for_Samarbejdende_familieterapi

Lieberman, M. D., & Ogi, O. (2015). *Shrinks: The untold story of psychiatry.* Little, Brown Spark.

Luhrmann, T. M. (2001). *Of Two Minds: An Anthropologist Looks at American Psychiatry.* Vintage.

Madigan, S. (2019). *Narrative Therapy* (2nd ed.). Washington DC: American Psychological Association.

Madsen, W. C. (2006). Teaching across discourses to sustain collaborative clinical practice. *Journal of Systemic Therapies, 25*(4), 44–58. doi:10.1521/jsyt.2006.25.4.44

Madsen, W. C. (2007). *Collaborative therapy with multi-stressed families* (2nd ed.). New York: The Guilford Press.

Maisel, R., Epston, D., & Borden, A. (2004). *Biting the hand that starves you: Inspiring resistance to Anorexia/Bulimia.* New York, NY: W.W. Norton & Co.

Malinen, T., & Anderson, H. (2004). Interview: The Wisdom of not knowing—a conversation with Harlene Anderson. *Journal of Systemic Therapies*, *23*(2), 68–77. doi:10.1521/jsyt.23.2.68.36646

Meuter, R. F. I., Gallois, C., Segalowitz, N. S., Ryder, A. G., & Hocking, J. (2015). Overcoming language barriers in healthcare: A protocol for investigating safe and effective communication when patients or clinicians use a second language. *BMC Health Services Research*, *15*(1), 371. doi:10.1186/s12913-015-1024-8

Morgan, A. (2000). *What is narrative therapy?: An easy-to-read introduction.* Adelaide: Dulwich Centre Publications.

Morgan, A. (2002). Discerning between structuralist and non-structuralist categories of identity: A training exercise. *International Journal of Narrative Therapy and Community Work*, *4*(4), 52–55. doi:10.3316/informit.662855987343361

Pearce, B. W. (1989). *Communication and the human condition.* Southern Illinois University Press.

Pedersen, E. R. G., & Huniche, M. (2011). Determinants of lean success and failure in the Danish public sector. *International Journal of Public Sector Management*, *24*(5), 403–420. doi:10.1108/09513551111147141

Pedersen, J. S., & Löfgren, K. (2012). Public sector reforms: New public management without marketization? The Danish Case. *International Journal of Public Administration*, *35*(7), 435–447. doi:10.1080/01900692.2012.679579

Phillips, L. (2011). *The promise of dialogue.* John Benjamins Publishing Company.

Rutter, M., & Stevenson, J. (2008). Developments in child and adolescent psychiatry over the last 50 years. In *Rutter's Child and Adolescent Psychiatry* (pp. 1–17).

Strong, T., & Sesma-Vazquez, M. (2015). Discourses on children's mental health: A critical review. In M. O'Reilly, & Lester, J. (Ed.), *The Palgrave handbook of child mental health* (pp. 99–116): London: Palgrave Macmillan.

Thapar, A., Pine, D., Leckman, J. F., Scott, S., Snowling, M. J., & Taylor, E. A. (2017). *Rutter's child and adolescent psychiatry.* John Wiley & Sons.

Thomas, L. (2002). Poststructuralism and therapy – what's it all about? *The International Journal of Narrative Therapy and Community Work*, *2*(2), 85–89. Retrieved from https://search.informit.org/doi/10.3316/informit.126462957543424

Usman, I. (2020). Lean Hospital management implementation in health care service: A multicase study. *Systematic Reviews in Pharmacy*, *11*(3), 361–367. doi:10.5530/srp.2020.3.45

White, M. (2006). Narrative practice with families with children: Externalising conversations revisited. In M. White, & Morgan, A. (Ed.), *Narrative Therapy with Children and their families* (pp. 1–56). Adelaide: Dulwich Centre Publications.

White, M. (2007). *Maps of narrative practice.* W. W. Norton & Co.

White, M., & Epston, D. (1990). *Narrative means to therapeutic ends.* W.W. Norton & Company.

1   A narrative family psychiatrist

Being met as a person worthy of respect

I was sitting in my tiny office as a young resident at the Child and Adolescent Psychiatric Hospital.

I was trying to keep track of what the mother, Sheila, was telling me. At the same time, I was desperately keeping an eye on her six-year-old son, Hans, who was climbing the furniture and getting into everything.

The mother was describing the troubles Hans faced at school, the complaints about him from people in their residential complex, the difficulties in raising him, and her fears for his future, which she already imagined being corrupted by crime and drugs.

By now, Hans had emptied the toys onto the floor and flipped the trash can so he could use it as a shed for farm animals and racing cars. He talked constantly about everything and nothing.

Despair invaded my brain, telling me that this mother was unfit, and her son was out of control. However, I tried to respond with empathy and common sense to invitations from Hans to play and, simultaneously, give my full attention to his mum.

Thoughts about the difficulties of my job were interrupted by other thoughts. How awful must it be for the mother and son here in my office? Does the mother expect me to see her and Hans as failures? What might they need most right now? Perhaps their biggest need is for respect and acknowledgement from a health professional like me?

Realizing that I needed to show Sheila and Hans my respect and faith in both of them, I said:

"Do you know the story of Emil of Lönneberga (Lindgren, 1963)? I am reminded of Emil and his mother. Do you remember all the troubles Emil made? Despite Emil's troubles, his mother loved him dearly and knew that his only goal was to make other people happy, even though his efforts often ended up all wrong. Emil's mother was the only person who understood him. Do you remember this?".[1]

To my horror and surprise, I saw tears in Sheila's eyes. She sat silently and nodded her head.

DOI: 10.4324/9781003171621-2

A narrative family psychiatrist   13

Luckily, Hans intervened. He sat on the floor in front of his mother, gave her legs a hug, looked at her with big, shining eyes, and said, "I love you too, Mum".

I asked if they remembered what Emil became as an adult in the story. They did not. I told them: "He became chairman of the local council".

My intention was to illustrate that I believed Sheila and Hans also had the potential for creating a good life. As a doctor, giving and holding onto hope is a calling. I view "hope as a practice, rather than simply an emotion or a cultural attitude" (Mattingly, 2010, p. 6).

Our talk about Emil of Lönneberga became instrumental to the success of our collaboration. The next time Sheila and Hans visited, Sheila handed me a huge pile of papers and said, "I have demanded and received access to all the records that the hospitals and social services have on me and Hans, here they are.[2] My social worker wants authorisation to remove Hans from our home. Nobody in the social services department has ever believed in me. Please read these papers. Then you will see why I need your help".

The records contained medical notes from hospitals and procedural notes from social services and the kindergarten dating from Hans' birth. Many interventions had been tried over the years. But the tone was the same throughout judgmental, arrogant, and condescending. The notes were written by professionals whose role was to offer help. These people, in their professional roles, had great power over this family, who were dependent on them for help. No one deserves to be seen through that kind of lens.

I marvelled at Sheila's courage in sharing the records with me. As I read, I thought, again and again, that help offered in such a condescending manner would not help.

I developed the deepest respect for Sheila and the battles she had fought. I felt terrified, imagining being in her position. I was certain that I would not have coped as well as her.

I assessed Hans with my colleagues and co-created an understanding with Sheila of his and the family's difficulties. Most importantly, we changed the narrative about Hans, from a boy being raised by a neglectful mother, to a boy whose Attention-Deficit Hyperactive Disorder (ADHD) was making parenting difficult.

We arranged a family community meeting with the social worker, school psychologist, and teacher and initiated several forms of assistance. Hans was provided with support in school and extracurricular activities. Sheila received support with her job and education. I provided her with psychoeducation on ADHD, and she was eager to learn.

Months later I received a thank you letter.

Sheila wrote that she had felt afraid before our first family community meeting. I had promised her there would be no surprises, and that I would say only what we had planned together. She had been sceptical, but I had kept my word.

14   *A narrative family psychiatrist*

Sheila also thanked me for seeing her as a mum of a child with problems, not as a mother causing the problems. She appreciated that I wanted to support her in creating a better life for her family and her son. I felt deeply humbled, receiving written appreciation for merely behaving like a decent person. All I'd done was to follow basic ethical principles of good conduct as a helper in a position that gave me great influence over another person's life.

Many years have passed since I met Sheila and Hans. I often share their story with younger colleagues and ask them to consider these questions:

Imagine, being that parent, how would you feel?

Imagine, living that parent's life; how tired would you be by now?

Imagine, what life like that might do to your parental self-esteem.

When we do this exercise, we feel overwhelmed at how difficult life must be for the parents of children with psychiatric problems and humbled by the love these parents manage to keep alive.

This insight compels us to acknowledge that parents deserve our respect and support. Giving correct scientific treatment is not enough; we must also deliver the treatment in the right spirit. A respectful, curious, trusting and hopeful spirit create the foundation for a mutual relationship necessary for treatment to be effective, and the best it can be (Sælør et al., 2014; Turns & Kimmes, 2013).

When one person suffers, everyone in the family suffers

A psychiatric illness is not solely an individual illness (Malla et al., 2015). As a narrative practitioner, I see it as mostly relational, because a person's experience of problems is shaped by stories, which are not individual constructions. We are all participants in each other's stories and thus in each other's psychological problems (Combs & Freedman, 2012, p. 1036, 2016).

This does not mean the psychiatric illness is not as real as somatic disease, and this book is not anti-psychiatric (Kendler, 2016). However, psychiatric illnesses are responses to trauma or unmet needs, too much pressure, or other reasons, and they carry a message about this, that we need to listen for (Hamkins, 2005, 2013). This makes them different. It is also important to acknowledge that one debilitating symptom, blame, is associated with psychiatric illnesses (Blum, 2007; White, 2002). This is why I use externalization (Morgan, 2000, pp. 17–31) in my language, according to the narrative mantra (White & Epston, 1990, p. 40):

The child is not the problem.

The problem is the problem.

And:

> The family is not the problem.
>
> The family has the key to solving the problem.

Families often experience that psychiatric illness drives them apart. These effects of the problems might lead us, and the families, to believe that their relationships and interactions were indeed dysfunctional before the illness, rather than a consequence of the illness (White, 2002).

Reflect on the patients you have met. How often have you thought that the parents have acted in illogical ways and wondered why they didn't behave differently? How often have you put some or all the blame on the parents? Don't blame yourself too much for having such a view. We are all governed by the same stories that have perpetuated our society for decades.

Mothers have been labelled "refrigerator-mums" (Bettelheim, 1967; Harris, 2018, p. 6) and explanations have centred on blaming the parents (Cohmer, 2014). Children have been institutionalized and isolated from parents who were thought to be the reason for their predicament (Eamon, 1994; Kerr & Bowen, 1988). Societal discourses (or stories) (Burr, 2003, pp. 63–80) continue to describe families as dysfunctional (Haefner, 2014, pp. 835–837).

The research and interest in biological explanations for children's predicaments have removed a lot of blame from the parents (Coleman & Gillberg, 2012). However, blame remains a "side-effect" from those theories in the 20th century (Silverman, 2012).

Changing discourses takes time, so being aware of their effects is important (Madsen, 2006, p. 47). For example, health professionals are taught to believe that we must, and can, do a better job than parents. This discourse still dominates whenever we focus on the effects of parental actions, instead of on the intentions and wisdom of the parents.

Health professionals are traditionally considered the real experts (Sutherland, 2007). For example, social workers are the experts on social aspects and psychiatrists are experts on psychiatric problems. But what about parents? They are experts on their child, their family, and their family life. Do we acknowledge this? Our position as experts puts parents and families in a non–expert-position, giving "expert" professionals the upper hand. This stance risks the obliteration of any knowledge and wisdom the family, parents, and children might have. How would we feel in their position? The experience of many families is that their knowledge is neglected and deemed unworthy of consideration.

We need to find a new way that is based both on the bio-psycho-social model (Borrell-Carrió et al., 2004) and collaboration with parents and children. Collaboration requires that we meet our patients and their families with respect and curiosity in order to incorporate their wisdom into the treatment. Treatment should not be something we do onto them, but with them (Ness, 2014).

16 *A narrative family psychiatrist*

How do we practice this? Our team uses negotiated dialogue (Strong et al., 2011). We offer ideas on what the problem might be, but only as our input to the conversation. This enables a genuine conversation and collaboration on how to move forward, away from the negative effects of the problem. However, the idea that health professionals can know what the parents might be thinking, and feeling, can still trick us. When we are unable to understand why people act or speak as they do, disrespect can arise. This is the point at which we must ask what we might not yet know, in order to better understand and help.

Blaming the parents, or the child, makes a bad situation worse. Meeting the whole family in a collaborative spirit is the best possible foundation for treatment to offer a person with psychiatric illness.

Joining forces with families

> I really am trying my best; I am here because I am lost and need help. I want to be able to shoulder the responsibility of helping my child. But I am powerless and have lost hope.
>
> Anna, Valiant's mum

Most apparent in our first conversation with Anna and Bertie, the parents of 16-year-old Valiant, was the suffering of these two parents. The grief from their experience of powerlessness and feelings of inadequacy filled our room. These parents even blamed themselves for having different perspectives on the reasons for their child's decline.

Parent blame can become so vicious it can suffocate any parental agency.

Valiant had been in a psychotic stupor for months and nothing seemed to be helping. The family came to us after a long and difficult treatment period, where misunderstandings between parents and professionals had been rife. The health professionals were deeply concerned that Valiant would become incapacitated by schizophrenia.

Anna and Bertie wanted to assist Valiant in a way that the treatment team interpreted as neglecting his severe symptoms, and communication deteriorated.

When we met the parents, they said: "We need to hold onto a hope that our child will get better. That is our intention for coming here. We do not need to be told he is very sick. We know that. But there is no reason to spend time away from him (i.e., having him admitted), unless the purpose is to get knowledge that can help him".

Doctors are taught not to deprive the patients of hope. This can be difficult, as we also want patients and parents to have realistic expectations of the prognosis. These conversations can be interpreted by families as relinquishing hope on healing (Mattingly, 2010, p. 4). However, the health professional does not have to be "tough", unempathetic or discouraging when delivering difficult messages.

A narrative family psychiatrist   17

To counteract the parents' previous experiences, my colleague and I began our conversations by focusing on hope, asking the parents what changes they could envision, if our conversations were helpful. Anna reflects on her experience of our collaboration, in this letter:

Dear Nina,

Overall, you helped us to ease the powerlessness we felt, and replaced it with curiosity, agency, even pride, and gumption.

At the hospital, Valiant was pulled out of our family and admitted for investigation. It seemed the doctors thought they could study him without affecting his condition, as if they didn't seriously consider that his condition was getting worse due to being isolated from his family. They did not have much time to talk with us parents. We often felt we were considered a troublesome, time-consuming attachment to Valiant.

Our confidence as parents was shaken. We had been led to accept that our previous experiences as parents were useless in the current situation. Therefore, for a long time we believed that we had to rely on the skills of the health professionals. We let go of our son, even though this felt completely wrong, because we trusted their authority and professionalism. However, the environment and situation were harmful to Valiant and his relationship with us.

The parental powerlessness must have been frightening for Valiant. He was in the biggest crisis of his life and had to experience and face our insecurities, desperation and despair. Powerlessness is not a good foundation for supporting a loved one.

With you, we were strengthened in our importance to Valiant. We were encouraged to believe we could do something to support and help him. You listened to us, inspired us, and focused on our strengths as parents. We felt better equipped to face the hard and difficult times.

We talked through difficult situations, became inspired to explore them, and sometimes obtained specific instructions on what we could do to manage the challenges. For example, asking curiously, "Why?", when Valiant would not get out of bed, instead of immediately entering a conflict, and finding middle roads so the choice was not either/or. We learned that when we were stuck, we could move forward by describing the situation soberly and calmly for Valiant. We learned to recognize when Valiant was under pressure and to reduce requirements during these periods.

Our greatest concern about the hospital ward professionals was their attitude. We repeatedly heard Valiant described through his failures and possible abnormalities. Our relationship with him was already affected

18 *A narrative family psychiatrist*

by the great change that had happened to him and, in the hospital, it seemed no attention was paid to the risk of increasing the distance and alienation between parents and child through disrespectful attitudes and behaviours.

It was beneficial for us to experience your empathy for us and with our son, and to hear you wonder what his motives and feelings might be. You helped us to unfold and understand what was going on. Your counsel was not alien and counter-intuitive, but insightful, giving us understanding. You helped us to feel our love for our son, and to be proud of him.

The situation with you was different from that at the hospital's inpatient ward, where the project was studying Valiant. Maybe the attitude there was due to time pressure and lack of resources, but respect, hope, and empathy were absent. These qualities don't cost extra time but, when absent, add to the sense of powerlessness.

Anna
PS: Valiant is doing well.

Becoming partners in un-messing a messy family life

My colleague, Kirsten, and I met with the parents of the Braveheart family, Dave and Em. They had two daughters, Flora and Gloria. The elder child, Flora, aged six, had autism. This was our third session, and I began by reading aloud our letter, written to the family after the second session. Our letter focused on the steps the parents had taken, their love for their child, their decisiveness and capabilities to take new actions, creating routines, systems, and rewards to benefit Flora.[3]

My first question was: Any thoughts about this?

Dave immediately spoke up:	Yes, this is all very good, but actually I am not that good, because I can become aggravated and vile towards my daughters and my wife. I sometimes leave them, not for good, but I get up and leave for a couple of hours when it becomes too much.

As we explored this further, the parents looked at each other, exchanged a smile and decided that they needed to talk about anger management.

Kirsten:	Okay! So, what things might cause the need for anger-management?
Dave:	When I interact with irrational people like Em, her emotional way of thinking can trigger my anger. Or if my sense of justice comes under attack, my anger will get easy access to me.

Dave had taken the externalizing grammar into his own language. He externalized some problems he struggled with and some values that were important to him, including anger, emotional way of thinking, and sense of justice.

Narrative therapists use externalizing language intentionally, based on poststructuralism (Thomas, 2002), but its use is common. Inspirational examples can be found in contemporary fictional literature[4] (Keyes, 1996) and fairy tales (LeBlanc & Marrissey, 2017).

Dave: When I am tired and have less energy, it becomes more difficult not to see things only through my own lens.

We asked Dave if seeing things through his own lens was a specific issue for him. Both parents laughed.

Dave: Yes, I am like our daughter that way – we only have our own point of view.

Em and Dave told a story about Dave taking Flora to dance class, and suddenly she did not want to dance. There was no rational reason for this, and Dave became frustrated and angry. He ended up having to call Em, who came and helped them to solve their conflict.

I used a long and convoluted sentence, to ask the next question about being able to see another person's point of view:

Nina: Would you, by any chance, ever have experienced just the slightest ability to find lenses other than your own to look through? Is there any story, or do you remember any experiences that tell you, that you are able to use some lenses other than your own?

By using Dave's own metaphor, "lenses to look through", this formulation provided him with a bigger platform to stand on when answering, and to think about abilities, experiences, and stories. I searched for unique outcomes (Morgan, 2000, pp. 51–58) in his response.

Dave: Oh, yes. At work, I do it all the time. I handle all the applications for building permits at our municipality. I know the laws and how to find the loopholes. I can stand on the other side of the table and imagine what the applicant wants. I know if the law will permit it or not, or if it is possible to find a loophole. I enjoy helping people and making them happy. I have a gene for service! It is not because I am a lovely person, but people are nice to me when I help them or give them what they want. Then I feel good.

20 *A narrative family psychiatrist*

Em: I see he is so much like Flora. She would love a job at the municipality office too, knowing the law, giving out permits, and feeling good about helping other people.

That spurred a long talk with heart-warming narratives about Dave being of service to his three women at home.

Kirsten: So, this gene for service is really something you use in the family! What about your ability to stand on the other side of the table at work, do you also use that in your family? What does that look like?
Em: The girls are more difficult to read than grown-ups, and at work Dave can read the papers, not the people.

This led us to explore difficulties in reading children and in showing feelings. We asked more about this and how the parents might see these difficulties and abilities in their children.

In this part of the conversation, we drew on our knowledge of autism. We spoke about difficulties of reading and showing feelings, not as a personality defect, but as an externalized capability, just like we externalize other things.

We also chose to share our expert knowledge that reading feelings can be difficult if a person has autism and this is seen as a defect by normal social norms. We suggested that if Dave also had difficulty in reading feelings, this might give him feelings of inadequacy and lead to feelings of anger. At this point, Dave expressed how this understanding made him feel acknowledged and helped him to realize that difficulties in reading feelings had a lot to do with feeling inadequate, which was a "door opener" for anger.

Em concluded that the best part of our session that day was being able to talk about anger without Dave "chickening out". This was the first time Dave had experienced any conversation about anger, where he was not berated for his anger, and Em was not criticized for accepting it. By externalizing the anger, we did not have to go into any kind of evaluation of the parents, their love, or their partnership. This gave us room for looking explicitly at the anger. Externalizing language gave the parents a way to communicate about anger.

For Dave, the most important outcome in this session was realizing that his daughters had difficulties reading or understanding him. He decided to go home and practice ways of expressing his feelings, like anger or tiredness, and even trying to communicate his feelings out loud to them. We asked what this endeavour might mean to the daughters. The parents were certain that it would help them to relax. They were certain that the girls used a lot of energy trying to "outguess" their dad.

Our hope was that this session changed the parents' narrative about Dave, from him having a vile temper to having some of the same problems they saw

A narrative family psychiatrist   21

in one of their daughters; not unsolvable challenges, but problems that took time to learn to solve. We heard later that those feelings of inadequacy ceased to trigger Dave's anger, as he progressively found healthier ways to signal and read his own and his daughter's feelings.

There were many venues to pursue with this family. Irrationality might throw the door open for anger, and we had already talked about how the demands of being creative could be stressful for Dave.

Irrationality and creativity are examples of concepts that are wonderful to externalize with families who struggle with autism.

This story illustrates how different family members can describe things from their own points of view and then share ideas on how to understand and manage their problems. Families can become allied in the plight for a better life, when the messy business of their different problems becomes exposed in a caring light. In this conversation, it was not Flora's autism, but difficulties in reading and showing feelings that were the problem. Family life had become messy, because it had been written into a narrative about anger management, that shifted the focus from the problem and put blame on Dave and Em. When we use externalizing language, search for unique outcomes and create alternative stories (Morgan, 2000, pp. 59–72), the problems execute less power over the families. In this case, Dave did not have to fight himself, and learn "anger-management". Instead, he learned new ways to understand the anger, and created a relationship with the problem of reading feelings that diminished the power it exerted over him.

With Dave and Em, and their daughters, we applied our knowledge about the genetics of autism and specific effects of autism from a non-blaming relational stance. Our main focus was not on the "designated patient" but on how the family lived.

Externalizing enables problematic behaviours or psychiatric illnesses to be viewed separately from the person. The externalizing language sets us free and apart from the social stories about mental illness and personal defects that can cause negative feelings like guilt, inadequacy, and weakness.

We work with the parents because they are responsible for handling life, and have more mental resources due to age, experiences, and reflective capability to change their thoughts and behaviour for the good of their family.

A new pathway of understanding opened for the parents when Kirsten asked, "What about this ability to stand on the other side of the table, do you also use that in your family? What does that look like?"

Kirsten listened for metaphors and for visual descriptions that were unusual, like "a gene for service" and "this ability to stand on the other side of the table". An ability that did not have a name but needed a whole sentence to be described. That was special. That was why Kirsten latched onto those sentences. She also became excited upon learning that Dave had a work-related ability and became curious about this ability being used at home.

We also listened for descriptions of the preferred self (Freedman & Combs, 1996; Madsen, 2007, p. 21). When Dave spoke about serving his women and

22 *A narrative family psychiatrist*

being helpful at work, we saw a proud and happy man. We wanted to expand these stories, to help him become aware of behaviours and situations that gave him agency. Those moments became strong antidotes to the self-blame we heard in Dave's first sentence, "I am not that good, I can become very aggravated and vile towards my daughter and my wife".

Kirsten had no idea where her questions would lead us in this conversation. She just knew that sentences with so much information had the potential for producing new wisdom.

With Em and Dave, we co-created a narrative about a family facing difficult struggles, but whose members were doing their best to adhere to their values, and to help and love each other.

We offer our expert knowledge in a collaborative spirit. We ask curious and hopeful questions to generate stories and co-create new narratives that make sense, give ideas and directions, for new and helpful actions.

Notes

1 Emil probably had ADHD, had the diagnosis existed then. https://www.astridlindgren.com/en/characters/emil-in-lonneberga.
2 In Denmark, the municipalities and regions are mandated to deliver all public records on a person, if they request it.
3 We write an e-mail to the family after each session, instead of long medical notes. We begin the next session by reading it aloud. Read more in Chapter 6: The therapeutic letter-writing team.
4 Marian Keyes: *Lucy Sullivan is Getting Married*, page 718: …if I had left then, I would have missed the arrival of my anger… I met it at the door…. "Sorry I'm late", it wheezed, ….".

References

Bettelheim, B. (1967). *The empty fortress: Infantile autism and the birth of the self.* New York, NY: Free Press.

Blum, L. M. (2007). Mother-blame in the Prozac Nation: Raising kids with invisible disabilities. *Gender and Society, 21*(2), 202–226. Retrieved 12 December 2020 from http://www.jstor.org/stable/27640959

Borrell-Carrió, F., Suchman, A. L., & Epstein, R. M. (2004). The biopsychosocial model 25 years later: Principles, practice, and scientific inquiry. *Annals of Family Medicine, 6*(6), 576–582. doi:10.1370/afm.245

Burr, V. (2003). *Social constructionism* (2nd ed.). Routledge.

Cohmer, S. (2014). Early infantile autism and the refrigerator mother theory (1943-1970). *Embryo Project Encyclopedia.*ISSN: 1940-5030.http://embryo.asu.edu/handle/10776/8149.

Coleman, M., & Gillberg, C. (2012). *The autisms.* Oxford University Press.

Combs, G., & Freedman J. (2012). Narrative, poststructuralism, and social justice: Current practices in narrative therapy. *The Counseling Psychologist, 40*(7), 1033–1060. doi:10.1177/0011000012460662

Combs, G., & Freedman J. (2016). Narrative Therapy's relational understanding of identity. *Family Process, 55*(2), 211–224. doi:10.1111/famp.12216

Eamon, M. K. (1994). Institutionalizing children and adolescents in private psychiatric hospitals. *Social Work*, *39*(5), 588–594. doi:10.1093/sw/39.5.588

Freedman, J., & Combs, G. (1996). *Narrative therapy: The social construction of preferred realities.* W.W. Norton & Company.

Haefner, J. (2014). An application of bowen family systems theory. *Issues in Mental Health Nursing*, *35*(11), 835–841. doi:10.3109/01612840.2014.921257

Hamkins, S. (2005). Introducing narrative psychiatry: narrative approaches to initial psychiatric consultations. *International Journal of Narrative Therapy and Community Work*, *1*(1), 5–17.

Hamkins, S. (2013). *The art of narrative psychiatry: Stories of strength and meaning* (1st ed.). Oxford University Press.

Harris, J. (2018). Leo Kanner and autism: A 75-year perspective. *International Review of Psychiatry*, *30*(1), 3–17. doi:10.1080/09540261.2018.1455646

Kendler, K. S. (2016). The nature of psychiatric disorders. *World Psychiatry*, 15, 5–12.

Kerr, M. E., & Bowen, M. (1988). *Family evaluation: An approach based on Bowen theory.* W. W. Norton & Co.

Keyes, M. (1996). *Lucy Sullivan is getting married.* Penguin Books Ltd.

LeBlanc, L., & Marrissey, C. B. (2017). Monsters in the closet. Narrative therapy and fairy tales. In L. Ormandy (Ed.), *The morals of monser stories. Essays on children's picture book messages*. MaFarland & Company, Inc.

Lindgren, A. (1963). *Emil and the Great Escape* (L. Seaton, Trans.). Oxford Childens.

Madsen, W. C. (2006). Teaching across discourses to sustain collaborative clinical practice. *Journal of Systemic Therapies*, *25*(4), 44–58. doi:10.1521/jsyt.2006.25.4.44

Madsen, W. C. (2007). *Collaborative therapy with multi-stressed families* (2nd ed.). The Guilford Press.

Malla, A., Joober, R., & Garcia, A. (2015). "Mental illness is like any other medical illness": a critical examination of the statement and its impact on patient care and society. *Journal of Psychiatry & Neuroscience*, *40*(3), 147–150. doi:10.1503/jpn.150099

Mattingly, C. (2010). *The paradox of hope* .University of California Press.

Morgan, A. (2000). *What is narrative therapy?: An easy-to-read introduction.* Dulwich Centre Publications.

Ness, O. e. a. (2014). "Walking alongside:" Collaborative practices in mental health and substance use care. *International Journal of Mental Health Systems*, *8*(55), 7.

Silverman, C. (2012). *Understanding Autism: Parents, doctors, and the history of a disorder.* Princeton University Press.

Strong, T., Sutherland, O., & Ness, O. (2011). Considerations for a discourse of Collaboration and Psychotherapy. *Asia Pacific Journal of Counselling and Psychotherapy*, *2*(1), 25–40. doi:10.1080/21507686.2010.546865

Sutherland, O. (2007). Therapist positioning and power in discursive therapies: A comparative analysis. *Contemporary Family Therapy*, *29*(4), 193–209. doi:10.1007/s10591-007-9050-2

Sælør, K. T., Ness, O., Holgersen, H., & Davidson, L. (2014). Hope and recovery: A scoping review. *Advances in Dual Diagnosis*, *7*(2), 63–72. doi:10.1108/ADD-10-2013-0024

Thomas, L. (2002). Poststructuralism and therapy – what's it all about? *The International Journal of Narrative Therapy and Community Work*, *2*(2), 85–89. Retrieved 2 December 2020 from https://search.informit.org/doi/10.3316/informit.126462957543424

24 *A narrative family psychiatrist*

Turns, B. A., & Kimmes, J. (2013). "I'm NOT the Problem!" Externalizing Children's "Problems" Using play therapy and developmental considerations. *Contemporary Family Therapy*, *36*(1), 3–15. doi:10.1007/s10591-013-9285-z

White, M. (2002). Addressing personal failure. In *Narrative practice and exotic lives: Resurrecting diversity in everyday life* (pp. 149–232). Dulwich Centre Publications.

White, M., & Epston, D. (1990). *Narrative means to therapeutic ends.* W.W. Norton & Company.

2 Collaborative family therapy

The aim of the Family Therapy Team is to be a co-traveller with the family on their journey towards a better future. We collaborate with, rather than "operate on", the family. Our stance is based on respect, curiosity, trust, and hope in co-creating treatment with our patient and their family. This chapter describes the structure of our collaborative family therapy, as described in our guide (Jørring & Juul, 2013, 2018).

Basic principles and practices of collaboration involve:

- Meeting the person with the expectation that they are worthy of our deepest respect.
- Sharing the power of decision-making with the family.
- Sharing expert and insider knowledge instead of prescribing it.

When I began training in child and adolescent psychiatry in the 1990s, I learned that patients should be assessed to determine if they could benefit from psychotherapy. I needed to assess if the patient had sufficient psychological mindedness for this treatment. Assessments that focus on the patient's ability continue to prevail today (Balkin & Juhnke, 2014) but a better approach is to co-assess with the patient and family to determine which treatment is most suitable for them (Anderson & Gehart, 2007; Corrigan, 2002).

Most evidence-based psychotherapy focuses on specific therapies for specific diagnoses (Carr, 2000; Fonagy et al., 2016). However, in Child and Adolescent Mental Health Services, we typically meet children with several diagnoses and complex issues. They live in families with problems and issues that do not exist in separate boxes. Family life is messy, and we have to create treatments that can handle messiness (Madsen, 2009, p. 104).

We co-create our treatment in line with the family's goals. Together, we design and evaluate the treatment with the family to create empowerment (Corrigan et al., 2012; Warner, 2010). This collaborative form of treatment is based on the basic ethics of respect, curiosity, trust, and hope and is tailored to each individual family (Ejbye-Ernst & Jørring, 2017; Ejbye-Ernst et al., 2015; Jørring & Gjessing Jensen, 2018; Jørring & Jacobsen, 2014; Jørring & Juul, 2013, 2018).

DOI: 10.4324/9781003171621-3

26 *Collaborative family therapy*

The basic structure of our collaborative family therapy course involves:

- Three phases: clarification, working, and conclusion.
- The family decides who shall attend the sessions, how often we meet, and if and when we meet with the school or social worker.
- We schedule five consecutive sessions followed by a "taking stock session" to co-evaluate progress and to make any adjustments.
- We strive for transparency. For instance, we write all of our notes on a paper chart[1] for everyone in the meeting to see.
- We share our thoughts and considerations, by sending a therapeutic letter by e-mail after each session instead of confining progress notes in medical records.
- We begin each therapeutic session with the family by reading the letter (sent after the previous session) aloud, as a ceremonious opening.
- The family decides with us when to conclude treatment.

Becoming the family's appreciative partner

Katja, the mother of Filippa, is my co-writer for this story.

Nina: I received a referral for Katja's daughter, Filippa, a 13-year-old girl. The referral described Filippa as having generalized anxiety disorder and early symptoms of anorexia nervosa that had been addressed unsuccessfully. Cognitive behavioural therapy for Filippa's anxiety had been effective but only temporarily. The conclusions were that Filippa and her mother Katja shared an unhealthy relationship (Freeman et al., 1997, pp. 75–93; Harrington, 2016). The referral indicated the mother might have her own issues with anxiety and depicted her as a sustaining factor for Filippa's anxiety. I called Katja to invite her to our first meeting. I described our context, our practices, and our values for treatment, to provide Katja with enough knowledge to make an informed and shared decision on the proposed treatment (White et al., 2003). This is our standard introduction:

> *Nina:* We are a small team that meets with families who have a child with one or more psychiatric diagnoses. Each family is very different. I think the only thing they have in common is that they haven't received enough help with those diagnoses and problems in order to live the life they have hoped for and want to live.
>
> We focus on the family's perspective. We can meet with you and any other family members you would like to be involved. We can also meet with Filippa's schoolteacher and the social worker, if you want.

Collaborative family therapy 27

We base our work on a special theory. We believe a psychiatric illness affects more than one person in a family, and when one person suffers, the entire family is impacted. We also believe that there is nothing wrong with the child; it is the problem that is the problem. We know for sure that the parents are essential to their child, and that parents will go through hell to help their child. Our job is to help everybody in the family to find ways to work together and get the upper hand on the problem.

We want to be the family's appreciative allies (Madsen, 2007, pp. 22–24), and we speak a special "language", to make it easier to talk about problems, without creating a lot of fighting. Initially, we meet with families once a week for an hour, and less frequently as treatment progresses, depending on each family's wish.

Our first conversation enables us to get to know each other. We want you to get a sense of who we are, and if we can be of help to you. Also, we will figure out whether we think we can help you. Some parents prefer to attend the first session alone, others want to bring their child or all of their children along. That's for you to decide.

Is this what you expected me to tell you?

Katja: Yes, I think so. What have you heard about us?

Nina: Well, Filippa's medical record is very thick, and I have not read it all. But let me tell you what I know from the referral. Filippa has been diagnosed with anxiety and has had many kinds of therapy that have been helpful for short periods only. Also, Filippa is not eating properly, and the doctor is concerned that her anxiety has transitioned to anorexia. Does this sound like what you would like me to know?

Nina: With this approach, I demonstrated that I expected the parent, Katja, to be a true participant in our collaboration.

Katja: My experience in meeting the family therapy team was very different from previous meetings with other health professionals. We had been given about 15 sessions with a psychologist for Filippa at the previous place, and I did not feel met or understood. Our psychologist never related well with us. I sometimes felt that she seemed a little unempathetic. A little thing that matters to me as a human being was that she never smiled at us. We felt like a task to be solved.

Katja: I would like to attend the first session with you alone, because Filippa has already met many people and I prefer to talk about some things with you first. Is this okay?

28 *Collaborative family therapy*

> *Nina:* Yes, of course. Many parents want to see who we are, before allowing their child to meet yet another stranger. Shall we try to find a date that fits for you?

Nina: Why did I speak to Katja this way? What was my purpose? In my experience, most families are weary of psychiatry. My hypothesis is, that scared thoughts occupy their mind, both in terms of meeting with us and of the outcome for their child's future. This might influence how they hear what I say.

Katja: This is true. I had previously met therapists who were quick to form opinions and make their own conclusion, based on ignorance, because the therapist hadn't understood the situation or listened properly to what I was telling them.

Nina: The Family Therapy Team's aim is to build a comfortable, egalitarian relationship with parents. This is a necessary step towards creating empowerment and personal agency (Corrigan, 2002; Corrigan et al., 2012). Katja and I found a date and time that worked well for both of us and exchanged e-mail addresses.

Making the first call to introduce myself is critical to our alliance with the families. Patients usually receive a notification by e-mail for the first appointment. Initially, we found that many families called our secretary to change the appointment and often shared their problems with her. This gave our secretary a lot of work, but she also obtained valuable information. We changed this, so the therapist calls the family to introduce our approach and agree on a date for the first session. This simple procedure helps us to build a stronger relationship with the family from the start, and the "no show" has dropped to zero.

The Worry Mum or the Mama Bear?

Nina: When Katja came to our first session, she initially seemed hesitant. I sensed Katja was trying to ascertain if I was trustworthy, even though she seemed burdened, talking about a daughter clearly suffering from both anxiety and an eating disorder. Her attitude earned my respect. Katja was not going to submit her daughter to yet another stranger unless she believed I could do the job.

Katja: One of the first things Nina said was that the trip, by train and bus, must have been terribly long for me. As if Nina had a crystal ball and had seen how my journey had been! I politely replied that the trip hadn't been so bad. I was more worried about whether I could ever persuade Filippa to go on that trip. Filippa suffered from anxiety about transport (if she saw a helicopter, for instance, she assumed it had been hijacked by a terrorist who wanted to hurt people, including us). Quite soon into our conversation, Nina said, "I'm pretty sure I can

Collaborative family therapy 29

help your daughter". Hearing Nina's words was a weight off my shoulders. I wondered if Nina heard the 30 kg fall to the floor. I was so relieved! I felt I could believe Nina!

Nina: Katja's comment speaks to the hope that health professionals must hold for families when their own hope has vanished (Acharya & Agius, 2017). During our first session, I began by introducing myself, describing my respect for parents, and my values for therapy. When children "fail" in therapy and health professionals describe the actions of parents as "sustaining factors for the illness", these derogatory judgments become obstacles to treatment and contaminate the therapeutic relationship with parent blame (Harrington, 2016; Jackson & Mannix, 2004; Jensen, 2018). Since I suspected Katja was heavily burdened by parent blame, I said, "In my experience, parents are the best allies for their children. I have never met a parent that wanted to hurt their child, but I have met many parents who have gone through great stress to help their children. So, you must know up front, that I expect to hear stories about how you have fought for your daughter, and I expect to be humbled by what you tell me".

Katja: As Filippa's mum, I was worried and did not know how best to help her. Finding help took a long time and there were many obstacles. For example, the school, which did not experience problems with Filippa in class, took one year to refer her to the school psychologist. As the single mother of two girls, I sometimes thought, "Am I the only one who can't figure it out?" I felt pressed and worn out because Filippa's anxiety consumed the family's energy, like a blood-sucking parasite! We needed help, but when the system you access responds with misunderstanding or inadequate knowledge, the feeling of hopeful support and trust can quickly turn to feel infinitely vulnerable and exposed. That's why I was pleased to meet Nina, in a relaxed, and accepting, and open-minded way. Everything about Nina signalled this positivity, verbally and non-verbally. Filippa was happy that I was allowed to participate, and I learned so much. Nina's office was decorated in a comfortable, child-friendly way. We sat around a small, low, round table. Even the shapes of the furniture matter and this consulting room was welcoming and comfortable. We did not need to spend a lot of time preparing for sessions, which was a relief as previous treatments had involved time-consuming homework. I never managed to do these homework exercises properly. Regardless of all the carrots in the world, and all the motivation or pressure, I could not persuade Filippa to do the exercises. I felt like an abuser every time. I was a mother, not a therapist. The problem then was that the anxiety had no respect for me, and sometimes it could scare me as well.

Nina: As the inherent hierarchal relationships that normally govern us would be counter-therapeutic and add to Katja's sense of being inferior,

30   *Collaborative family therapy*

I wanted to ask Katja for permission to see her daughter. I wanted to flip the power hierarchy around intentionally, for the purpose of building Katja's feelings of self-worth (Madigan, 1992). This standard, often-used question usually leads people to share their dreams and provides directions and "lighthouses" to aim for:

> *Nina:* If you allow me to meet with your daughter together with you, and if what we do together is to be helpful for both of you, what differences or changes do you imagine will be good in your daily life, that are impossible right now?

Nina: Katja didn't respond as I had expected, so I let it go and followed her lead. I knew I could circle back to the question later.

> *Katja* I would like to tell our story first, so you know why I am here. Is that okay?
>
> *Nina:* Of course, I gather more knowledge from parents sharing their stories than from reading medical records, so go ahead.

Nina: Parents are often burdened by the knowledge that health professionals are in a hurry, and typically, they don't want to waste our time. But when we rush, try to cut corners, stick to checklists and demand a family's history in record time, we miss the most important information. Building reciprocal trust takes time. Listening to a parent's story, told at their own pace, is a good investment. As Katja shared her story, I was amazed by how two different versions of the same story competed to be the true and dominating story (Morgan, 2000, pp. 5–16). One story described a woman who had stood up for herself and her children, had shouldered responsibilities on her own, had a keen sense of her child's needs, and came up against authorities, who were negligent to her reasonable pleas for help. The other story described Katja as a failure, a woman who hadn't made wise decisions, was needy, scared and had transferred her worrisome nature to her children. I liked the first story and thought it could be helpful for Katja by giving her confidence in herself, providing strength to carry on and supporting her in striving for a better life. Katja's second story seemed to shackle her with self-blame, insecurity, and feelings of disability. Katja looked confused when I wrote sentences that supported and acknowledged each story on my paper chart. She seemed to expect me to support the more negative story, but nevertheless, wanted me to hear both stories. I wanted to acknowledge both stories, respecting that no story ever holds all the truth and nothing but the truth. But I also wanted to explore Katja's relationship with

Collaborative family therapy 31

each story. I imagined that she would have more options for actions and experiences, and more personal agency, when describing herself as the Mama Bear, rather than as a Worry Mum.

Katja: I was relieved to feel understood when I met Nina. At times, I had felt exposed and feared that the authorities might deem us a dysfunctional family. I feared being labelled a Worry Mum and being considered the reason why Filippa was not getting rid of her anxiety. The assertions were frustrating and felt evil. Such prejudices can have fatal consequences for a mother, child, or whole family.

Nina: After this first session, Katja wanted to return with Filippa as soon as possible. She knew that getting her daughter to take the necessary transport would be hard work, so I suggested that I would write a letter to Filippa if Katja thought doing so may be helpful. Katja agreed this was a good idea. I began the letter by asking Katja to decide whether this letter would be good for her daughter as a therapeutic stance, acknowledging that she has expert knowledge about her daughter and will know best. This is an example of "not-knowing" (Anderson, 2005):

Dear Katja,

As promised, I have written a letter addressed to Filippa. I want you to decide if you want to read it to Filippa. I look forward to seeing you again and meeting Filippa.

Dear Filippa,

I met your mother for the first time last Tuesday. It was an exciting meeting where I heard your mother's story about your upbringing, a little about your sister, Isabella, and a lot about what a powerful mother you have. In fact, I got a picture of a mother who has an iron will. I wondered, after your mother had left, if you also have an iron will and whether you are also a take-action person?

I probably get these thoughts because your mother told me about the special bond you two share. You were the first-born and were tiny at birth. So, it was important that your mother had both an iron will and was vigorous, to help you survive those first months of your life, and to grow up to become the lovely girl you are today.

Your mother used expressions like "the invisible navel cord that cannot be cut" and "telepathy" between the two of you. I imagine that you might not look robust on the outside, but that you are strong and powerful inside. Your mother looks gentle and sensitive, but I quickly got the feeling that she has fought like a Mama Bear for her two daughters. She described how she's

32 *Collaborative family therapy*

promised you that if she must crawl all the way to my office on her knees, she will do so to help you fight your anxiety. That has impressed me!

I also heard about the many ways you have struggled with anxiety; how you have had to shoulder it all on your own. I heard that there are always worry-thoughts that you might be coming down with some dangerous illness. I didn't get to ask your mum much about this, but I got curious to know if your anxiety not only gives you ugly thoughts but also can create unpleasant feelings in your body? Everyone knows about having butterflies in their stomach, when they are nervous. But some people can get heart palpitations, so they think their heart is racing out of their body, others get pains in their muscles. I imagine your anxiety is one of the bad ones, is that correct?

I would love to meet with you and hear about your anxiety. But first, I want to hear more about who you are when the anxiety is not in your life or when it doesn't ruin too much of your life.[2] I want to hear about what you use your powers for, if you also have an iron will; what you like best about your school, and what you do in your spare time, who the most important people are in your life, do you have any close friends? Do you have a favourite hobby? How do you feel about Isabella?

I hope to see you soon,

Nina.[3]

Nina: Filippa agreed to attend the next appointment and later, I also met her younger sister, Isabella.

Katja: Although Filippa's anxiety was severe, she liked that it wasn't "heavy and severe" when we talked about it at Nina's place. Our conversations helped us to understand what mechanisms were at play when the anxiety came. We talked about it together, and sometimes Nina gave Filippa suggestions on how to deal with the anxiety. Filippa really liked it when Nina occasionally added some humour. Filippa has quite a sense of humour. Nina wrote and drew on her large paper chart in front of us. Visually, we saw our own story, and sometimes she asked Filippa to come up and draw on the paper (how Filippa experienced it in her thoughts). Our life story took shape and often connections were made…giving us a visual "aha" experience, especially about how anxiety affects people. At times, Nina referred to the experiences of other children in therapy and their

Collaborative family therapy 33

mothers. It was interesting, and we felt relieved to hear we were not alone. There were others "out there" like us.

Can we join you in your struggles?

As we saw in Chapter 1, Valiant's parents felt deep despair when the health professionals did not understand their view of their son's problem. Our first conversation had focused on hope, and this led to descriptions of how each parent dealt differently with their hopes. They kept repeating that they were scared but were hoping to find ways to help Valiant. They described different situations where they felt lost. Valiant had once talked about tigers he saw on the street, and the parents had no idea how to respond to this. Anna's biggest hope was that she once again would be able to shoulder her responsibility of helping her son.

Being scared and trying to hold onto hope are two different ways of looking at the same situation. Narrative therapists attend to the absent but implicit (Freedman, 2012; White, 2000), telling us that holding onto hope gives a lot more agency than feeling scared. This is what we built on in our letter to Valiant's parents after our first conversation:

Dear Anna and Bertie,

This is our first letter to you. We would like you to know that if we write anything you cannot recognize, if you feel misunderstood, or if our letter in any other way seems useless, please ignore it. You are welcome to write back, but we do not expect you to, and we may not have time to reply. We will begin our next conversation by reading this letter aloud. We will not read this letter if you bring your son Valiant, as he was not with us today. We always read aloud a letter that has been written to those people who attended the session. Does this make sense?

After you left, Kirsten and I talked about Anna's hope. We think you are hoping that if you could understand what is going on inside Valiant's brain, this would provide ideas about how best to help him. So, we each thought about books, written by people who have had schizophrenia in their lives. Kirsten remembered a nurse who wrote that she learned to become curious about each concrete word. For example, what did "tigers on the street" mean for Valiant exactly on that day and at that time? Not because we want to interpret, but because we are curious. Are tigers monsters? Something dangerous? A cat? Something to cuddle?

This got my thoughts going. I remembered a book by Norwegian psychologist, Arnhild Lauveng, who developed schizophrenia as a young girl (Lauveng, 2012). I believe she described that it was as if her ability to hold onto her own thoughts had disappeared, and the thoughts tumbled around inside her brain. As she was unable to control her thoughts, they changed from words to pictures, took on weird shapes and colours, and

34 *Collaborative family therapy*

became creepy or soft without meaning. Arnhild described how, late one night, she got scared of wolves following her on her way home. Later, when she became well again, she suddenly understood that it had been her thoughts taking form as wolves that had been tormenting her. She had tried to run from the wolves in the night, but we can't run from our own thoughts, and Arnhild had experienced the wolves as hunting her. I am trying, in a few sentences, to retell something Lauveng has used many pages to describe.

I have no idea whether the book will be helpful for you to read. What I remember best is Lauveng's interpretation of mental illness:

> Mentally ill people are just as different as others. We must ask in each case, how does this person want to be helped? As a patient I was told that I should be patient, humble and resigned. But when I received an award for my work, the reason was that I was strong, courageous and defiant. Precisely the qualities that were prerequisites for me to recover.[4]

You told us that since you know the healthy Valiant, you can see his fabulations reminding you a little of his once charming humour. You can see that his wish for being in your bed cuddling the dog, fits well with the loving and very physical boy who, even though fairly big, still likes to hold hands with you when you walk in the woods.

You can find meaning in some of those things that others view only as symptoms of disease. I get the sense that this speaks to what Bertie spoke of. Can you support Valiant by expanding these positive narratives about who he is?

Maybe you are on the right path?

Best wishes,
Kirsten and Nina

True collaboration demands that we expect the people we collaborate with to have knowledge that we do not have, that their knowledge will have an equal value to ours, and that they will be equally essential to the success of the project.

Notes

1 The paper chart is an easel with a paper roll. That's our "notepad". We make notes on a big board, so the patient and family can see what we write. The paper chart and "public note-taking" are explained in Chapter 5.
2 Read more about wonderfulness-interviewing before we get to the problem in Chapter 3.
3 This was not a standard invitation letter. Find an example of a standard invitation letter to children with autism in the Addendum.
4 This is my translation from an interview with Lauveng in a Danish newspaper in 2008: https://jyllands-posten.dk/kultur/anmeldelser/litteratur/ECE4358466/arnhild-lauveng-i-morgen-var-jeg-altid-en-loeve/

References

Acharya, T., & Agius, M. (2017). The importance of hope against other factors in the recovery of mental illness. *Psychiatria Danubina*, *29*(Suppl 3), 619–622.

Anderson, H. (2005). Myths about "Not-knowing". *Family Process*, *44*, 497–504.

Anderson, H., & Gehart. D. (2007). *Collaborative therapy. Relationships and conversations that make a difference.* Routledge.

Balkin, R. S., & Juhnke, G. A. (2014). *The theory and practice of assessment in counseling.* Pearson.

Carr, A. (Ed.) (2000). *What works with children and adolescents?: A Critical review of psychological interventions with children, adolescents and their families.* Routledge.

Corrigan, P. W. (2002). Empowerment and serious mental illness: Treatment partnerships and community opportunities. *Psychiatric Quarterly*, *73*(3), 217–228. doi:10.1023/A: 1016040805432

Corrigan, P. W., et al. (2012). From adherence to self-determination: Evolution of a treatment paradigm for people with serious mental illnesses. *Psychiatric Services*, *63*(2), 169–173. doi:10.1176/appi.ps.201100065

Ejbye-Ernst, D., & Jorring, N. T. (2017). Doing it collaboratively! Addressing the dilemmas of designing quantitative effect studies on narrative family therapy in a local clinical context. *Journal of Systemic Therapies*, *36*(1), 48–66. doi:10.1521/jsyt.2017.36.1.48

Ejbye-Ernst, D., Jorring, N. T., & Jacobsen, C. B. (2015). Klientperspektiver på anvendelsen af sporgeskemaer i opstartsfasen af et psykoterapeutisk behandlingsforlob. *Fokus på familien*, *43*(2), 109–125. doi:10.18261/ISSN0807-7487-2015-02-

Fonagy, P., Cotrell, D., Phillips, J., Bevington, D., Glaser, D., & Allison, E. (2016). *What works for whom?: A critical review of psychotherapy research.* Guilford Press.

Freedman, J. (2012). Explorations of the absent but implicit. *The International Journal of Narrative Therapy and Community Work*, 4 (4), 1–10.

Freeman, J., Epston, D., & Lobovits, D. (1997). *Playful Approaches to Serious Problems.* W. W. Norton.

Harrington, A. (2016). Mother love and mental illness: An emotional history. *Osiris*, *31*(1), 94–115. doi:10.1086/687559

Jackson, D., & Mannix, J. (2004). Giving voice to the burden of blame: a feminist study of mothers' experiences of mother blaming. *International Journal of Nursing Practice*, *10*(4), 150–158. doi:10.1111/j.1440-172X.2004.00474.x

Jensen, T. (2018). *Parenting the crisis: The cultural politics of parent-blame.* Bristol, UK: Policy Press.

Jørring, N. T., & Gjessing Jensen, K. (2018). Treatment efficacy of narrative family therapy for children and adolescents with diverse psychiatric symptomatology. *The Scandinavian Journal of Child and Adolescent Psychiatry and Psychology*, *6*(2), 107–114. doi:10.21307/sjcapp-2018-012

Jorring, N. T., & Jacobsen, C.B. (2014). Narrative Therapy in CAMHS: Creating Multistoried Treatments. *Journal of Systemic Therapies*, *33*(1), 89–101. doi:10.1521/jsyt. 2014.33.1.89

Jorring, N. T., & Juul, J. (2013). Collaborative Family therapy with psychiatric multi-stressed families. Retrieved 8 June 2021 from https://www.researchgate.net/publication/336512754_English_manual_rev_October_2013

Jorring, N. T., & Juul, J. (2018). Manual for Samarbejdende familieterapi. Retrieved 8 June 2021 from https://www.researchgate.net/publication/329269185_Manual_for_Samarbejdende_familieterapi

36 *Collaborative family therapy*

Lauveng, A. (2012). *A road back from Schizophrenia: A memoir* (S. S. Østtveit, Trans.). Skyhorse Publishing, Inc.

Madigan, S. P. (1992). The application of Michel Foucault's philosophy in the problem externalizing discourse of Michael White. *Journal of Family Therapy, 14*(3), 265–279. doi:10.1046/j..1992.00458.x

Madsen, W. C. (2007). *Collaborative therapy with multi-stressed families* (2nd ed.). The Guilford Press.

Madsen, W. C. (2009). Collaborative helping: A practice framework for family-centered services. *Family Process, 48*(1), 103–116. doi:10.1111/j.1545-5300.2009.01270.x

Morgan, A. (2000). *What is narrative therapy?: An easy-to-read introduction.*Adelaide, Australia Dulwich Centre Publications.

Warner, R. (2010). Does the scientific evidence support the recovery model? *The Psychiatrist, 34*, 3–5.

White, M. (2000). Re-engaging with history: The absent but implicit. In *Reflections on narrative practice: Essays & interviews* (pp. 35–58). Adelaide: Dulwhich Centre Publications.

White, M. K., Keller, V., & Horrigan, L. A. (2003). Beyond informed consent: The shared decision making process. *JCOM*, 10 (6), 323–328. Retrieved 5 June 2021 from https://www.researchgate.net/profile/Maysel-White/publication/252846413_ Beyond_Informed_Consent_The_Shared_Decision_Making_Process/links/56982fd908aea 2d74375ecaf/Beyond-Informed-Consent-The-Shared-Decision-Making-Process.pdf

3 I am not the problem! We are the heroes!

What makes a parent feel warm inside when they think about their child?

This chapter presents examples of how we greet families who are heavily burdened with problems. The first conversation is crucial to our future collaboration with both children and adults. We seek to get to know people as they are, separate from their problems, before we hear about the problems. In the first interview and in every subsequent interaction, we seek to find the magical wonderfulness in their intentions and actions to awaken our own curiosity (Marsten et al., 2016).

The first part of this chapter's title comes from a note scribbled by a young child during their first meeting with us. Imagine how the children of these families might benefit by changing the family narrative from one of negativity to, "We are the heroes!"

The wonderfulness interview

You may have taken a patient's history as part of a medical assessment many times. But have you wondered about the effect on the family of how you do this assessment?

We believe it is unprofessional to ask about problems and illnesses before creating a relationship built on respect, curiosity, trust and hope (Madsen, 2006, p. 49). Therefore, interviewing the child and parents about the child's wonderfulnesses is a cornerstone of our treatment.

David Epston was the first therapist to use wonderfulness interviewing to get to know patients before getting to know about their problem(s) (Marsten et al., 2016). The intention is to "team up" with the child and their parents against the problem (Epston, 2016, p. 63; Freeman et al., 1997, pp. 34–46). Wonderfulnesses are all those things that make you feel warm inside, proud and grateful about your child, your child's values, competences and dreams.

We ask wonderfulness-questions to get to know the best possible version of the patient and the family, before we learn about the problems. We seek to help our patients and their families to find or regain their moral voice and speak through that to the sources of their sufferings, whether a psychiatric illness or other problem (Epston, 2008, p. 175). This procedure gives the

DOI: 10.4324/9781003171621-4

38   *I am not the problem! We are the heroes!*

family a platform to stand on, when they describe the externalized problem (Madsen, 2007, pp. 28–32; Marsten et al., 2016, pp. 27–47).

Most families wonder why we want to interview them about the wonderful traits that define their child or family unit. We explain how these interviews provide information that can counteract the problems their family is facing. For example, we might say:

> You are probably very wise and can talk easily about the problems you have, but I wonder if you are as wise about how wonderful you are, as well. How brave and courageous, loving and creative, caring and conscientious you are. We want to know all about how wonderful you are, because that's the information we need to help you find your way towards the better life you dream about. Okay?

Alternatively:

> Most people expect to tell us about the problems right away. But is it okay if we first get to know you as you are, when you are not troubled by problems? We want to get to know you as you are when mastering life in the best way you know. This will help us help you to outsmart your problems.

A standard approach is followed for these wonderfulness interviews. We start by drawing a stick figure of a boy or girl in the middle of the paper chart, and explain to the child:

> I'm going to ask your parents how wonderful you are. I'll ask them to speak to me, so you do not have to respond to what they're saying. Of course, if they say something you don't agree with, you can correct them. But all you really have to do, is sit back and enjoy being praised.

Experience has revealed that most of the children who come to our clinic have heard too much about how problematic they are. So, we tell them:

> I want to give you one hour of feeling good about yourself, to feel praised and cared for, to know you're worthy of being loved dearly, as I know that your parents love you. Is this okay with you?

We then say to the child's parents:

> Dear Parents, imagine standing at the door to your child's room, when your child was a baby. Your baby is peacefully asleep. Do you remember experiencing the feeling of gratefulness, for having this child in your life? Can you feel the love in your stomach and your heart? It's quite overwhelming, right? Can you describe what is so special about your child, that creates these wonderful feelings?

Most parents respond by saying their child is "caring", "loving", and "humorous".

We choose one of their words, and ask:

> Can you tell me a specific story, that illustrates this "caring" (or the word they have said) that you appreciate so much?

In our mind we have different scenarios that we perform during our lives. We could be at home, school/kindergarten, with the extended family or friends (parental or the child's), participating in extracurricular activities (sports, hobbies) or religious activities (church, synagogue, mosque, temple, customs at home) and engaging in future dreams (lovers, the family the child will create, our job). Sometimes we are inspired to add other scenarios. As the parents speak, we draw lines in a star-like fashion and fill the pages with scenarios, values and qualities about the child.

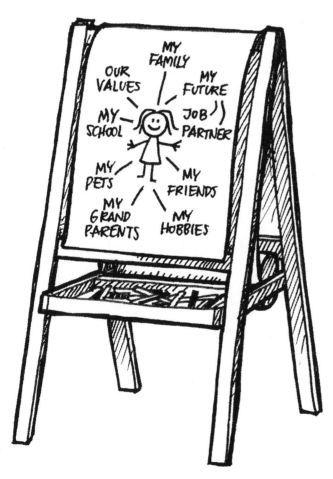

The scenarios gradually become more illuminated and detailed by asking questions such as:

- Is this something you have heard from teachers?
- Do you see this when your child is with their grandparents, or do they act differently then?

We also ask the parents about intentions and values, and broaden the narratives to include the family, so the child is connected to their parents. For instance, we ask the parents:

- Do you have any idea about what your child hopes to achieve or why this is important?
- Is this a family-value?
- A trait that they got from you?
- Do you also value this?

When we take time to do this, we create thick descriptions opposed to thin descriptions about values, dreams, and competencies. The thick descriptions become the resilience that will stand up against the negative dominant stories about a child being the problem (Ungar, 2005).

The wonderful stick girl

When we met Angie, we said, "We want to start by getting to know you outside the influences of the problem because this knowledge will help us find ways to 'outsmart' your problems".

Angie had been in the mental health system since she was 11-years-old and had been diagnosed with anorexia. When we met her for the first time, she was 14. Angie's anorexia was extremely powerful and would only allow her parents Mary and John to feed her nutritious drinks, her sole nourishment, through a straw when she was in bed under her duvet. My colleagues thought Angie should be admitted to a treatment facility away from her parents. But Mary and John didn't believe this approach would help Angie. They also were reluctant to allow Angie to meet yet another doctor.

With Mary and John, we explored how we could begin the creation of a positive relationship with Angie. The parents were certain Angie would refuse to participate in any meetings. I could have viewed this as parental resistance, but I chose to explore what knowledge they had, that would explain their prediction. This led me to suggest that I could get to know Angie outside the influences of her problem (Madsen, 2007, pp. 172–173) by interviewing Mary and John about how wonderful they found Angie, when she was listening. She could be silent during the entire session if she chose. The parents liked this idea but said they didn't believe that I would be able to only ask about the wonderfulnesses of their daughter.

I am not the problem! We are the heroes! 41

To reassure the parents, I wrote a letter that they could show to Angie about my plans, and I promised not to ask Angie any unpleasant questions. When I met Angie for the first time, I drew the stick-girl on my paper chart and asked her parents to describe the ways in which their daughter was wonderful. Angie's reaction was overwhelming because she not only chose to stay for the entire meeting, but she also took the paper chart home. Her parents later said Angie had shown the paper to her grandmother, which demonstrated how important the experience had been to Angie. This may have been the first time anyone had explored who Angie was when she had reason to be respected and proud about herself.

The paper chart that Angie took home that day described:

- Angie as a committed handball player, and her father and younger brother as committed soccer players.
- Family traits as focused, detail oriented and academically ambitious.
- Angie's small dog (given to her during her illness) with a focus on how Angie trained it and the love between the dog and girl.

I often reflected on this first meeting in subsequent years as Angie continued to struggle with her relationships with anorexia and Asperger's syndrome, social phobia, self-harm and other insecurities. My hope was that Angie never doubted my great respect for her, that I saw her as much more than a girl with diagnoses, and that I wanted the best for her.

As we continued working together, we found the best narrative to explain Angie's struggles was that her anorexia had tried to help her cope with the problems that the undiagnosed Asperger's syndrome had presented (Nickel et al., 2019). Angie, Mary and John had been unaware of the Asperger's syndrome, until several years after the arrival of anorexia and self-harm.

When Angie was 16-years-old, the anorexia yet again tried to steal her life. This time it destroyed her dream of enrolment at a residential sports college. At this point, my knowledge about the pet dog's love and de-pendence on her enabled the creation of a pathway away from a slow suicide, inspired by David's and Tom Carlson's article, *There's Always a Puppy* (Carlson, 2016).

The combination of an eating disorder and autism-spectrum disorder is difficult to live with. However, Angie slowly progressed supported by the collaboration between the parents, a school for autistic children, the social worker, a psychologist who specialized in working with children with autism, and our team. We all met regularly, focusing on creating a mutual under-standing of how Angie and her parents fought to change her relationships with anorexia and Asperger's syndrome to get her life back. My aim was to hold Mary's and John's knowledge and goals as our guiding lights.

Angie achieved a healthy weight at age 18 and began engaging in the social life of a healthy young adult. She continued her therapy with her parents to find ways to better cope with her Asperger's syndrome, that she never saw as

42   *I am not the problem! We are the heroes!*

an illness. Angie created a calm and mutually respectful relationship with her Asperger's syndrome.

> The way you used the paper chart to record the positive things we talk about has been very useful. It has helped us to remember and hold onto those messages.
>
> Your letters with follow-up from the conversations were valuable, especially for us parents, because your messages were always appreciative, positive and encouraging. This meant a lot when we were going through difficult times.
>
> We benefited from your direct and honest approach, while at the same time, feeling encouraged to give feedback when we did not share the same view as you. It was also great when you brought yourself and your own experiences into play, as this made the conversation more secure and transparent.
>
> Mary

I'm often humbled by parents mentioning how much they appreciate the personal inclusion, transparency, honesty and the opportunity to disagree (Besley, 2010). Seeing disagreement as an invitation and responding openly and respectfully is necessary for true collaboration. Mary's words speak to the ethics of our practices, meeting people as wonderful heroes in their own lives and stories.

The wonderful children, parents, and autisms

One day, Em and Dave (see Chapter 1) brought both their daughters to meet us. We had met with the eldest daughter, Flora, before but this was our first time meeting with Gloria. By now, Flora was six-years-old, and Gloria was four-years-old. Their younger ages shaped our approach. Flora had autism, and her problems included imagining what others may be thinking, and that others may think and feel differently to her. From previous meetings with Flora, we hypothesized that she would benefit from short, concrete sentences. So, we focused on narratives about actions.

My colleague, Kirsten, and I introduced ourselves with few words and sentences, focusing on things we thought may interest the girls. I said:

> I have three boys. When one was in first grade, just like you, a girl wanted to come home with him for a play date, but my son became scared. He said, "Mum, what should I do? We don't have any girls in our house, we don't know anything about girls!"
>
> I replied, "In my work I meet a lot of wonderful girls who are your age. I know all about girls. I was a girl myself, when I was younger. It's going to be okay; I can help you".

I am not the problem! We are the heroes! 43

This story always generates a lot of laughter. It sets a good tone, the children know that I have children, and that I'm probably a pretty normal and non-scary person (Roberts, 2005).

We then told the girls we wanted to know about how wonderful they are:

> You probably know that we meet with families who have problems. We help parents to create a more pleasant family life, with less fighting or anything else that is making life more difficult. When we meet a family for the first time, we want to learn how wonderful that family is. How the parents love their children and what they are most proud of. We ask them to brag about their kids and if the children want to share what they are good at, we want to hear all about that too.
>
> But there are rules. When we ask you something, you're allowed not to answer. Or you can ask your parents to answer for you. If this happens, then it's our fault, as we have asked something you don't feel comfortable answering. Also, unlike at school, here, you can interrupt whenever you want to. If you don't agree with the answers your parents give, you can correct them. Okay?

The rules are paraphrased differently depending on whether the child is more inhibited, and needs encouragement, or has a wild Attention-Deficit and Hyperactivity Disorder (ADHD) that will wreak havoc in the room. We may also talk about taking turns to speak, and about how we can avoid interrupting each other.

We knew that Em and Dave felt bad about how Flora's autism meant it was difficult for her to fulfil the role of being an older sister, taking into account her younger sister's age and wishes. The parents felt sad and burdened because their girls did not seem to be able to play together. Their dream of their daughters being best friends did not look promising. We were interested in exploring how much and how little the girls were able to do together, so we formulated questions to explore this. We hoped to identify any exceptions, however small, that could challenge the belief that the girls were unable to do anything together.

We were searching for unique outcomes that could lead to re-authoring their narratives. We wanted to create a counter story to the dominant story about the family being considered a failure because the girls could not play together (White, 2007, pp. 61–128). Our theory was that if we could find small exceptions, they might provide a starting point for developing these new stories. We also wanted to better understand Flora's challenges in addition to autism. If autism-related, what specific problems did they present? This knowledge would be valuable for us when meeting with Em and Dave in other sessions, enabling us to guide them in providing an autism-friendly environment for Flora's development, so she could learn at her own pace.

44   I am not the problem! We are the heroes!

An exciting breakthrough came when the family told us about an invention we had not heard about before, a "Children Decide Day". This was Em's own creation, whereby on a Saturday or a Sunday, when the parents had no plans, their daughters were placed in charge. There were clear guidelines for the things on which they could make decisions, such as when and what to eat, what games to play and when to sleep. Clear guidelines also were provided on what the girls could not decide, for example, when Mum or Dad needed to go to the toilet. This conversation created many opportunities for laughter.

This is the letter we e-mailed afterwards to Em and Dave:

Dear Flora and Gloria, and your mum and dad,

Thank you so much for visiting us, Flora and Gloria. You helped us to create an impressive list about all of the things you two like to do together. You are both helpful and caring towards each other.

While we spoke, we got to see how skilful Gloria is at writing her own name with Flora's help. Flora, you are a clever big sister for knowing how to help Gloria in that way. No wonder Gloria is so fond of you. We are impressed that a four-year-old girl can write her own name!

Here are some of the things we heard you both like:

- To play make-believe roles together. For example, you like to be mermaids, shopkeepers and ghosts.
- The water park – both of you love to play in the water.
- To tease each other in a fun way (we wonder if Dad needs a little help in understanding why you enjoy the teasing).
- "Children-Decide-Day": On these days, it is totally clear what one may decide and what one may not decide.
- Recalling the happy experiences, you have shared together.
- Helping your granddad.
- Watching television together.
- Knowing exactly what is going to happen, when this will start and stop, and who will be involved.

We also heard that Flora:

- Is a competent big sister because she reads aloud for Gloria.
- Teaches Gloria to read and draw.
- Is good at lending her things to Gloria.
- Shows Gloria how to do things correctly.
- Is good at helping Dad when picking up Gloria at the kindergarten.

I am not the problem! We are the heroes! 45

We also heard that Gloria:

- Looks to Flora and tries to mimic Flora.
- Wants to play more with Flora. It's hard for Gloria to stop without becoming sad or angry. Gloria will learn to stop soon, when she is a little older.
- Is always on Flora's side, when Dad or Mum is angry with Flora.
- Loves to imitate her older sister, such as reading, drawing and making the same choices as Flora.
- Says "yes" to everything that Flora says "yes" to.
- Looks forward to doing more things together with Flora, when Gloria is a little older.

We want you to know, that we enjoyed seeing your loving family. We saw how you, Flora, showed your drawing to your dad, and how he saw right away that you drew an eye. Flora, we think you know that it is good to sit on Dad's lap, because we saw you crawl on his lap during our conversation, and both you and Dad appeared to enjoy this closeness.

Many greetings,
Kirsten and Nina

We concluded our letter with a comment about Flora and her dad, because several times prior to this session, Dave spoke about not understanding little girls. Em was a schoolteacher and had more expertise to draw on in relating to the girls. Remembering, noticing and writing about Flora sitting on her dad's lap, telling him that we enjoyed this and that it meant something to us, was a tiny witnessing practice, aimed at reducing his doubt about being a good enough parent (Carey & Russell, 2003, pp. 3–16).

This letter differs from many letters we write as it needed to be easy to read for a girl with autism. Children with autism do not favour long, convoluted sentences, metaphors or "wonderings". They like facts and data (Bulhak-Paterson & Ferguson, 2015; Frith, 2003). But in other letters, we might include messages to be read "between the lines".

Wonderful family post-it notes

If the first session with a family involves more than one child, wonderful descriptions of the entire family unit can be utilized. To do this, we write the names of participating family members on the paper chart before handing out palm-sized post-it notes, using a different colour for each person. Then, we ask three consecutive key questions:

- What are three things you really like about yourself?
- What is one thing (or three things) you really like about your family members?
- What is one thing you really like about your family?

46 *I am not the problem! We are the heroes!*

When everyone has written their answers, we place the post-it notes on the paper chart. We then take time to unfold the stories behind the statements, and gather stories about everyone's values and dreams, to make those stories important and nurturing for the family. This may take longer to complete than the first session, if there are many stories.

Making this activity a joyful experience is essential. It may seem to be very difficult, if participants cannot think of anything positive to write. Helping people to position their stories and providing ideas and explanations about the purpose of this exercise is extremely important.

Here is an excerpt from a letter that I wrote to a father, Jon, and his two children Mattis and Mary:

> I asked what future you might imagine, if the problems magically disappeared, and Jon answered, "I have no idea, because I feel like the problems have erased all the good". How unfair, that psychiatric illness can do that!
>
> I then asked you all, what you love most about each other, and we discovered a whole other story. You spoke about all of the things you find wonderful about each other.
>
> At the end of our conversation, I asked you all what words you would prefer to remember from our time together. Mattis and Mary chose "fanciful", "laughter-bubble" and "Nutella sandwiches".

Mattis and Mary's chosen words ignited ideas about how they could approach their Obsessive-Compulsive Disorder and anxiety. These words from our first conversation became their guiding lights and the starting points for reminding their dad, Jon, about everything that was good in their life and for the re-writing of their family's story (Aman, 2007; Marsten et al., 2016, pp. 49–72).

Another family of four taught me the brilliance of asking the third question, "What is one thing you really like about your family?" The parents, Alice and August, and their twin sons, Michael and Marcus, were referred to us after Michael was diagnosed with ADHD. This diagnosis didn't relieve Michael of being considered the problem in the family. We first met with the parents, who described the communication in the family as being full of discord. Alice and August saw Michael's refusal to acknowledge his problem and to take his medicine as the "root of the problem". We agreed to explore who or what was the root of the problem, and how this related to the family's communication, as the parents said they hoped to improve their communication (Strong & Tomm, 2007).

We began the first conversation with the boys, Michael and Marcus, exploring what they liked about each other. The boys became extremely animated when talking about what they liked about their family. They told us about building a shelter to sleep in and having campfires in their backyard.

I am not the problem! We are the heroes!   47

This became a story that contained more than warm feelings. The story illustrated their handling of crises, both big and small, in ways where everyone felt acknowledged and included in the family unit. This story became the family's guiding light for their family life.

The campfire story became our foundation for exploring and deconstructing many narratives that had led to Michael being considered "the problem". Soon, the family began to find new ways of relating to the diagnosis and the discourses about acknowledging ADHD. As Marcus said, "Nobody wants to be the scapegoat".

This inspired Alice and August to ask for conversations without the children. August was very creative and had recognized some traits in himself that were now named as ADHD traits in his son. August had spent his youth combatting these traits as perceived faults. He had become scared, frustrated and enraged whenever he saw Michael being unable to combat these same traits. By unfolding and deconstructing his own narratives, through the lens of the campfire-narrative, he not only forgave himself but also embraced and acknowledged his creativity as part of his ADHD traits. From this position, August could begin to treat Michael with proud compassion (Ingamells, 2016a, 2016b).

Health professionals can learn to know who people are, without their problems (or diagnoses) obscuring the picture. From this point, they can then elicit narratives about how wonderful the family and family members are (Madigan, 2019, pp. 118–121). Narrative therapists use this information to create cracks in a family's walls of despair, enabling light to shine on the knowledge and wisdom that problems and illnesses do not have to rule their lives.

As health professionals, we step into decentred yet influential positions with this approach (Morgan, 2006, pp. 57–84). We use the children's imagination, their metaphors and stories as alternative plots to the dominant stories. Narrative therapists call these unique outcomes. They give us starting points for re-authoring conversations (White, 2007, pp. 61–128) and "re-membering" conversations. "Re-membering" differs from "remembering" in that the focus of re-membering is on helping the families or patients to create imaginary "clubs". The members of these clubs are specific people, memories and values that will support the person or family in their endeavours (Epston, 1998, pp. 69–72; White, 2007, pp. 129–164).

There are endless ways to proceed when we ask ourselves what we really like about a family, and when we focus on how wonderful they are. When we meet children, not as victims of an illness, but as creative members of wonderful families with loving magical powers, we create healing moments in our sessions (Marsten et al., 2016, pp. 27–47).

This chapter concludes with a quote from a mother who had been struggling for years not only with her daughter's psychiatric illness but also with the health system:

48   *I am not the problem! We are the heroes!*

I became the worst possible version of myself, while my daughter was hospitalized. I wish the clinicians had met me before, so they knew my other, "better side". Then we might have been able to cooperate more readily.

Carol

References

Aman, J. (2007). Linking families together: Narrative conversations with children, adolescents, and their families. *The International Journal of Narrative Therapy and Community Work*, *4*, 27–37. https://search.informit.org/doi/10.3316/informit.059688074744169.

Besley, A. C. T. (2010). Foucault and the turn to narrative therapy. *British Journal of Guidance and Couselling*, *30*(2), 125–143. doi:10.1080/03069880220128010

Bulhak-Paterson, D., & Ferguson, T. (2015). *I am an Aspie Girl: A book for young girls with autism spectrum conditions.* London, UK and Philadelphia, USA: Jessica Kingsley Publishers.

Carey, M., & Russell, S. (2003). Outsider-witness practices: Some answers to commonly asked questions. *The International Journal of Narrative Therapy and Community Work*, 2003(1), 3–16.

Carlson, T. S. E. A. (2016). There's always a puppy (and sometimes a bunny): A story about a story about a story. *Journal of Systemic Therapies*, *35*(3), 73–82.

Epston, D. (1998). *Catching up with David Epston: A collection of narrative practice-based papers, published between 1991 and 1996.* Adelaide, Australia: Dulwhich Centre Publishing.

Epston, D. (2008). *Down Under and up and over: Travels with narrative therapy.* Karnac Boks.

Epston, D. (2016). The dirty pants problem and a wonderfulness interview. *Journal of Systemic Therapies*, *35*(3), 63–72. doi:10.1521/jsyt.2016.35.3.63

Freeman, J., Epston, D., & Lobovits, D. (1997). *Playful Approaches to Serious Problems.* New York London: W. W. Norton.

Frith, U. (2003). *Autism. Explaining the Enigma* (2nd ed.). Wiley-Blackwell.

Ingamells, K. M. (2016a). Learning how to counter-story in narrative therapy (With David Epston and Wilbur the Warrior). *Journal of Systemic Therapies*, *35*(4), 58–71. doi:10.1521/jsyt.2016.35.4.58

Ingamells, K. M. (2016b). Wilbur the worrier becomes wilbur the warrior: A teaching story for narrative family therapists. *Journal of Systemic Therapies*, *35*(4), 43–57. doi:10.1521/jsyt.2016.35.4.43

Madigan, S. (2019). Recent development and future directions in narrative therapy. In *Narrative Therapy* (2nd ed., pp. 117–160). American Psychological Association.

Madsen, W. C. (2006). Teaching across discources to sustain coillaborative clinical practice. *Journal of Systemic Therapies*, *25*(4), 44–58.

Madsen, W. C. (2007). *Collaborative therapy with multi-stressed families* (2nd ed.). New York, London: The Guilford Press.

Marsten, D., Epston, D., & Markham, L. (2016). *Narrative therapy in wonderland. Connecting with children's imaginative know-how.* New York, London: W. W. Norton & Co.

Morgan, A. (2006). The position of the therapist in working with the children and their families. In M. White, Morgan, A. (Ed.), *Narrative Therapy with Children and their families* (pp. 57–84). Adelaide: Dulwhich Centre Publications.

Nickel, K., Maier, S., Endres, D., Joos, A., Maier, V., Tebartz van Elst, L., & Zeeck, A. (2019). Systematic review: Overlap between eating, autism spectrum, and attention-deficit/hyperactivity disorder. *Frontiers in psychiatry*, *10*(708). doi:10.3389/fpsyt.2019.00708

Roberts, J. (2005). Transparency and self-disclosure in family therapy: Dangers and possibilities. *Family Process*, *44*(1), 45–63. doi:10.1111/j.1545-5300.2005.00041.x

Strong, T., & Tomm, K. (2007). Family therapy as re-coordinating and moving on together. *Journal of Systemic Therapies*, *26*(2), 42–54. doi:10.1521/jsyt.2007.26.2.42

Ungar, M. (2005). A thicker description of resilience. *The International Journal of Narrative Therapy & Community Work*, *2005*(3/4), 89–96. doi:https://search.informit.org/doi/10.3316/informit.247303462342985

White, M. (2007). *Maps of narrative practice* New York, London: W. W. Norton & Co.

4 Mattering is at the heart of the matter

It's the mattering, that matters. But how we matter, matters a lot

Mattering is a practice with the purpose of engaging with families in ways that make them feel welcomed, respected, knowledgeable, interesting, and worthy of being present in the room. Mattering enables families to participate on equal grounds with the professionals. Our purpose is to make collaboration work in a relationship that, from the starting point, is inherently hierarchical.

Mattering is the art of seeking ways to engage with people labelled as clients that honour their experience and knowledge, combine their wisdom with our professional expertise, and collaboratively invite their influence in our work with them (Madsen et al., 2021, p. 20).

Traditionally, the therapist is in charge of deciding what will signify a good outcome. Mattering is in line with the recovery movement that disputes this approach. Treatment goals set by the clinician often focus solely on symptoms and problems. Mattering involves the creation of treatment goals that are based on the person's own dreams, hopes and values, accepting and embracing that each treatment goal will be unique and idiosyncratic (Slade, 2009, p. 370).

Some patients describe their experience of the hierarchical distancing in this way, "I am just a patient, but you are the doctor/psychologist", or "I am the illness, you are a person". Or "We feel like we are just another case", "Like she couldn't get rid of me fast enough", "Like she didn't really care one way or the other". These phrases reveal that it matters a lot to our patients when we express interest in their point of view.

We want the families to experience us as appreciative allies, who are standing in solidarity with them to help them develop preferred directions in life (Madsen, 2007, 2014).

Ask yourself:

What is it that I do, when my patients feel that I am helpful?

What is it I do, when the patients feel I am unhelpful?

DOI: 10.4324/9781003171621-5

Also ask your patients and families:

What do I do, that makes you feel that I am helping you?

What should I do more, do less, or change in order to be more helpful?

You might experience similar answers, such as, "You care about me and what I want". A literature review (Sommer et al., 2017, p. 3) explored what people with mental health problems experience as a helpful support to promote their participation in education and work. Some of the answers related to health professionals practicing mattering:

- Health professionals' expressions of valuing the person and belief in their potential.
- Collaboration and being trusted as a person who is competent and has potential.
- Relations that reflect equality and friendship.

These practices create feelings of being together on a shared project instead of being evaluated and judged. These findings emphasize the importance of focusing on how we are together with others, instead of which role we have as professionals (Sommer et al., 2017).

The relationship or alliance between patient and therapist is described as a "common factor" in psychotherapy and is regarded as one of the most influential factors in this form of treatment (Duncan et al., 2004, 1999).

We focus on two aspects of mattering:

Making the person feel that it matters to us how they fare in life.

Making the person feel that it matters to us what they want.

We often use the narrative idea of creating resonance. When a person creates emotions in another person, for example by telling a story, that resonates with that person's own emotions, we share this resonance. The storyteller experiences being seen, valuable, and connected to that other person. This idea is used as a specific step in a technique called definitional ceremonies, that creates an audience to the person's rich descriptions of preferred narratives (White, 2007, pp. 191, 165–218). We can become that audience, the families' appreciative allies, in all conversations by expressing our personal understanding and response to what is said.

We create resonance in our letters and in the conversations, when we respond by:

- Naming what the patient or family has just said.
- Telling what we are reminded of in our personal or professional life in relation to what they have told us.
- Explaining which of our actions will be affected by that conversation.

52 *Mattering is at the heart of the matter*

You may ask:

> What if I don't like the patient or family?

My answer:

> What is it, that you do not yet know about them?

We often use this opening question in supervision:

> What do you most respect, or what do you really like about this family?

This question helps us step into a position or a relational stance of respect, curiosity, trust, and hope (Madsen & Gillespie, 2014).

When in a session, and we find ourselves appalled by a parent's outburst, or we dislike a person, or the pain is too much, we practice mattering. This is achieved by bringing out our values of respect and curiosity and stepping closer to "the fire". We argue that if something seems illogical to us, it must be because there's something we don't know.

No matter how incomprehensible or awful the situation we expect that, if in this person's position, we probably would not cope as well, since the sum of the problems is probably bigger and more complex than it seems. We express amazement that this person is still alive (or the couple is still married, the patient is still trying to get better, and so on). We keep asking and keep trying to understand. We end up admiring and liking people. This process is actually rather fun and fulfilling.

When we admire our patients, it's easier to feel their pain, because we also see the things that make us impressed and respectful of them. We marvel at how wonderful they are. This counteracts the pain and disrespect that psychiatric illness otherwise instils in us. This allows us to shoulder and holds hope for our patients and their families, simultaneously, without feeling burnt out (Figley, 2002; Morse et al., 2012).

These practices make the people we meet with feel mattered, so they can participate and collaborate with us, to the best of their ability.

There was no ultimatum with you

Katja, whose struggle with her daughter Filippa's anxiety is described in Chapter 2, reflects on what was helpful and mattered to her:

> One thing you did that really mattered to Filippa and I, was when Filippa refused to come to you because the public transport made her anxious.
>
> I came alone and feared you would finish our treatment. I knew that there were queues for children to come to your therapy.

Mattering is at the heart of the matter 53

Without knowing what I feared, you said, "If you are interested, we will continue without Filippa! If you come and tell me how Filippa is, then I can write letters to Filippa that you both can read".

That's how it sometimes happened. There was no ultimatum with you, and this approach worked. I was the messenger if Filippa failed, and she got the therapy through the letters. It was so good, although I would wish with all my heart that she had joined in.

I also got a lot out of reading your letters to us after our conversations. The stories made sense and could be accessed as needed – we could read them several times, as a personal "therapy guide" tailored to us!

That first day I had no idea that Katja feared we would terminate the treatment early because she came alone. I assumed she knew we expected the parents to be in charge of deciding who would attend the sessions. Obviously, I had not explained this properly.

I am also astonished by the observation, "There was no ultimatum with you". How often do health services put forward ultimatums for people who need help? (McCarthy, 2001). Such an approach contrasts starkly with the values of equality and empowerment.

Being genuine or putting on a facade of seriousness?

A final conversation with the "Messy" family comprising Ariana the mum, Tom the dad, and two daughters Eva and Taylor, was revealing. They had come to me with an anorexia that had attacked them all in different ways. Our work had been based on their values and dreams for their family unit. This changed their narratives from, "Taylor's case of anorexia nervosa", to a shared story about more complex and interconnected problems. The family was ready to move on and, as part of this last session, where we were to say goodbye, I said:

Can I ask you one thing? I normally ask the families for help at our last meeting. Can you tell me what I have done, that you believe would be helpful for other families like yours? What should I do more, do less, or change, in order to become a better therapist and psychiatrist for the next family? This is the best way I can improve myself, learning from families like you, on how you experience things and get their evaluations. Do you have time for this?

Eva: YES! You stop and say, "Are we talking about the right thing?" This is helpful.

Nina: Okay, I can do more of that. It's good to know that you have noticed and appreciate that I ask that.

54　*Mattering is at the heart of the matter*

Taylor:　When you are impressed and say, "That was really impressive", or "That's interesting, tell me more about that", then we feel like we are on the right track. That is nice. Then I feel optimistic.

Nina:　Let me explain why I do that, so you don't have to wonder. I also want you all to be aware of these techniques, because you can use them at home and help each other in this way. We know that families who come to us are burdened and feel very sad. We can imagine that there's a scale: the more burdened the family is, the more happiness we must bring into the room. We can never truly imagine or comprehend how big a burden it is to have a psychiatric illness in your home. But we can be as curious as possible. I also know that nobody needs to be told that a situation is serious and sad, because they already know that. Most people need someone to hold their hopes up for them. Am I right?

Tom:　Yes! We don't come to therapy to be told that we have a terrible life. We know we have a terrible life.

Eva and Taylor began telling stories together about the different therapies they had endured, where one psychologist had nodded, like a doll bobbing its head up and down for no reason whatsoever, and another had looked deeply sad all the time. Eva and Taylor tried to make light of how the experiences had been for them. They had witnessed the professionals putting on a façade and pretending, instead of being genuine. They also emphasized the difficulties for a child being confronted with so much seriousness and so many heavy feelings.

Ariana:　I know we have said this before, but I really like what you write on the paper chart. It helps to keep us on track. Also, you keep going back to the purpose of the conversation, asking if what we are talking about is relevant.

Taylor:　I like that you are curious about what I am thinking. You don't act as if you already know and are judging what I am saying. You seem genuinely interested in understanding my point of view, as if my opinion has equal value. I think it's about being warm and having empathy, is that right? (Looking at her mum).

Tom:　I don't know if it makes sense, and this might sound too solemn, but you seem to care about us. Could that be a good word? Is it too big a word? Caring?

Nina:　Wow! I love that! I must tell you about a concept, called Mattering. It means, if our patients do not matter to us, then our therapy cannot be effective. We have to care about our families; how you fare in life must matter to me. This is not hard; it's about finding those things that I like about you, and then I cannot help being involved in how well you are doing. Thank you for using such big words.

Tom:	You know what? Every time we leave here, we feel uplifted. When we left previous forms of treatment, we were in uproar, fighting, feeling bad as parents, and as a family.
Eva:	Can I say something else? I like when you tell stories, like the one about the little girl when Taylor mentioned she had trouble eating when something was not right.

I had told this story to Taylor:

I wonder if your family realizes, that when something happens, eating becomes difficult for you? I wonder if you can tell your family, or not? Because it might be difficult to explain this. This reminds me of a very young girl I once met. She might have been nine years old, or maybe only seven. She was so young, that when I asked her all those questions at the assessment, you might remember, that you were asked: Is it important to have an empty stomach? Do you count calories? And so on, she just looked at me, like I was speaking a foreign language. I thought to myself, *this little girl doesn't have anorexia, because she doesn't even understand my questions.* Eventually I asked her, "What happens for you when you are about to eat?". She answered, "I look at the plate and I have to eat a little less than the day before". Then I asked, "But the next day, what then if you ate a little less the day before?" She replied, "I must eat less than I did the day before". Can you imagine? This little girl had no idea about calories; she didn't have any words for what was happening to her. So, we had to teach her to eat a little more every day, than the day before. I am glad you are older, but I respect that putting these feelings into words is difficult.

Eva continued:	When you tell stories like this, we feel we are not alone with this problem, and if others got better, then we can get better too. And it feels more personal, like you care about us and the others you meet with.
Eva:	It's like you are sharing your knowledge with us.
Ariana:	You give us fresh perspectives on what we are experiencing.
Eva:	You give us hope, and we can see there is a way through all this.
Taylor (looking at her family):	Do you remember the previous place? They would ask, "Have you been through this module or that module?" Or "Well, you have been through all the modules, so you are done". But Nina makes her treatment specific for each person.
Nina:	Yeah, this is what I try to do. I have some ideas about things that might be good to talk about, and what questions to ask. But I need to tailor it to what you want and hope for. You see, I think our task is different from surgery on a knee. Knees are probably fairly identical. The surgeon can do the same operation on many different knees and use the same kinds of

56   *Mattering is at the heart of the matter*

	tools every time. But each family's mental health challenges are very different from the next family, so I must be flexible and do what you need me to do.
Eva:	But that's why it seems like you really care about us!
Ariana:	It's not a prescription you give us. It's specifically for us.
Tom:	I think there's a balance. You ask questions like many other psychologists. But you also share many of the facts, that biomedical knowledge. It's like there's a balance between the number of questions and the amount of wisdom that you give us. Sometimes you say things like, "I know, as a child and adolescent psychiatrist, this is how it is with anorexia, or this is how the body works, or this is how psychiatric illness operates", and we can listen and learn.

At this point, I felt excited and said, "Thank you! I believe we can all provide a better treatment, if we combine the therapy approach and the biomedical approach".

Taylor:	I think that's why you are not only talking about the eating disorder. You are interested in helping us with the real causes. It's not only symptomatic treatment; you care about helping us to understand why the illness came, and what we can do about the real problems.
Nina:	You are right. I believe that mental illnesses come as responses to problems, and that we can only really help if we become detectives together, searching for those "other real problems", and figuring out how to handle them in better ways.

This conversation left us all tired and excited. Getting the family's help had been beneficial for me, and they experienced the effects of mattering practices even more, because we put it into words.

Holding onto our values

Mattering is about seeing each patient as a person trying to do their best. It is also about seeing problems as frustrated dreams (McAdam & Lang, 2003).

The following story illustrates how illness is often only treated with life-long self-blame. In this family, an illness became a controversy between two parents and an obstacle to their child's well-being. It could have evolved and caused more damage, if we had not intervened with mattering practices.

Olga and Oluf's daughter, Aurora, had struggled with "classic" Obsessive-Compulsive Disorder (OCD) for many years and had received a lot of in-dividual cognitive therapy with only partial relief. As we learned about the parent's backgrounds, it became clear that OCD could be understood as part of a more complex system of problems. But these complexities could not be

Mattering is at the heart of the matter 57

addressed in an individualized setting, and so had been seen only as diffuse, disturbing problems, that nobody had tried to untangle and understand. We decided that if we were to help Aurora, these complexities had to be addressed together with the OCD.

One of the many complex problems was whether Oluf also had a severe and troublesome OCD, and whether Oluf had any chance of changing something he had tried to live with, and hide, since childhood. This problem had been a source of frustration and controversy between the couple. There were other problems, but this was one of the most pressing.

Olga and Oluf only told us about Oluf's struggles after several months into treatment. Being seen as a good dad, and especially one that might be able to understand his daughter in ways that his wife did not understand, gave Oluf the strength to acknowledge and address his own OCD, instead of continuing to try hiding it. This change became possible when we co-created with Olga and Oluf new narratives about him. Until then the one "true" and very negative story he had about himself, and his problem, had obstructed his chances of finding fresh possibilities for actions.

This is the letter my colleague Janni, a psychologist, wrote after the session, where we unpacked and named Oluf's problems as OCD. She did not use the term "OCD" in the letter. She wanted to use her mattering practices, highlighting her respect for Olga and Oluf's aspirations for their parenthood. She focused on their movement from fighting over who possessed the right truth, to acknowledging the partner's dreams, intentions, and actions, as the best foundation for better parent collaboration and new ways to progress.

> Dear Olga and Oluf,
>
> What a wonderful conversation! We are impressed by you because amidst all sorts of problems, concerns, and frustrations over things your daughter Aurora cannot do, you manage to stay focused on how she can best be helped. You examine the problems from several sides, and you complement each other well with your different ideas and experiences.
>
> Your attitudes emphasize for us, that there is rarely only one truth, but several ways of perceiving a situation. These different perceptions complement each other and provide us with an understanding of how complex it is to help a child, and of the difficulties in knowing what "is right".
>
> We will remember Oluf's focus that this challenge must never become a battle between you and your daughter.
>
> Best regards,
> Nina and Janni

58 *Mattering is at the heart of the matter*

We received this reply a few days later:

> It is so nice to have our thoughts "translated" through you and your questions. A bit like a Google translator – just better ☺ It is wonderful to be made aware of what we do that is good, and to know that you appreciate it.
>
> To hear you say that what we do is good, that we are good parents, means a lot! Because generally that gets lost in all the problems. You give me strength to be a dad.
>
> Olga and Oluf

Drawing on Foucault's ideas about power issues and mental health issues (Foucault, 1979), I am mindful of power when I meet with families. I am in a position of power. I have the power to give diagnoses, to give empowerment, to build up people, and to break them down, depending on how I act. I also carefully consider the fact that my actions can negatively affect people who are already vulnerable (Paré & Lysack, 2004).

Empowering our patients and their families demands that health professionals give power away and accept less power than previously accustomed to (O'Hagan, 2009; Oedegaard et al., 2020). Mattering is the stance we take to make this happen. It is a precondition for treatment to be helpful and empowerment to happen. When it really matters to us how the other person fares in life, we give them power over our feelings. This makes mattering more powerful and empowering.

Everyone matters in a mattering team

Two parents described their experience with our program. They said they knew from the first minute they entered the waiting area that this would be a good place for them because of the way our secretary had greeted them. I felt bewildered. What did our secretary have to do with clinical conversations? The parents said the secretary had greeted them like long-lost friends, as people she had looked forward to meeting and expected to like. "When Jette (the secretary) behaved in this way, we knew that people in this workplace would be good people", the parents said.

Jette makes mattering an art. She lets every person who enters our consulting rooms know that they matter to her. She cares deeply about each family member we see. Jette can do this because she is part of our team. She participates in our meetings and clinical conferences. She has the same legitimacy to speak up, ask questions and voice her opinions as the therapists.

We acknowledge that Jette spends time with our families in the waiting room. We recognize that she makes observations and engages with family members in ways that leave them feeling treasured and important. She often has conversations with a parent or a child that she can relate to us later. She contributes to the nuanced and multicolored understandings we hold of the families we meet. However, if we did not let Jette know that she and her work matter to us and to the families we serve, her ability to matter to the families would be lessened (Madsen et al., 2021, p. 29).

The following summary of our first four chapters is presented in an externalized language that describes the psychiatric illness as a person or a creature with intentions and goals:

- Psychiatric illness wants to take over a child's or adolescent's life and ruin it (Fryers & Brugha, 2013; Maisel et al., 2004). The illness tries to obliterate whatever personality the child has and replace it with its own, making it close to impossible for the child, the parents, or anybody else to separate the two (Lock et al., 2005; Maisel et al., 2004).
- Psychiatric illness blames the parents (Blum, 2007; Jackson & Mannix, 2004; Maisel et al., 2004). Telling everybody in society that the child is the problem, and the parents are to be blamed.
- Psychiatric illness directs health professionals to look for and focus on only negative effects of actions (Anderson & Gehart, 2012; Bentley et al., 2016), claiming those effects are equal to the person's intentions behind the actions.
- Psychiatric illness has allies in societal stories emphasizing the glory of hierarchy, claiming that doctors are rightfully at the top of society and children are at the bottom (Bentley et al., 2016; Combs & Freedman, 2012). These stories support the faulty ideas that health professionals possess the true knowledge, shall have all the power, and are entitled to judge children and their parents on their actions while under the influence of psychiatric illness.

Narrative family psychiatrists are aware of these tactics (Maisel et al., 2004; Marsten et al., 2016) and seek to develop the ethics and skills to counteract the effects of psychiatric illness (Carlson et al., 2017; Epston, 1999, 2014; Hankins, 2005, 2013, 2019; Ingamells, 2016a, 2016b). Narrative family psychiatrists:

- Know that the child is not the problem, the problem is the problem.
- Know that the parents are not to blame, they are the child's most important people.
- Use externalizing language that separates the child and family from the disease.
- Use wonderfulness interviews to get to know the child and family separate from the disease.
- Ask questions to learn about the most loving aspects, hopes, and values of each family.
- Use dialogue and mattering to minimize the negative effects of hierarchy.

60 *Mattering is at the heart of the matter*

- Ask questions about intentions, separating these from the effects of actions.
- Position themselves, so the families and their wisdom matter to the collaboration.
- Practice respect, curiosity, trust, and hope.

References

Anderson, H., & Gehart, D. (2012). *Collaborative therapy: Relationships and conversations that make a difference*. Routledge.

Bentley, K. J., Cohen-Filipic, K., & Cummings, C. R. (2016). Approaching parental guilt, shame, and blame in a helping relationship: Multiple methods for teaching and learning. *Journal of Teaching in Social Work, 36*(5), 490–502. doi:10.1080/08841233.2016.1238024

Blum, L. M. (2007). Mother-blame in the Prozac Nation: Raising Kids with invisible disabilities. *Gender and Society, 21*(2), 202–226. Retrieved 20 may 2021 from http://www.jstor.org/stable/27640959

Carlson, T. S., Epston, D., Haire, A., Corturillo, E., Lopez, A. H., Vedvei, S., & Pilkington, S. M. (2017). Learning Narrative therapy backwards: Exemplary tales as an alternative pedagogy for learning practice. *Journal of Systemic Therapies, 36*(1), 94–107. doi:10.1521/jsyt.2017.36.1.94

Combs, G., & Freedman J. (2012). Narrative, poststructuralism, and social justice: Current practices in narrative therapy. *The Counseling Psychologist, 40*(7), 1033–1060. doi:10.11 77/0011000012460662

Duncan, B. L., Miller, S. D., & Sparks, J. (2004). *The Heroic Client: A revolutionary way to improve effectiveness through client-directed, outcome-informed therapy* (1st ed.). San Fransisco: Jossey-Bass.

Duncan, B. L., Miller, S. D., Wambold B. E., & Hubble, M. A. (1999). *The heart and soul of change* (2nd ed.). American Psychological Association.

Epston, D. (1999). Co-research: the making of alternative knowledge in narrative therapy and community work. In P. Moss (Ed.), *Narrative Therapy and Community Work: A conference collection*. Adelaide: Dulwich Centre Publications.

Epston, D. (2014). Ethnography, co-research and Insider Knowledges. *Australian and New Zealand Journal of Family Therapy, 35*(1), 105–109. doi:10.1002/anzf.1048

Figley, C. R. (2002). *Treating compassion fatigue*. Brunner-Routledge.

Foucault, M. (1979). *Discipline and punish: The birth of prison*. Middlesex: Peregrine Books.

Fryers, T., & Brugha, T. (2013). Childhood determinants of adult psychiatric disorder. *Clinical Practice and Epidemiology in Mental Health: CP & EMH, 9*, 1–50. doi:10.2174/1745017901309010001

Hamkins, S. (2005). Introducing narrative psychiatry: Narrative approaches to initial psychiatric consultations. *International Journal of Narrative Therapy and Community Work*, 40 (3), 5–17.

Hamkins, S. (2013). *The Art of Narrative Psychiatry: Stories of Strength and Meaning* (1st ed.). New York, USA: Oxford University Press.

Hamkins, S. (2019). Narrative psychiatry and family therapy: Promoting resilience and collaboration with persons with intense mental and emotional experiences at risk of causing violence. *Australian and New Zealand Journal of Family Therapy, 40*(3), 295–307. doi:10.1002/anzf.1380

Ingamells, K. M. (2016a). Learning how to counter-story in narrative therapy (With David Epston and Wilbur the Warrior). *Journal of Systemic Therapies, 35*(4), 58–71. doi:10.1521/jsyt.2016.35.4.58

Ingamells, K. M. (2016b). Wilbur the worrier becomes Wilbur the warrior: A teaching story for narrative family therapists. *Journal of Systemic Therapies, 35*(4), 43–57. doi:10.1521/jsyt. 2016.35.4.43

Jackson, D., & Mannix, J. (2004). Giving voice to the burden of blame: a feminist study of mothers' experiences of mother blaming. *International Journal of Nursing Practice, 10*(4), 150–158. doi:10.1111/j.1440-172X.2004.00474.x

Lock, A., Epston, D., Maisel, R., & Faria, N. (2005). Resisting anorexia/bulimia: Foucauldian perspectives in narrative therapy. *British Journal of Guidance & Counselling, 33*(3), 315–332. doi:10.1080/03069880500179459

Madsen, W. C. (2007). *Collaborative therapy with multi-stressed families* (2nd ed.). The Guilford Press.

Madsen, W. C., & Gillespie, K. (2014). *Collaborative helping: A strengths framework for home-based services.* John Wiley & Sons Inc.

Madsen, W. C., Roth, E., & Jørring, N. T. (2021). Mattering as the heart of health and human services. *Journal of Contemporary Narrative Therapy, 1*, 19–31. Retrieved 20 May 2021 from https://www.paperturn-view.com/?pid=MTY161367&p=21

Maisel, R., Epston, D., & Borden, A. (2004). *Biting the hand that starves you: Inspiring Resistance to Anorexia/Bulimia.* New York, NY: W.W. Norton & Co.

Marsten, D., Epston, D., & Markham, L. (2016). *Narrative Therapy in Wonderland: Connecting with children's imaginative know-how.* W. W. Norton & Co.

McAdam, E., & Lang, P. (2003). Working in worlds of children: Growing, schools, families, communities through imagining. *The International Journal of Narrative Therapy and Community Work, 4* (4), 48–57. doi: https://search.informit.org/doi/10.3316/informit.661365349642706

McCarthy, I. C. (2001). Fifth providence re-versings: The social construction of women lone parents' inequality and poverty. *Journal of Family Therapy, 23*, 253–277. doi:10.1111/1467-6427.00183

Morse, G., Salyers, M. P., Rollins, A. L., Monroe-DeVita, M., & Pfahler, C., 39(5), 341–352. https://doi.org/10.1007/s10488-011-0352-1. (2012). Burnout in mental health services: A review of the problem and its remediation. *Administration and Policy in Mental Health 39*(5), 341–352. doi: 10.1007/s10488-011-0352-1

O'Hagan, M. (2009). Leadership for empowerment and equality: a proposed model for mental health user/survivor leadership. *International Journal of Leadership in Public Services, 5*(4), 34–43. doi:10.5042/IJLPS.2010.0110

Oedegaard, C. H., Davidson, L., & Stige, B. et al. (2020). "It means so much for me to have a choice": A qualitative study providing first-person perspectives on medication-free treatment in mental health care. *BMC Psychiatry, 20*(399). doi:10.1186/s12888-020-02770-2

Paré, D., & Lysack, M. (2004). The willow and the oak: from monologue to dialogue in the scaffolding of therapeutic conversations. *Journal of Systemic Therapies, 23*(1), 6–20.

Slade, M. (2009). The contribution of mental health services to recovery. *Journal of Mental Health, 18*(5), 367–371. doi:10.3109/09638230903191256

Sommer, M., Ness, O., & Borg, M. (2017). Helpful support to promote participation in school and work: Subjective experiences of people with mental health problems. A literature review. *Social Work in Mental Health, 16*(3), 346–366. doi:10.1080/15332985. 2017.1395778

White, M. (2007). *Maps of narrative practice.* W. W. Norton & Co.

5 Not untidy scribbles but a beautiful illustration of my life

When we ask families what they find helpful in our sessions, they most often mention our public or shared note-taking. Note-taking is instrumental in our therapy, helping us to be transparent, collaborative, curious, focused, and respectful. This chapter describes how we write our notes in collaboration with the families and how we can organize the notes we take.

Few therapists can remember all that is said during a session, so most take notes when meeting with families. However, who are those notes for? Narrative therapists consider the notes to be the property of the families (Morgan, 2000, p. 96).

Family conversations need to be helpful, first and foremost, for the family members. This is why we engage in transparent public note-taking on big paper charts.

We use a timber easel covered with a paper roll to write on.[1] We do our best to write the exact words and sentences spoken by each member of the family. Our aim is to honour their words and language, highlight their wisdom, and make visible what is most helpful.

The notes on the paper chart help us, like notes on a paper pad help us, to keep track of what we are talking about, and to ensure we are talking about the right subjects. But the notes on the paper chart are more than this. Such note-taking becomes a device for our collaborative practices.

We take a digital picture of the paper chart after each session. This picture can be stored in the electronic medical record. Thereafter, we only need to write a brief account about the session, since the important words are already stored in the picture.

The family is given the original paper chart to take home. Some families prefer to take their own digital pictures. We use the picture to support our memory when writing the therapeutic letter, but more about that later.

I also use the technique of public note-taking in other contexts such as conferences, assessments, anamneses, notes at meetings and supervision, because this is an effective way to co-record and share thoughts.

DOI: 10.4324/9781003171621-6

Untidy or beautiful illustrations of life   63

The others always hide their notes from me

Marlene came to our consulting room with her mum. She was 14 years old and a patient in a high-security inpatient ward for adolescents. Reluctantly sitting down, Marlene's countenance signalled, "This was not my idea to come here". A colleague had asked our team to meet Marlene and her mum for a few sessions to help them break Marlene's pattern of self-harm, and to help them accept Marlene's admission to a long-term residential treatment institution.

Unsure what Marlene and her mum were expecting, we began by asking what they hoped to get from this first session and what they had been told about us.

Mum: They[2] want me to give up on Marlene. But I am her mother and I want to be here for her.

Marlene: I want to go home, but Mum can't take care of me. I am suicidal all the time and she doesn't know how to restrain me.

Nina: Okay, so when I write on this paper, what should I write that you hope for?

Marlene: I want to be with my mum.

These were the first words placed on the paper:

Marlene's hope I want to be with my mum

Our conversation continued and, when we stopped, I asked Marlene and her mum what had been most important for them to talk about at our meeting that day, and what would be most helpful for them to remember and think more about.

Mum: Most important is Marlene's hope to be with me.

Nina: It seems that Marlene's statement was a surprise to you, am I right? Is this why you want to hold onto her hope?

Mum: Yes, I had no idea that we shared the same hope and dream for Marlene to come home, so we can live together. I am very grateful for this because now I can begin to believe in this dream.

Nina: Marlene, is this also what you would like to remember from today? Or does something else stand out for you?

Marlene: I want to remember that you wrote all your notes on that big paper, so I could see them all, and that you only wrote things that I agree with.

Nina: What? What's the big deal about how I take notes?

Marlene: You are the first person to take notes so I can see them. All the others hide their notes, and I use much energy trying to figure out what they are writing. I am certain they write about how crazy I am.

Nina: Wow! I am impressed. I hadn't thought about how stressful that

64 *Untidy or beautiful illustrations of life*

would be for you, if I wrote on note-paper that you could not see. I share my notes with you because I want to make sure I write the right stuff, and to have your help in getting it right.

Marlene: No, it's more than that. You know what? I did not want to come today, and Mum promised me that it would only be once if I did not like you guys. But now I want to come back. I think this conversation could be helpful for me.

I carry this conversation with me because it demonstrates and clarifies the many benefits of public note-taking. I believe it was because Marlene suffered from paranoia, that she could phrase the beneficial effects so clearly. Probably many patients, like Marlene, have justified reason to feel paranoia due to unpleasant experiences resulting from hidden note-taking practices.

But for me, the collaborative practices remain my main reason for using this technique.

Organizing notes on the paper charts

Our handwriting, how we choose which colours to write with, and where we choose to write on the paper chart, is often a personal choice, but each decision influences the progress of the session. It's a real joy when our actions help us to summarize, and locate unique outcomes and startling insights, so the family moves forward towards their chosen vision.

Learning the different ways to structure the scribbles, so they will create the most helpful patterns, takes time. But don't worry. The act of writing the notes so they are visible for everyone is most important.

The subject and the purpose of the conversation dictate the note-taking. But one element is constant with every conversation, and this is the use of many different colours. The colours help the treatment team and the family to give substance and depth to the scribbles. The most basic way is to change colour several times during the conversation, so the colour shift helps everyone to remember the sequence of the sentences and provides a timeline. Sometimes we have a colour for each person. When we do this, we invite each person to choose their own colour. I often shift back and forth between colours, so a colour can signify different themes or individual perspectives. I reserve a special colour (sometimes yellow, but yellow is hard to see on digital pictures) for putting star stickers on specific sentences at the conclusion of the session.

We start each session by reading our therapeutic letter and asking:

"How did you experience listening to me reading this letter? Do you have any comments? Is there something we should talk about in relationship to the letter?"

Untidy or beautiful illustrations of life 65

Next, we ask one of these questions:

- For this conversation to be helpful for you, what should we talk about today?
- What would you like to be smarter at, better able to cope with, or manage better, when this conversation concludes today?
- What would you like to be the "lighthouse", giving us a guiding light for our conversation today?
- Did you speak about what you would like to talk about today, on your way here?
- Shall we write an agenda for today?

These questions often lead us to write a vision, hope, or dream, that will become our guiding light for the conversation. This guiding light will be something that we can keep returning to, point at, and ask:

- Are we talking about the right thing?
- Is this conversation still leading us towards your hopes for today?
- Is this relevant for what you want from the conversation today, or have we digressed from our plan?

We strive to achieve transparency, by telling the family what we are doing, and to share power over the conversation, by asking the family for help. Sometimes we explain we are trying a new technique, to make the conversations more valuable for the family, and we ask, "Do you find this method disturbing or helpful for you?"

We also ask:

- I want to write this down, but where should it go (on the chart)?
- Should I write it this way or that way?
- Does what you say relate to this (pointing to a sentence) or to that (pointing to something else)?
- Wait a minute, what did you say? It's important, right? Can you repeat it?
- Did I write this right?

We do not want to ask questions while we are writing on the paper. The conversation process slows when we are writing, and we have learned that these pauses provide the patient and their family with time to think. This is not an unpleasant quiet, but a contemplative quiet that arises from thinking and looking at the words on the paper (Epston, 1998, p. 97).

Many people have difficulty looking directly into another person's face, and some people experience therapy as "inquisitory". This tendency is lessened when we all look at the paper.

The paper also serves as a "common third". The common third is a concept in pedagogy, describing an activity or project that two people carry out

66 *Untidy or beautiful illustrations of life*

together without it being something that one does for or by the other. The common third changes a hierarchical therapist-patient relationship to one that is more equal. It activates, involves, and opens doors in the relationship (Christiansen, 2015, p. 125; Hadi, 2018; Husen, 1996; Storø, 2013).

Writing on the paper chart is a physical and tactile way of externalizing the thoughts of the family. The thoughts are "out there" on the paper, not just inside the head of the patient or family members. The words stay on the paper instead of disappearing into the air, the second they have been said. Writing the words on paper makes them easier to examine and "delve into".

The play with words becomes a poetic and fruitful exercise. We can write the same message in several ways, and consider our perception, depending on how the message was expressed. By writing the message on the paper, we can examine the effects without it becoming a personal critique.

We enjoy encouraging younger children to draw pictures on the paper, while we take notes, and rejoice when an adolescent or grown-up asks to take over and draw something to demonstrate what they are trying to convey but lack the skills or confidence to express verbally.

Useful guidelines:

- Remember to interrupt the flow. For instance, summarize the conversation so far by pointing to the sentences on the paper charts. Then ask what subject or direction it would make sense to talk about next. Do this whenever in doubt about what to do, or what to ask, or to confirm you are talking about the right subject.
- Remember to ask the family to explain why, repeatedly. Don't act like a disinterested friend, who nods their head and agrees. Be genuinely curious and step into a real not-knowing position. A curious question to what seems an obvious answer often leads to the most fascinating developments. Point to the sentence and ask for a qualification for that statement.
- Ask each family member to choose one element (a sentence or a metaphor, for instance), that is most important to remember. Put a star and a name next to it. Remember to invite an explanation for the choice.
- The last words to be added to the paper chart comprise the name of the family and the date. The dates and names become important for later use.

Public note-taking is an essential building block in the overall structure of a session:

- Start each session by reading the e-mail from the former session.
- Invite comments on this e-mail.
- Ask the family for their goal for the session and decide on an agenda with the family.

Untidy or beautiful illustrations of life 67

- Write all notes on a big paper chart and never take private notes.
- Summarize regularly and ask the family for direction according to their vision for the current session and their overall visions for the treatment.
- Ask the family members to choose their preferred part of the conversation at the end of the session.
- Write a date at the top of the paper chart, take a photo, and give the original chart to the family.
- Use the photo with your co-therapist after the session to prepare the therapeutic letter together.
- Send the e-mail to the family within a few days.

There are different ways to structure questions and "scribbles" in each session, depending on the focus of the conversation. The wonderfulness interview, for example, is described in Chapter 3 and another technique, the collaborative helping map, is described in Chapter 6.

This chapter describes three other techniques – that of documenting a problem-focused conversation, taking a family's history, and creating stars. The use of metaphors and learning this technique in collaboration with the family, is also discussed.

Let's map that problem

When setting out to expose a problem, by being detectives and unpacking "the thing" that is bothering the child or/and the family, we follow the standard structure for a narrative interview about problems. This is called the "statement of position map" and has four categories (White, 2006, pp. 17–18; 2007, pp. 54–59). Michael White, David Epston's co-founder of narrative therapy, explained that he used the metaphor of a map, because he was an avid amateur pilot, and liked to look at maps. When he spoke with families, these maps were pictured inside his head.

Art Fisher, a Canadian psychologist, was inspired by White's maps and created a visual, collaborative externalization of discourses rather than problems. Working collaboratively with his clients, he wrote on large paper charts. I met Fisher at two workshops in Copenhagen in 2006 and 2007.[3] I have since explored and applied this visual approach when working with families, mostly to externalize problems.

Make a cross in the middle of the paper chart to create four quadrants that comprise:

1   The problem with detailed descriptions.
2   Effects of the problem on everyone, and on relationships.
3   Evaluations and judgments of the effects of the problem's activities.
4   Justifications of the evaluations, that give us visions/dreams/hopes/values.

68 *Untidy or beautiful illustrations of life*

There is no need to write all this explanation on the paper chart. I usually write "Problem" and "Hopes and Dreams", "Evaluations" and "Effects".

Let me give an example:

In the top-right quadrant, write about the problem, its name, and intentions, and how the problems influence or impact on the person and the family. This could be:

> I'm always scared of being in the wrong. It's like an extra radio program running all the time, talking to me....

In the lower right quadrant, we note the problem's effects on the person and relationships with other people, on the person's abilities to pursue their aspirations, and so on.

> It makes me irritable; I get into fights. My mum hates me. I can't concentrate....

In the bottom left quadrant, we write the person's evaluations of what's on the right side.

It has way too much power, it's too loud. I can't trust that program....

In the top left quadrant, we write the person's justifications of their evaluations. These are often a person's dreams, hopes, and values.

I want to live happily in my family.

I want my mum and me to love each other.

Headlines are inserted in the two top quadrants. Insert on the Right: Problems; and on the Left: Hopes and Dreams. Remember that keeping to the system is impossible because the conversations never go linear. This is just a guideline.

Here's the basic quadrant with the sentences from our imaginary conversation:

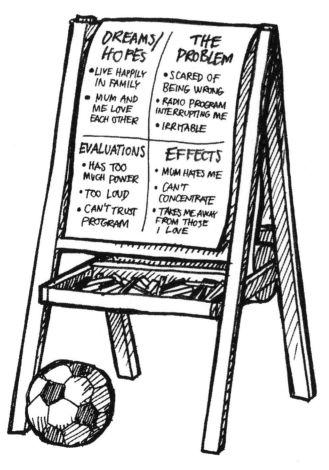

70 *Untidy or beautiful illustrations of life*

Radio Program is noted in capital letters and bold, to signify that this is a metaphor that can be used for externalization.

Note: The same system can be applied for a preferred value, a dream, hope, a competence, and so on. Don't limit externalization to problems. The internalizing of problems is hurtful, so we need to externalize the problems, but it is also fun and therapeutic to externalize the positive and preferred aspects of life.

Tracking a story

We all want to get the full story at the beginning of a treatment, and our story-tracking technique can also be used for documenting a medical history. The idea is to illustrate the family story as a road journey on the paper chart. Many families have said that seeing their life unfold in this way on paper is very helpful. To start, I go to the lower left corner of the paper chart and make a timeline that snakes upward on the paper. As the paper is on a roll, the timeline can become as long as necessary.

Assign each person a specific colour at the outset, to reduce messiness. Also, allow space for extra notes; many important memories will pop up throughout the conversation, as it is difficult to describe one's life chronologically.

Remember to ask questions, so you can finetune the wording to enable the problems, values, intentions, and dreams to become externalized, as they are put onto the paper. You can make this more poignant by writing the externalized phenomena with capital letters, giving them names. Here are examples of questions that can be asked in response to statements from the family, before noting the stories on the paper chart:

> "We were too busy". Would you say that Business ruled you?
> "She was so depressed and down all the time". Did Depression tie her down?
> "He was so unruly". Was Unruliness running havoc in your home?
> "He should obey us". What would you call this? Is it a Rule, an Ambition, or a Value you have for your parenthood?
> "I ended up shouting at her". Do you remember what your intentions were before this Shouting-match took over?

This technique helps the family to form relationships with their problems, values, intentions, and dreams, and it has a great therapeutic effect, as they also begin to evaluate these relationships.

Untidy or beautiful illustrations of life 71

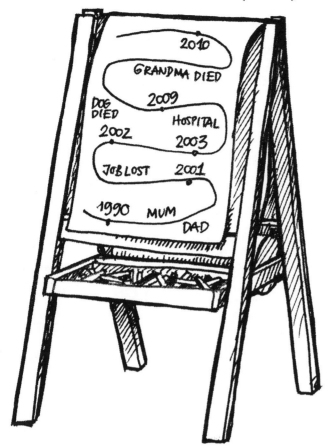

We also often use this story-tracking technique for the last session, to track the family's development of what has happened during the course of therapy and note what new or old values, skills, and wisdom have been created, incorporated, or rediscovered in the family during the time we have known each other. We start by asking, "Where were you, when we met?" As well, we talk about how different conversations were helpful. We ask questions like:

- What do you want to remember from our conversations?
- Do you remember what gave you that insight? What were we talking about?
- Why do you think this is important for you to remember?
- What have you or others done, that you attribute to this new perspective?
- What might you envision will happen in the future, if you keep this insight close to your heart?

72 *Untidy or beautiful illustrations of life*

Metaphors

We focus our attention on asking about and writing the family's descriptions of their values, hopes, and intentions on the paper, so we can come back to them. This is an effective way to create shared knowledge and understanding.

Many of us remember pictures and metaphors more than individual words because pictures and metaphors transfer a conglomerate of information. Pictures and metaphors often solve a problem of describing something unnameable with too many characteristics, bringing it closer to personal experience, and making it more vivid and memorable (Ortony, 1975). When a family member uses an expression that contains something visual or a metaphor, write it on the paper chart. If any sentence or use of a word is out of the ordinary, use it.

Let me give an example. Mandy and Andy have four sons with different diagnoses: autism, Attention-Deficit Hyperactivity Disorder (ADHD), and schizophrenia. Mandy herself has autism and ADHD. Two of the sons were referred to us with problems and received family treatment in our team for more than two years. I visited them when researching for this book, five years after they had ceased family therapy. I invited their insights and reflections on what had been helpful and not helpful. They offered to re-visit the family sessions with me by looking at their paper charts.

Joel, now 16, had no recollection of any words on the paper charts. However, a drawing of a raft and a canoe sparked a recollection, and he said, "I remember the friendship-canoe!"

> Andy joined in, excited: I remember that drawing! Joel's friendship canoe, yes, that was good. This painted a strong picture of how much friendships meant to you. At the time we didn't see how socially pressured you were, and how much you needed friends.

> Andy pointed at the old drawing on the paper charts and said: The others had a raft; they pushed each other into the water. Yes, that was the power struggle that was going on in the class, which was totally insane. We still talk about this in the parent group when we meet in town.

Mandy turned to Joel: Didn't you and Dad use the friendship-canoe afterwards? I think, I remember you talking about it, right?

Andy: Those were some nice metaphors! The canoe moves, but the raft remains still. You can fight your way up on the raft, but you get pushed back down. However, you can sail the canoe towards something. That's what you did, and still do, Joel!

Joel: I do not want to stand still. That raft didn't move. Today I have friends in my canoe, and we go places.

Reach for the stars

Visualizing stars as guiding lights is a wonderful metaphor that we use as a ceremonial ending to each conversation.

We aim to help the family members focus on and increase their knowledge about aspects of the conversation that they have found most helpful, by asking them to discuss the aspect that appeals most to them.

We say: Now, you must each answer the final question (and then we can express the rest in different ways):

- If you were to remember only one thing from today (remember we will give you the paper chart to take home), but if you really would remember only one thing from today, what would you choose?
- What did you find most fascinating or interesting from our time together today, that you want to think more about?
- What point in the conversation touched you the most, or felt most intense?
- What would you hate to forget from our conversation today?
- What struck you as most significant today?

We place a star and the name next to that sentence. Sometimes a sentence is not on the paper chart, so then we write it.

Once we did a taking-stock session with a family, who said they would like us to stop a little earlier to allow more time for these "closing-questions". They had noticed that the answers to these questions often led to new interesting questions, and they themselves got interested in understanding why the others chose what they chose. That taught us the importance of making time for questions like:

- Why did you choose to put your star there?
- If you remember this, what might that help you to do, or influence how you think about…?
- Wow, that's interesting, it reminds me of what you mentioned earlier about…: Is there a connection between that and this star?

Experiences have taught us that when we make time for these questions, the "star-questions" become more powerful and helpful.

We often use these sentences as the primary inspiration for our therapeutic e-mails.

74 *Untidy or beautiful illustrations of life*

Becoming a better "scribbler"

Putting a patient's own words about themselves, their problems, hopes, and dreams, about their lives, onto a paper chart, makes it possible to stand together and look at the problems or the illness from the outside, and this puts the patient in a powerful position.

The patient starts to see that they (not us) are able to create relationships with the problems and their dreams, analyse, evaluate, judge, get ideas, and make decisions about their own lives from a position where they feel good about themselves.

The public note-taking becomes more than shared note-taking; it becomes therapeutic in itself.

Looking at the paper charts I have often exclaimed, "What a mess I have made!" Sometimes I feel embarrassed by the messy paper charts, full of circles and lines connecting sentences, exclamation marks, and stick drawings. But once when I apologized for the mess, a young male patient, with whom I was trying this new technique, said, "No it's not messy. This is how my life is, and

Untidy or beautiful illustrations of life   75

it gives me a good overview. Of course, in some ways, life is messy, right? But I like it! It's a beautiful illustration of my life".

Having the messy scribbles described as "beautiful" provided powerful encouragement to pursue this technique. This and other responses inspired me to work hard on becoming a better "scribbler".

We become better at public note-taking, and better therapists, when we:

- Remember the therapeutic effects of the slowing down of the tempo in the sessions. We and the families get time to think, creating a calm and caring atmosphere that is essential for the creation of feelings of togetherness and collaboration. Sometimes people find the quietness to be eerie, but this is avoided when we look together at the shared notes.
- Use the notes as "templates" or "memory cards" for writing our therapeutic letters.
- Use the paper chart technique in different contexts, such as sharing photos of our paper charts at conferences to describe the process or to introduce the family at supervision.
- Observe our different writing techniques and inspire each other.
- Remember to ask those with whom we speak, how and what they think ought to be written on the paper, and what we can do to improve. We can only learn to do this, when in collaboration with the family (Ostrander, 2017).

Inspiration for poetical descriptions, metaphors, and drawings can be found in many places and especially by reading other therapists' stories about their experiences. Such stories provide a bottomless well of inspiration (Aman, 2006; Carey, 2002; Fox, 2003; Linnell, 2004; Marsten et al., 2016; Ncube, 2006; Torneke, 2017).

I hope you will find your own "easel" and experience the joy of sharing your notes with your families.

Notes

1 A well-known Swedish furniture company has an easel in their children's department, that we find helpful. It is the right size for sitting around a "tea table", children can play with it, and the paper can be continuous.
2 They: The doctor in charge at the inpatient ward and their social worker.
3 Workshops by Art Fisher, arranged by Narrative Praksis, November 2006: Visual narrative therapy and community work: Level II Intensive. November 1–5, intensive, Copenhagen, Denmark. 2007, September: Advanced narrative therapy practice: Supervision III. Level III Intensive, September 27–30, Copenhagen, Denmark.

References

Aman, J. (2006). Therapist as host: Making my guests feel welcome. *The International Journal of Narrative Therapy and Community Work*, 3, 3–10. doi: https://search.informit.org/doi/ 10.3316/informit.197553429083591

76 Untidy or beautiful illustrations of life

Carey, M. (2002). What the wildman, the dragon-arguing monster and camellia chameleon taught me about externalising conversations. *The International Journal of Narrative Therapy and Community Work*, *4*, 3–11. doi:https://search.informit.org/doi/10.3316/informit.662315631176874

Christiansen, M. (2015). A deliberate pedagogy. Introducing the hidden curriculum, social pedagogy, and the common third. In L. Pyles, & Adam, G. (Ed.), *Holistic engagement: Transformative social work education in the 21st Century*. Oxford University Press.

Epston, D. (1998). *Catching up with David Epston: A collection of narrative practice-based papers, published between 1991 and 1996*. Adelaide, Australia: Dulwhich Centre Publishing.

Fox, H. (2003). Using therapeutic documents: A review. *The International Journal of Narrative Therapy and Community Work*, *4*, 26–36. doi:https://search.informit.org/doi/10.3316/informit.661328083700189

Hadi, J. (2018). Viewpoint the common third. It ain't what you do it's the way that you do it. *Professional Social Work Magazine*. Retrieved from 10 December 2020 http://www.sppa-uk.org/wp-content/uploads/2018/09/It-aint-what-you-do-its-the-way-that-you-do-it.pdf

Husen, M. (1996). Det fælles tredje – om fællesskab og værdier i det pædagogiske arbejde. In B. Pésceli (Ed.), *Kultur og Pædagogik*. Copenhagen, Denmark: Munksgård/Rosinante.

Linnell, S. (2004). Towards a "Poethics" of therapeutic practice: Extending the relationship of ethics and aesthetics in narrative therapies through a consideration of the late work of Michel Foucault. *The International Journal of Narrative Therapy and Community Work*, *4*, 42–54. doi:https://search.informit.org/doi/10.3316/informit.262899259286099

Marsten, D., Epston, D., & Markham, L. (2016). *Narrative therapy in wonderland. Connecting with children's imaginative know-how*. W. W. Norton & Co.

Morgan, A. (2000). *What is narrative therapy?: An easy-to-read introduction*. Adelaide, Australia:Dulwich Centre Publications.

Ncube, N. (2006). The tree of life project. *The International Journal of Narrative Therapy and Community Work*, *1*, 3–16. Retrieved 13 December 2020 from https://search.informit.org/doi/10.3316/informit.197106237773394

Ortony, A. (1975). Why metaphors are necessary and not just nice. *Educational Theory*, *25*(1), 45–53. doi:10.1111/j.1741-5446.1975.tb00666.x

Ostrander, C. (2017). The chasing of tales: Poetic license with the written word in narrative practice. *The International Journal of Narrative Therapy and Community Work*, *2*(2), 55–63. doi:https://search.informit.org/doi/10.3316/informit.960099553781207

Storø, J. (2013). *Practical social pedagogy. Theories, values and tools for working with children and young people*. Policy Press and Bristol University

Torneke, N. (2017). *Metaphor in practice: A professional's guide to using the science of language in psychotherapy*. Context Press.

White, M. (2006). Narrative practice with families with children: Externalising conversations revisited. In M. White, & Morgan, A. (Ed.), *Narrative Therapy with Children and their families* (pp. 1–56). Adelaide: Dulwich Centre Publications.

White, M. (2007). *Maps of narrative practice*. W. W. Norton & Co.

6 The helping map as a guiding light

A helping map is one of our preferred collaborative methods for creating new knowledge and this chapter describes how to use it. We base this practice on William Madsen's collaborative helping map (Madsen, 2009, 2011, 2016). There are focal differences between using the helping map, and the externalized problem-map described in Chapter 5.

Traditionally the patient is asked, "What's wrong with you?" The expectation is that if their problem is revealed, it will be fixed. This is why people talk about "getting to the bottom of it", wanting to "go deep", and "finding the origin of the problem". In contrast, narrative therapists ask the patient, "What's wrong with your problem?" or "What's wrong with your relationship with your problem?"

Narrative therapists step away from the idea of "getting to the bottom of it" by employing externalizing language to create a relationship between the problem and the person. Using the helping map, we take an extra step and focus on the preferred future. We ask, "What might your future be, if you were to decide?", "What gets in the way of this happening?", and "What will support you to go in that direction?"

If we explore something and talk about it a lot, we can become wise about it. If we talk a lot about the problem, we can learn a lot about the problem, but that doesn't necessarily help us to solve the problem. Most of the families we meet have difficulties imagining a different life, so we help them to discover fresh perspectives and possibilities. We might say, "If we have no compass and no knowledge about where we want to go, how can we get there? When we know what we want to do differently and we talk a lot about that, and paint it in vivid colours, we can more easily take steps towards this preferred way of life".

Focusing on preferred family-life stories, the times when family members are happy about themselves, is also more productive and fun. That's why I am passionate about this way of working.

If you are familiar with externalizing conversations, but unfamiliar with using the helping map, you can imagine that the helping map is like starting at the end of the externalized problem-map and reversing. The justification of

DOI: 10.4324/9781003171621-7

78 *The helping map as a guiding light*

the evaluations leads you to the dreams and hopes. The helping map allows you to focus on these dreams and visions in a more direct manner.

We begin by drawing lines on the paper chart to make four quadrants. But it looks a little different to the externalized problem-map in Chapter 5.

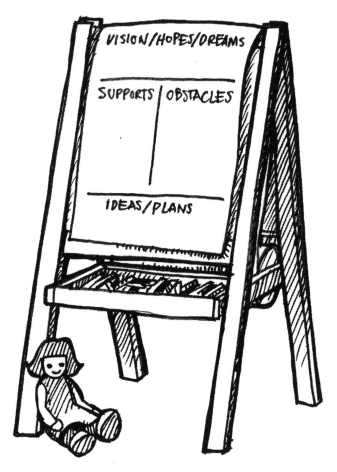

We want to guide the conversation according to a vision, dream, or hope, so we write these words at the top of the paper. Next, we put obstacles or problems on the right side, and supports, values, and preferred descriptions on the left side. We create a new category at the bottom: ideas and plans.

These conversations include questions like:

- What would you be doing if the problem wasn't there?
- If I had a magic stick and waved the problem away, what would you be able to do, that you cannot do now?

The helping map as a guiding light   79

- Has there been any small event, where you could do even a tiny bit of what you just described?
- Are there differences in your family life, where some days the problem is more powerful than other days? What is special about those days when it has less power? What would I notice about those days? What happens on those days when the problem has less power?
- What might you be doing differently on those days, that lessens the problem's power over you?

We ask the patient and their family if talking about the problem this way is helpful for them and most often the answer is, "Yes". When we ask why it makes sense to talk about the problem in this way, the response is often because it gives energy, hope, or ideas about how to move away from the problem-saturated daily life. Many of these questions are inspired by solutions-focused therapy that concentrates on the non-problematic future (Berg, 1994) and especially on magical questions (de Shazer, 1994).

This supports the theory that we do not need to focus on the problem and become experts on it. Rather, we need to become experts on how to live the preferred life. We might ask:

- What might help you to live this preferred way of life?
- What might stand in the way of doing what you want to do?
- What stories are in your family that supports our belief that you can do these wonderful things?
- What stories, values, or discourses might there be that could be obstacles, that could prevent you from moving in this direction you want to move?

That said, I do not advocate ignoring the problem. We need to explore the problem, to get smarter at understanding why it is an obstacle, and learn about its purposes, tricks, and lies, so we can cope with it more easily, and focus on the preferred way of life.

We often use the metaphor of joining the family on their life-journey, as stepping onto their train, and travelling through the plains or desert. In this way, the family is moving towards the new, instead of moving away from the problematic old (Madsen, 2007, p. 126). We ask what landscape they see through their train windows and ask them to describe the countries and train stations we are visiting. This process is like we cannot see, and the family is describing what they see, to enlighten and inform us.

If you are a seasoned narrative therapist, you can envisage the square called "Obstacles" as the statement of a position map, and the square with "Supports" chartering preferred stories, either as unique outcomes, re-membering, or re-authoring conversations. All of them lead to the top with the "Values, Dreams and Hopes" for the future.

80 *The helping map as a guiding light*

Creating a unified story about our family

Our colleagues were concerned about Iris, 16, who had been admitted to the adolescent inpatient ward due to psychosis. When discharged, Iris refused to comply with advice to pursue an educational program designed for young people with special needs. She went straight from inpatient care to living at home and starting college. Her younger sister, Karen, had recovered from anorexia several years earlier but, when Iris became ill, Karen's eating disorder flared up. The purpose of the referral to us was "for family therapy to support the parents, Hella and Jon, in making better decisions for their daughters".

The beginning of our collaboration with this family illustrates how we use the helping map. When I initially spoke with the mother Hella, on the phone, I was mindful of the helping map and explained the vision that we could offer conversations with all four family members about what kind of family life they would like to live. I said, "Our aim is to help you cope and become the family you have hoped to be, despite struggling with at least two psychiatric illnesses that we know can destroy families".

Hella said she was self-employed and had stopped working so that she could support her daughters full-time, and because she herself felt too burdened to work. At first, I only heard the latter part of her sentence, that the mother stopped working because she felt too burdened. This led me to think that the mother was having problems herself, and I placed this information in the box of obstacles. Only later did I hear her decision was made proactively to help her daughters, despite the sacrifice causing a drop in their income. This led me to see Hella's actions in another light and the parents as more resourceful than my first impression. This information, therefore, belonged in the support box. This experience caused me to wonder if I often judged parents as more burdened than they wanted me to see them, and if I adequately acknowledged their sacrifices.

Hella described her family as "worn out" and doubted her daughters would agree to more therapy. Karen had attended family therapy at an eating disorder unit and Iris had received individual therapy. They were both tired of being "problems". Accordingly, we agreed that the parents would come alone to our first session.

Hella and Jon had spoken with their daughters prior to our meeting. They already had some answers for the vision box: "We want help for our family; we want a unified narrative about our family, not four separate stories about who we are".

We suggested that Hella and Jon share the parental story about their family. This family had experienced many traumas, somatic and psychiatric illnesses, serious diseases with grandparents, and problems at work. We used colours to signify if an event had been a struggle or a sustaining factor in their lives. They observed our note-taking on the paper chart and commented several times, "That was a hard year!" This led the parents to conclude that they had too many stories about traumas and problems compared with sustaining and positive stories. At the end of this session, they said, "We would like to create a new balance in our family".

Now we had at least two, slightly different, hopes to put in the vision box.

Co-creating the treatment plan

The entire family came to the next meeting. We suggested we focus on getting to know each family member outside the influences of the problem and introduced the idea of a wonderfulness-interview. However, the girls were expecting and wanted us to speak about the problems, so we added:

> "It's also possible to begin by speaking about your problems, or how your family life could improve if your conversations with us become helpful".

First, the family wanted to talk about their visions and hopes for doing family therapy.

I wrote these visions on the paper chart:

Visions

How can we help each other better?

- Improve communication; verbalize the problems.
- Dad to become better at telling us when things are hard for him.

We asked questions, for example:

- What might stand in the way of you helping each other?
- What will change if Dad gets better at telling you things?
- What obstacles might make it hard to share feelings when things are difficult?
- What have your efforts at communication been like so far? Can you tell a story about a communication experience, that indicates a small step in the right direction? Can you provide an example of what you consider good communication?
- What are some examples of unhelpful communication?
- When people can articulate that they hope to help each other, it's because they know something about helping. Can you tell us about your experiences with giving and receiving helpful help?

We documented the family members' words on the paper chart and organized the information according to themes. We placed the struggles and obstacles on one side of the paper, and inserted competencies, positive experiences, and knowledge on the other side. As the conversation developed, the family's descriptions became more concrete with descriptive stories about the girls

82 *The helping map as a guiding light*

doing things together, their values and hopes as a family, and ideas on how to proceed towards a better future.

The family's stories led us to ask questions like:

- Can you describe some of your sisters-doing-things-together experiences? What does this tell us about you and your family values?
- Is your idea about being responsible a new thing or have you had this idea for a long time?
- Is hug-giving an important thing in your family?
- Seeing your parents hug each other, is this important for you to witness?
- What are your worries urging you to do, as a mum?
- Does "worry" want to help you to prevent the eating disorder from returning?
- How do you experience your mum's "worry-actions"? Did you know that worries are dictating her actions?
- What might be helpful for you as a mum in relationship to worries?
- You said the word "blame". We are "big on blame": parent-blame, sibling-blame, and so on. We believe blame is one of the biggest allies to psychiatric illness (Bentley et al., 2016; Jensen, 2018). We believe that blame also might be one of the biggest causes of family unrest (Harrington, 2016). Have you thought about blame in this way? If so, what do you think about blame now?
- Will your dad become a role model for you, if he improves at describing how he is feeling? Or will this mean something to the ambience in your family? Why do Dad's feelings matter to you?
- You have mentioned feeling bad, and also that your dad is finding things hard. Is "feeling bad" and "finding things hard" the same thing, or something different?

Answers to questions like these often lead family members to give descriptions and tell stories that become metaphors and family narratives about their family's identity and their values (White, 2004). Psychiatric problems often erase the valuable memories in a family. Since the mother Hella had described her family as worn-out, we wanted to help her family to recollect narratives that could sustain them in striving for their goal, which was to find a new balance.

Several times during the conversation we asked:

- Are we speaking about the right stuff?
- Is this relevant in relationship to your vision about helping each other/ improving communication?

These two curious, standard questions are aimed at creating collaboration and giving the family members agency by handing them the power to evaluate the process (Madsen, 2014b). Such questions also help us all to take a "helicopter view" of the therapy and evaluate if we are going in the right

The helping map as a guiding light   83

direction. If we just get a "yes" as a response, we might ask family members to justify their evaluations, so making it possible to express specific values that inform their hopes and dreams (White, 2007, pp. 263–290).

By now the paper chart contained loads of information, so we made a summary of what we had talked about and focused on the following items:

Vision/hopes/dreams

How can we help each other better?
Improve communication, verbalize the problems.
Dad to become better at telling us when things are hard for him.

Obstacles

Worries: eating disorder returns
Karen finding things hard
Mum's "worry-actions"
Blame
Hiding worries

Supports

Value: being helpful to each other
Sisters-doing-things-together
Parents hugging
Value: taking responsibility for my self

Ideas/plans

Try telling others if feeling bad
Being open about worries

We next asked the family:

*   What direction might we take now? Shall we talk more about the visions, or the problems that stand in your way of your visions, or more about what you are already doing, that is assisting you in that direction?

Two items were added to the "Visions" list. Iris added to the last sentence about her dad:

Being able to say it without getting angry.

The parents inserted:

Worries for the girls shall become smaller.

84   *The helping map as a guiding light*

Colleagues had been concerned that the parents had too few worries and were failing to protect Iris the way the worries told them they ought to (like advising her against going to college). But the family experienced the situation differently. Who were the experts here? We decided to explore this issue with the family, and they described their experiences with the negative effects of worries. To them, worries increased rather than reduced psychotic symptoms, family disputes, and mutual distrust. We supported their conclusion, in keeping with our ethics of empowerment and mattering.

When the time ran out for this session, we concluded by saying, "Time is running out! We must stop. But first we invite you to answer these questions:

- How was the conversation for you today? What worked well, what worked less well for you?
- Would you like to talk in the way we have been talking today when we meet again?"

All four members of the family responded positively, and this conversation became the template for our treatment plan.

We explained that the family could take the paper chart home, so they could look at it whenever they wanted to do so. We then asked our traditional concluding questions, "If you could remember only one thing from today, what would you choose? What do you find most important to think more about? We will place a star and your name next to that sentence, and if it's not already on the paper, we will write it on".

Karen was the first to answer. She chose words from the plans box, something she could work on by herself. It was also an action that would lead her and the family closer to one of their visions, that of improving their communication. She said, "I will try to practise telling the others, if I get hit by sadness or otherwise feel bad".

Iris and her mum focused on the visions box and chose the same thing, "That the worries for the girls shall become smaller". They agreed that this was possible, "If we can become better at communicating".

The dad said, "I was really touched by Iris's remark, that she thinks we parents fit well together, like Lego blocks. Even though I am not sure I like to be compared with Lego blocks, I like the metaphor, that we are two very different people but fit together like two Lego blocks". This comment, also written in the supports-box, had been made by Iris after we heard answers to these questions:

- What have your efforts at communication been like so far?
- Can you tell a story about a communication experience, that would be a small step in the right direction?
- Do you have an example of what you consider good communication?
- Seeing your parents hug each other, is this important for you to witness?

When preparing to write to the family after this conversation, my colleague Kirsten and I talked about our intentions for writing this letter. We focused on the idea of a proactive vision for the family (Madsen, 2007, pp. 125–154). We wanted to clearly state the visions from the helping map and also focus on the wonderfulnesses of the family members. We wanted to give the family members knowledge about themselves that they could build on, when they wanted to find ways to achieve their vision of becoming better at helping each other, better at communicating, and reducing worries about the girls.

Our intentions were to shine a bright light on those utterings and actions that we observed during the conversation, that showed the supports, the family's values, intentions, and actions that could give each person power to move forward in their preferred direction. We wanted to paint a picture comprising those pieces that we thought the family would prefer to be defined by – a picture describing some of "the best possible versions of our family".

Kirsten wrote:

Dear Karen, Iris, Hella, and Jon,

Thank you for the conversation.

This is an e-mail with a mix of your words and our words, thoughts, and tales from our conversation. We hope you will all feel seen and heard in this e-mail. If, in any way, we write something that doesn't fit well with you (and that does happen now and then), please let us know. As we told you, you do not have to reply to this letter, but you may do so, if you feel like it. We won't have time to respond, though. At our next meeting, we will start by reading this letter, and then we would like to hear your thoughts in relation to what we have written and anything else important to you.

We were captivated by the many resources in your family. We think, for example, of how you all tried to do your best to help each other and create change. We see this attitude as a great strength for a family.

For you, supporting each other may feel natural, but it is not so in many of the families we meet. Often there may be one or more members in the family who think, "The problem has nothing to do with me", and that the others must deal with it.

We were surprised, for example, when you, Karen, said that what you wanted to remember from the conversation was, "I will try to practise telling the others, if I get hit by sadness or otherwise feel bad".

We were surprised by this, because in our experience people who have been affected by an eating disorder, are often prevented by the eating disorder from saying that kind of thing out loud – anorexia, especially, tends to make you think that you should stay quiet and get a little thinner.

86   *The helping map as a guiding light*

We wonder if this was a big counter-eating disorder step? We thought it did lessen some of the worries we might have about the eating disorder and might be a kind of first step for us away from those types of worries. We wonder what each of you think about this, and what experiences you have with this?

Next, like you Jon, we were moved by Iris saying she thought her parents fit well together – we all know that children are nurtured by their parents' love for each other!

As you will notice, we both got immersed in the conversation and were inspired by what you said – not least by your desire to help each other to lessen worries – and that you found that communication could be a step in that direction.

We wonder if you will be inspired to use this same approach to counter the feelings of blame that we heard had affected all of you?

The communication we heard from you yesterday brought many nuances forth – for example the talk about what it means to have a bad time. It could mean many different things and this knowledge made room for varied options for actions. We would call that helping each other! Cool!

And we wonder how you each experienced the communication yesterday – was it different from what you are used to? If so, how was it different?

Talking with you inspired us, and we look forward to next time.

Many greetings Nina and Kirsten

Later, when we wrote up a treatment plan, the Visions from this conversation were incorporated in the plan, as was the long story from the first conversation with the parents. The parents appreciated that they got a shared story of the family's struggles, instead of four different stories, and they also appreciated having family goals, rather than individual goals, for their treatment.

The helping map provided a way for us to structure a conversation, so we could return to the purpose of the conversation and jump back and forth between problem-saturated and preferred narratives on the same piece of paper, in the same map, without it becoming too complicated.

The taking-stock session

Together with the family, we decided on the structure of the treatment course, as part of the treatment plan. This family chose a sequence of sessions comprising two sessions with all four family members, and one session for the parents only. We took stock with all four family members after two sequences, totalling six sessions. We brought a printed version of the

The helping map as a guiding light   87

treatment plan to the taking-stock session and looked at the visions after we had read the therapeutic letter.

We used that session to ask family members about their evaluation of the progress towards their goals and visions. We also asked specific questions about what each family member experienced as being helpful. These questions were asked in ways that allowed the family members to give constructive criticism, which was not easy due to the power hierarchy.

We did not ask, "What was good and what was bad?", because it is unpleasant to criticize. We wanted the family to step into a position of being our consultants. Therefore, we focused on inquiring what could be better, what benefits might flow from a certain change or restructure, and what we did not need to do as much (Madsen, 2014a, p. 13).

We asked, "What should we do more of, less of, or change?"

In the letter we sent to the family after the taking-stock session, my colleague Kirsten pointed out the family's evaluations. They had specific ideas about how we should proceed, with the family choosing the theme beforehand, writing specific actions on the paper chart, and giving each other ample time to unfold a preferred narrative for all to comprehend and appreciate the beauty of the development. The idea of deciding on a theme and telling us beforehand was different from our normal session structure, and therefore the family taught us how best to help them.

We used the letter to emphasize the contribution of family members to the collaborative work in the session and in their daily life at home. We also told them how we felt about them, not as an evaluation but as an appreciation. We were transparent. We shared our thoughts and used naming of knowledge and actions, to unpack and make their knowledge and actions more prominent in their lives. As well, we stepped into a position of inviting their evaluation of the treatment process, by asking if what we wrote made sense to them.

Dear Karen, Iris, Hella, and Jon

This was our first taking stock conversation and we talked about how we are doing and where we are going. It was very helpful for us to hear your thoughts and reflections on what works well for you:

- That the conversations are specific and focus on what you can do about the problems.
- That everyone in the family listens to each other describe what is going on for them.

You found that this approach shows you are a family where everybody has compassion for each other – even if you sit in different rooms watching a movie, doing homework, or are busy with other things. In our opinion, your care and respect for each other is a great and valuable thing that makes you strong together.

88   *The helping map as a guiding light*

As we heard it, you all appreciate making time to listen to each other's concerns about both big and small things, for example:

> "What was it with Karen's homework today?" Or "Why was Iris home from school today?"

> Making time to listen could also extend to the illnesses that have caused you all great concern and have affected you all. The girls have illnesses, but there is also your grandparents' somatic diseases and parental stress.

> For example, you asked each other, "How was it for Karen when Iris was admitted to hospital?"

> We thought about this session after you had gone home, and we realized that this taking stock session also became a taking stock session on the progress each of you has noticed. As we heard it, there have been many new steps. But we wonder if perhaps you each only see glimpses of this progress unless it becomes the focus of attention?

> Concerns and grumpiness demand attention. However, signs of progress can often kind of hide in the shadows. Is this how you see it?

> You pointed out that you have difficulty in forgiving each other for never being perfect, and in accepting the fact that you will always commit some small stupidities. But that old sense of divisiveness, that you know so well, seems to have been replaced by:

> *We're the "we-take-care-of-each-other" family.*
> Do we understand correctly?

> You chose to jointly decide and plan a specific theme for us all to discuss at our next conversation and we understand you will mail the theme to us beforehand. Is this right?

> Many greetings,
> Nina and Kirsten

To achieve the best outcome, the guidelines and framework that are created for any psychotherapeutic treatment need to be both specific and flexible to use. They need to encompass everything from the detailed questions we ask in every little encounter with a patient or a family we want to help, to the organization of the team's work.

In our team, the helping map is a cornerstone of our framework based on the narrative practices, including co-research, ethnographical work, and the use of insider knowledge, as described by David Epston (Epston, 1999, 2014; Maisel et al., 2004) and William Madsen (Madsen, 2007).

References

Bentley, K. J., Cohen-Filipic, K., & Cummings, C. R. (2016). Approaching parental guilt, shame, and blame in a helping relationship: Multiple methods for teaching and learning. *Journal of Teaching in Social Work*, *36*(5), 490–502. doi:10.1080/08841233. 2016.1238024

Berg, I. K. (1994). *Family based services: A solution-focused approach* .W.W. Norton.

de Shazer, S. (1994). *Words were originally magic*. W.W. Norton.

Epston, D. (1999). Co-research: The making of alternative knowledge in narrative therapy and community work. In P. Moss (Ed.), *Narrative therapy and community work: A conference collection*. Adelaide: Dulwich Centre Publications.

Epston, D. (2014). Ethnography, co-research and Insider Knowledges. *Australian and New Zealand Journal of Family Therapy*, *35*(1), 105–109. doi:10.1002/anzf.1048

Harrington, A. (2016). Mother love and mental illness: An emotional history. *Osiris*, *31*(1), 94–115. doi:10.1086/687559

Jensen, T. (2018). *Parenting the crisis: The cultural politics of parent-blame*. Bristol University Press.

Madsen, W. C. (2007). *Collaborative therapy with multi-stressed families* (2nd ed.). The Guilford Press.

Madsen, W. C. (2009). Collaborative helping: A practice framework for family-centered services. *Family Process*, *48*(1), 103–116. doi:10.1111/j.1545-5300.2009.01270.x

Madsen, W. C. (2011). Collaborative helping maps: A tool to guide thinking and action in family-centered services. *Family Process*, *50*(4), 529–543. doi:10.1111/j.1545-5300. 2011.01369.x

Madsen, W. C. (2014a). Applications of collaborative helping maps: Supporting professional development, supervision and work teams in family-centered practice. *Family Process*, *53*(1), 3–21. doi:10.1111/famp.12048

Madsen, W. C. (2014b). Taking it to the streets: Family therapy and family-centered services. *Fam Process*, *53*(3), 380–400. doi:10.1111/famp.12089

Madsen, W. C. (2016). Narrative approaches to organizational development: A case study of implementation of collaborative helping. *Family Process*, *55*(2), 253–269. doi:10.1111/famp.12212

Maisel, R., Epston, D., & Borden, A. (2004). *Biting the hand that starves you: Inspiring Resistance to Anorexia/Bulimia*. New York, NY: W.W. Norton & Co.

White, M. (2004). Narrative Practice and the unpacking of identity conclusions. In *Narrative practice and exotic lives: Resurrecting diversity in everyday life/by Michael White* (pp. 119–147). Adelaide: Dulwich Centre Publications.

White, M. (2007). *Maps of narrative practice*. W. W. Norton & Co.

7 Therapeutic letter writing

Therapeutic letter writing can expand the focus of medical records on diagnostic assessment and legal documentation to one of sharing thoughts and curiosity with the family. This chapter explores how therapeutic e-mails expand the role of documentation to one of sharing information with each family. The goal is to improve the treatment by practicing therapeutic transparency and collaboration with those we want to help. This process is empowering for both families and therapists.

As noted in Chapter 5, a narrative family therapist writes notes on a paper chart visible to all. When note-taking becomes shared public knowledge, and the families can take their paper charts home, they are given ownership of the process and can collaborate.

The literary approach to narrative therapy has been a cornerstone of David Epston and Michael White's work. Their first book, *Narrative Means to Therapeutic Ends,* contains many examples of letters that invite the patient to have authorship and re-authorship of their own experiences. Epston and White wrote the letters to narrate their therapy instead of documenting their therapy. This difference in methods can be compared with the difference between quantitative and qualitative research (White and Epston, 1990, pp. 77–187). The fundamental practice of therapeutic letter writing has been expanded and described by many narrative therapists. One way to learn therapeutic letter writing is to read books and articles describing and demonstrating this practice. I have been especially inspired by Jennifer Freeman's book, *Playful Approaches to Serious Problems*, David Nylund's article, *Poetic Means to Anti-anorexic Ends,* and Ann Epston's letter to a girl attacked by anorexia in *Biting the Hand that Starves You*, in which Ann takes a moral stand against anorexia (Freeman et al., 1997; Maisel et al., 2004, pp. 160–162; Nylund, 2002).

The endurance of written words has therapeutic potential because the written word can be kept and read again, minutes, days, or many years later. The spoken word lasts but a second and disappears (Epston, 1998b, p. 95).

Likewise, all written documents, treatment plans, and medical record notes can potentially have positive effects on treatment, when we write in a way that enables the patient and their family to experience respect.

DOI: 10.4324/9781003171621-8

Even though writing therapeutic letters is a cornerstone in narrative therapy, many therapists have difficulty making time to write an e-mail letter after each session. However, our team members write letters after every session, in the same way, that therapists or doctors document each of their sessions in the medical records. Our letter-writing practices make the paperwork and legal requirements less tedious and help us to create transparency, equality, collaboration, and hope.

> My experience with these e-mails is that they frame the sessions and help us to remember more perspectives on those problems we are working on – and they also give us a starting point for the next session.
>
> One must remember, our family is experiencing a chaotic period in our life, and the therapeutic letters, by providing firm, essential working points, help us to get more out of each session.
>
> A mother

Creating e-mail-writing practices collaboratively

To support our learning and implementation of letter writing before it became a routine practice, our team created guidelines and goals which included:

1. Sharing an "after-talk" after each conversation. The two therapists composed the letter together.
2. Starting the first letter to a family with a disclaimer and asking for feedback.
3. Keeping the first letters brief and including just one question, metaphor, reflection, or reference to the family's "stars".
4. Signing the letters on behalf of both co-therapists, demonstrating our collaboration.
5. Reading the letter at the start of each session.
6. Developing and using templates that we can learn from and be inspired by.

The purpose of the "after-talk"

The "after-talk" between the two therapists is an important part of the e-mail writing practice.

The "after-talk" focuses on:

- What might be helpful for the family to read in the letter.
- Specific aspects of the therapy that have moved the family forward (therefore also creating a self-supervisory focus).
- Questions our therapist partner asked in the session, that have most intrigued us (therefore also focusing on developing our techniques).

92 *Therapeutic letter writing*

- Remembering metaphors that the family mentioned, and exploring how a metaphor might be beneficial, if we expand on it in the letter.
- Asking each other what we are most intrigued by in the conversation and using the witnessing technique to develop a poetic tale or metaphor when writing to the family.

Standard questions that therapists ask each other may include:

- What did you really like/appreciate about today's conversation?
- What (and who) were you impressed by today?
- What do you think the family would most appreciate our writing/asking them about?
- What metaphor pops into our mind?
- What are we curious about now, that we wish we had asked about?

The role of the disclaimer

A disclaimer is a paragraph stating that the e-mail letter comprises our thoughts and reflections (not scientific-based truth) and might not be experienced as helpful by the family. The disclaimer is another way of honouring the family (Pilkington, 2018, p. 29). Our letters may begin with:

> "If there is anything you disagree with or cannot recognize, just ignore it".

We emphasize the family's expertise and knowledge by using sentences such as:

> "Please let us know next time, what you think".

> "If I am way off with my understanding, just tear the letter up or delete it".

> "Can this letter be of use to you?"

We aim to use the family's own words and language (i.e., concrete, factual, or reflective), and we are especially attentive to the children's vocabulary. We pose our ideas as questions, not as interpretations. Often, we write:

> "Does this make sense?"

> "I might be totally wrong, …".

> "Did we get that right?"

The posing of questions has become a fertile ground for reflection in our e-mails. By reading our questions the family has an opportunity to nurture their hopes and dreams and explore their motives and intentions. The family members are inspired to examine their own life, and the resulting movement and developments can be therapeutic.

Importantly, the family members have the opportunity to correct or deepen our understanding of what was talked about during the interview. This enables the family members to disagree with us without feeling they are criticizing the very people they depend on for help. Collaboration and empowerment demand that the family members feel secure enough to criticize us. Reading the letter allows us to externalize the therapy, so the therapy itself can be scrutinized, questioned, and reflected on (Epston, 1998b, p. 97).

The reading of the letter aloud is a powerful means for creating a context, enabling patients and families to voice their thoughts and disagreements. Accordingly, we invite comments after the reading, before discussing the agenda for the next conversation.

Making the project of writing un-daunting

Starting small and being unambitious, is important. David writes:

> Whenever I find myself stuck in writing a letter, I often end up including my concern about this in the letter, "I am wondering if you got anything out of this therapy. Where did I go wrong? The only glimmer was... but did it have enough substance for you to merit a therapy session?" (Epston, 1998a, p. 100).

Having each other's back

Sharing responsibility and success is important when a team embarks on a new practice. Helping and supporting each other, even when only one therapist writes and signs the letter on behalf of both therapists, is essential.

A colleague remembers creating and learning the e-mail-writing practice this way:

> We mailed each other "boasting-mails". We amplified the successes – not only what the families succeeded in, but also what we thought we had succeeded in. It was great! We celebrated when we succeeded and were immensely happy on each other's behalf.
>
> Hanne, a psychologist

Being witnessed as worthy

We read aloud the e-mail that we send to the family, at the start of the next conversation. The reading has become our ceremonial way of starting each session. It sets a calm tone of trust, acknowledgement, hope, and reflection.

94 *Therapeutic letter writing*

The experience of reading aloud in this way can become very moving for both the family and us, when we feel the ambiance from the letter fill the room. This is because the physical experience of being witnessed as a worthy person and family, by us reading the letter for the family, has therapeutic effects when the focus is on their moral values, competencies and actions of which they can be proud (Epston, 2009; Meyerhoff, 1986; Moules, 2009).

The letter reading also assists us and the family in recalling what happened in the previous session. The family members might comment about the letter, on content that they appreciate, or on our questions that have inspired or given them solace. They have the opportunity to update us on new developments that have happened since our previous meeting. The letters help to move our therapy into the everyday life of the family and help both the family and us to stay on track.

> The written language becomes a team player. An important advantage is that e-mails can be read again and again, whereas a verbal conversation is elusive. The e-mails are especially helpful when a person's world is falling apart, and stress has given way to panic and despair.
>
> E-mails combined with notes on paper charts create lasting, palpable prints of what happens in those rather condensed therapy sessions.
>
> They help to create the experience of being welcome with one's whole person, by making room to formulate and provide input and to send, for example, photographs and articles, that substantiate what is being communicated.
>
> To me, these e-mails enable reciprocal dignity and life-giving forth-comingness.
>
> They also contribute to empowerment.
>
> Nelly, mother of Charlotte, (Chapter 9), on therapeutic e-mails

> I am one of those parents who keeps an e-mail printout inside my wallet – an e-mail message that has ongoing importance for me and in my role as a parent.
>
> A mother

Using letters as templates

Since we share our letters with each other, we can use these letters as templates. A letter of invitation (see Chapter 2, the letter for Filippa) becomes a template that can be revised to make it appropriate for each new child.

All e-mails are written in an externalizing manner. Our most common techniques are:

Therapeutic letter writing   95

- Quoting the family's stars or metaphors.
- Retelling the family's favourite points from the conversation.
- Summarizing the most important parts of the conversation.
- Referring to the helping map (vision/objectives, support, obstacles, plan).
- Expressing our reflections as questions and wonderings.
- Witnessing the family's favourite stories and favourite life stories.
- Using poetic narratives inspired by their stories.
- Employing metaphorical narratives, based on our reflections or on an image that emerged in the conversation.

Making fun of anxiety

I wrote about Katja and her daughter Filippa in Chapters 2 and 4. Katja brought Fillipa for a session, but Filippa's anxiety prohibited her from participating at the next session, so Katja came alone. That led me to write a letter to both of her daughters, externalizing the anxiety and describing what Katja had shared about their struggles. I hoped to give Filippa a sense of personal agency, and to make the problems seem less powerful:

> Dear Fillipa and Isabella,
>
> I write this letter to both of you. I have met Fillipa once, so I know what a lovely girl you are. I have only heard about you, Isabella, but I have agreed with your mother that the next time she comes to talk, she will bring you both.
>
> Your mum told me about how amazing Fillipa was after your visit with me. To me it sounded almost like an adventure, because what your mother told me is so impressive. Maybe you think it's a little weird what I'm writing, and maybe Fillipa needs to explain to Isabella how we talked together when you were here? Do you want to do that, Fillipa?
>
> This is the adventurous tale I heard from your mother:
>
> When Fillipa and her mother began their homeward journey, they left the evil anxiety in the parking lot outside Nina's office. They did not make a big deal out of it, and perhaps that is why the evil anxiety did not even realize that they were quietly returning home by bus and train.
>
> But Fillipa felt the freedom of not having to drag that heavy and troublesome evil anxiety. It gave her freedom to dream and imagine a future with completely different possibilities to those she had envisaged before. As two buses passed each other on the street, Fillipa could see the two bus drivers greeting and laughing at each other, from one bus to the other. Fillipa saw how happy the drivers were, helping to transport people around the city. Fillipa got the idea that a job where you can help, and

96   *Therapeutic letter writing*

smile, and laugh, and greet your colleagues in the other buses, was a job she would like to do, when she grew up.

Fillipa's little sister Isabella looks up to her lovely big sister and wants to be just as loving and skilled as her. When Isabella heard about this new dream Fillipa had of becoming a bus driver, Isabella thought, "Maybe I can become a bus driver too? And maybe one day I will ride a big, beautiful bus around town. I will take care of the people on the bus and maybe I will pass the bus my sister is driving, and we will greet each other and smile and laugh together".

I also heard that the evil anxiety slowly discovered that it had been left behind. It was exhausted and had lost power being alone; it became very angry and spent many days cursing and swearing as it crawled and slid into the city, looking for the mother and two daughters it thought it was entitled to rule.

When Fillipa and Isabella's mother went for their next meeting with Nina, the evil anxiety did everything to prevent them from leaving home. Anxiety was afraid of being abandoned again, because if this happened, it would be further weakened and would have less power over Fillipa. It did everything it could to avoid that. It made Fillipa stay home. But it couldn't prevent the girls' mother from attending the meeting.

That little bit of anxiety that retained power over Fillipa and Isabella's mother faded during the meeting. In contrast, the love that the mother had for her daughters grew and took up more room in her life. Now the mother could feel her love blossom without the anxiety constantly getting in the way, making it difficult for her to see her lovely daughters.

See, this is an adventure that is not yet finished, but which is about a battle between evil and good. I am sure the good will win, because your mother has so much love, drive, and willpower, that she will do everything to ensure that the evil anxiety does not gain power over your family.

I am grateful that you have chosen to make me your partner on this adventure, and I look forward to seeing you next week, meeting Isabella for the first time, and hearing you describe your battles with the evil anxiety.

Many anti-evil-anxiety greetings, Nina

Katja later reflected:

I remember this letter because you managed to change something that was very "heavy" (because Filippa was always anxious about riding a bus. She feared, "What if the bus driver is an evil person who has hijacked the bus and wants to drive us to death?"). You managed to change the story into something easy and humorous for Filippa, for all three of us, with Filippa and Isabella each driving a bus and waving to each other.

I remember how Filippa and Isabella burst out laughing because they saw that picture in their heads – it was so paradoxical to imagine for them, but they were amused and I was, too.

When we read the "bus letter", (while sitting on our couch), Isabella was the first to jump into the role as a bus driver. She laughed and pretended that she was a bus driver and, as she passed Filippa, she was shouting, "Hello, hello".

Filippa immediately jumped into the role of the other bus driver (verbally and acting out with her hands on the big steering wheel) and there was a fun ping-pong between the girls. A little play. Right there, while we read your letter.

You are welcome to use the letters

Inspired by David's archives of resistance to anorexia (Epston, 2013), I asked patients and families for approval to use their e-mail letters for educational purposes. Lielle, 17, responded, "You are welcome to use my letters", and reflected on her experience:

> You made prints of all our letters and gave them to me in a folder at the end of our therapy. These letters have been good for me because they provide a timeline of my personal development.
>
> I have been able to look in this folder when things have been insurmountable, and just knowing that the letters are there, in my drawer, is calming. To me it has been good to have something tangible, that describes something from the past and helps me to understand today.

Lielle was 13 when she began to experience psycho-somatic symptoms, and she was diagnosed with depression. She was referred to us a year later with psychotic symptoms and was prescribed antipsychotic medicine. The family received family therapy for a year, and then a second and final year of treatment involved Lielle meeting me fortnightly, plus parental meetings monthly.

Lielle's evaluation at our final meeting included this advice:

- It's more important to have the e-mail letters read aloud than reading them alone.
- Hearing you read the letters helps me to remember where we were.
- Your tales resemble a mirror, inspiring me to think alternative thoughts.
- Don't ask questions in the letters because I find such questions too confusing. They might be good for others, but not for me!

98   *Therapeutic letter writing*

- Don't make the letters too detailed. We each have different recollections. If you include too much detail, I'll remember how you experienced it, not how I experienced it.
- I like the resumes.
- When your letters focus on the future, this is helpful.

Lielle's suggestions underline the importance of asking each patient for their evaluation, so letter writing can be tailored in the same way that therapy is tailored to each individual patient.

Studying letters from other therapists is a powerful tool for learning this practice. When asked, most therapists reply, like Lielle, "You are welcome to use my letters" (Bjorøy et al., 2015; Fox, 2003; Freedman and Combs, 1996; Marner, 1988; Moules, 2003; Pilkington, 2018).

Counterbalancing those problems

Siblings, Karen and Iris, described in Chapter 6, each struggled with anorexia and psychosis. The family was worn out and wanted help to reduce the power of the worries. We were amazed by how the girls' family worked on counteracting the problems that were causing their worries. Our job became one of highlighting the family's determined focus. Our e-mails became a tool for sustaining family members in their plight and fight for a better life. We asked at the end of each session what they wanted to remember and invited them to place a star next to the most pertinent sentence on the paper chart (see Chapter 5). Those stars were often used in our letters. Here is an example:

Dear Karen, Iris, Hella, and Jon,

This time we were captivated by Karen's choice for a star. Karen, your star is about things that you can do differently at home, that can benefit the whole family, not just yourself, but all of you.

We get a picture of a girl walking around sharing gifts, quietly, almost hiding it. Karen is listening, thinking, and then finding ways to contribute. We understand these gestures as being like small gifts to the family, nurturing family life.

We are intrigued that Karen chooses to use lists and practices telling her parents how she is doing. We have a notion that you choose your stars based on a great desire to make the other three people in your family happy. Can this be true?

Iris chose to place her star next to the sentence, "Dad is happy that the cleaning was done without quarrels", because she was pleased that her dad had acknowledged this effort. We imagine that this star is an expression of how important it is to hear others are happy and content with the things you do. Are these small gifts you give to each other?

Therapeutic letter writing 99

Maybe we are wrong, but we get the idea that both Iris and Karen must have done something special for the bathroom cleaning to succeed. What did you two do to achieve this task without quarrels? Isn't this another kind of gift?

Is it possible to be detectives on family gift-giving? How will that be for you?

Will your father's focus on finding and using his "husband- and dad-cap" become small gifts for the rest of you? How will you notice if the "boss-cap" is placed on a shelf at work (before Dad goes home at night)?

We think you told us, that you want to focus on these two challenges:

1.   To notice what cap your dad is wearing.
2.   To notice all the ways you give each other small gifts.

Is this right?
Many greetings, Kirsten and Nina

As "giving gifts" and "Dad's cap" were written down, read, re-read, and retold, the terms became important and helpful externalized concepts in this family's shared language, narratives, and family life. Had we not written about these observations they might have been forgotten on the same day they had been spoken.

The therapeutic letters are inestimable!

Therapeutic e-mails are a time of reflection and become the finest mirror of what can be understood in a conversation between different partners – therapist and client.

Nelly, mother of Charlotte

Our team continues to reflect and develop our techniques. When reflecting on our letter writing practices, my colleague Kirsten, a nurse, said, "We are gentle with our words! We can get away with writing almost anything today. This is because we avoid making conclusions and instead pose our wonderings as questions in the most respectful ways. We use the family's words and read them aloud, and then we express curiosity if any of it makes sense".

Our team describes our e-mail practice with a metaphor:

We step into the circle and present our expert knowledge, then step out and invite the family members to look at it with their expert knowledge, evaluate, and decide if there's anything there that they can use.

100 *Therapeutic letter writing*

> My colleague Camilla, a psychologist, describes our team's practices: The practice develops every time we write our mail after every conversation. Reading the e-mail letter aloud works beautifully as the conversation opener and it helps to set the mood. One of the first things a new colleague noticed was how the letters contribute to setting a good tone in the team, when we talk about the families. For instance, if something strikes us negatively in the families, our language is characterised by wonder and curiosity, rather than attributing negative intentions and dysfunctional behaviours to them. Our e-mails help to send us in the wonder and curiosity direction in our relationship with the families. The style of our e-mail letters has remained constant since we began in 2014. Maybe they have become little longer, because we are quicker to follow our immediate streams of thought, as they move us. We often talk about e-mails writing themselves. We have developed the "go-to" e-mail, when time is short. We write words and phrases from the paper chart (like a poem), but we start or finish by writing a little about why those sentences have stood out to us.

The use of financial terms like "efficiency" and "production" instead of "patients" and "quality" can detract from the value of letter writing. Several aspects can be addressed if these issues come up. Most importantly is the fact that the letter-writing process makes treatment more effective for the patients and their families (Nylund and Thomas, 1994). Another small but significant advantage is that medical journal notes become shorter. Either the e-mail or the digital picture is placed into the record and serves as the primary note. Our team's guidelines create an infrastructure that makes the letter-writing process more efficient and the letter-writing practice becomes self-supervisory, with team supervision improving the therapeutic skills of each team member.

American psychologist, David Nylund, surveyed 40 clients and found the average worth of a letter was 3.2 times face-to-face interviews and that 52.8 per cent of gains from therapy could be attributed to the letters (Nylund and Thomas, 1994). Our team invited families, who had experienced collaborating with our team both before and after we began letter writing, to help us. We explained that we needed their help in deciding whether to continue or cease this practice. We composed an Internet-based survey and questioned the value of e-mail letters. The families were asked to compare the value they would put on a therapeutic e-mail letter with that for a session. The average number was that one e-mail equalled between 1.5 and 2 sessions. This result was achieved in our early stage of writing e-mails.

One mother wrote that such a calculation was impossible because she had kept all her family's letters and continued to read them now and then. She said, "Ask me again in another 10 years".

Therefore, the effects of the letter-writing process are numerous, but most importantly:

- The e-mails create a common thread between conversations, enhancing the therapeutic effect. When the family reads in the e-mail that we have been touched personally or learned something from them professionally, they experience being important for other people. This mattering practice increases a family's agency and self-esteem.
- The practice helps the therapist-family relationship become more curious and respectful. Our after-talks become small private supervisions that improve our competencies, since we focus on things that can help families move forward therapeutically. E-mail writing helps therapists to process the therapy session constructively and put it aside before leaving for home. The letter becomes an externalization of the family's problems and those feelings they invoke in us, enabling us to become wholeheartedly interested in their stories. The sharing of e-mails allows us to trace and follow each other's work and our own development in relation to the form and content of our e-mails.
- Reading the e-mail aloud creates a sense of calmness and ambience for becoming present in the room. It provides a common ground to start the conversation. It focuses the therapy. The effect might be similar to the mindfulness technique that therapists use when starting a therapy session with a small mindfulness exercise (Kabat-Zinn, 2005; Linehan, 1993).

The extra effort that is required to create an e-mail letter is like an investment that pays high rewards. Therapeutic e-mail writing is a fun and liberating practice that greatly increases the effectiveness of therapeutic treatment.

References

Bjoroy, A., Madigan, S., & Nylund, D. (2015). The Practice of therapeutic letter writing in narrative therapy. In B. Douglas (Ed.), *The Handbook of Counselling Psychology* (4th ed., pp. 332–348). SAGE Publications Ltd.

Epston, D. (1998a). *Catching up with David Epston: A collection of narrative practice-based papers, published between 1991 and 1996.* Dulwhich Centre Publishing.

Epston, D. (1998b). Expanding the conversation. In *Catching up with David Epston. A collection of narrative practice-based papers* (pp. 95–110). Dulwich Centre Publications.

Epston, D. (2009). The legacy of letter writing as a clinical practice: introduction to the special issue on therapeutic letters. *Journal of Family Nursing, 15*(1), 3–5. doi:10.1177/1 074840708331150

Epston, D. (2013). The history of the archives of resistance: Anti-anorexia/anti-bulimia [article]. http://www.narrativeapproaches.com/resources/anorexia-bulimia-archives-of-resistance/457-2/.

Fox, H. (2003). Using therapeutic documents: a review. *The International Journal of Narrative Therapy and Community Work, 4*, 26–36. doi:https://search.informit.org/doi/10.3316/informit.661328083700189

102 *Therapeutic letter writing*

Freedman, J., & Combs, G. (1996). *Narrative therapy: The social construction of preferred realities.* W.W. Norton & Company.

Freeman, J., Epston, D., & Lobovits, D. (1997). *Playful approaches to serious problems.* W. W. Norton.

Kabat-Zinn, J. (2005). *Comming to our senses: Healing ourselves and the world through mindfulness.* Piatkus Books.

Linehan, M. M. (1993). *Diagnosis and treatment of mental disorders. Skills training manual for treating borderline personality disorder.* Guilford Press.

Maisel, R., Epston, D., & Borden, A. (2004). *Biting the hand that starves you: Inspiring resistance to Anorexia/Bulimia.* New York, NY: W.W. Norton & Co.

Marner, T. (1988). *Letters to children in family therapy: A narrative approach*: Jessica Kingsley Publishers.

Meyerhoff, B. (1986). "Life not death in Venice": Its second life. In V. W. T. E. M. Bruner (Ed.), *The anthropology of experience* (pp. 261–286). University of Illinois Press.

Moules, N. J. (2003). Therapy on paper: Therapeutic letters and the tone of relationship. *Journal of Systemic Therapies, 22*(1), 33–49.

Moules, N. J. (2009). Therapeutic letters in nursing: examining the character and influence of the written word in clinical work with families experiencing illness. *Journal of family nursing, 15*(1), 31–49.

Nylund, D. (2002). Poetic means to anti-anorexic ends. *Journal of Systemic Therapies, 21*(4), 18–34.

Nylund, D., & Thomas, J. (1994). The economics of narrative. *Family Therapy Networker 18*(6). Retrieved 4 June 2021 from http://therapeuticconversations.com/wp-content/uploads/2014/05/The-Economics-of-Narrative-in-the-Networker.pdf

Pilkington, S. M. (2018). Writing narrative therapeutic letters: Gathering, recording and performing lost stories. *Journal of narrative family therapy*, 20–48.

White, M., & Epston, D. (1990). *Narrative means to therapeutic ends.* W.W. Norton & Company.

8   Telling stories that make sense and inspire

> Why did this happen to us? We need to make sense of it and create a story that explains what happened in a way that is helpful for our entire family.
>
> Valiant's mother

People explain themselves and their lives through story-telling, and doctors use scientific explanations to understand illness (Thapar et al., 2017). However, narratives can provide powerful techniques for making sense of meaningless events in our lives, through borrowing from fairy tales, and exploring family-specific metaphors (Frank, 1995). Being witnessed through a story as a person with a beautiful soul and courage at a time when despair tries to steal all the energy, can be empowering. We also learn through stories about coping with illness and problems within the families (Ingram and Perlesz, 2004).

This chapter describes how to listen for unusual words voiced in a session and expand on them in therapeutic letters, maybe by creating a story or describing the family in a colourful or adventurous metaphor. This can bring energy, hope, and joy into a family. Examples illustrate the process of finding, creating, or rediscovering counter-stories to dominant stories that otherwise hold a family in a tyrannic grip of despair, and robs them of personal agency.

Being recognized and witnessed as the best version of yourself

Katja, the mum of Filippa who battled with anxiety, is described in Chapter 2 as experiencing two stories about her role as a mother. I was mindful of how different discourses about good parenthood could run havoc with Katja in her search for being the best version of a mother. We had known each other for a while, when Katja sent an e-mail just prior to a session. The gist of her letter was:

> I am so tired, like metal that finally breaks down. It's like trying to turn the Titanic around; I cannot do it. I never told you this before, but my

DOI: 10.4324/9781003171621-9

104 *Tell stories that make sense and inspire*

dad probably had anxiety like Filippa. He never got any help, always denied his problems, and finally nobody in the family wanted to visit him because he was so terrible. Filippa refuses to take public transportation, so she is not coming to our next session. Now Isabella also has many checking behaviours. I am bringing Isabella because she needs help. I am tired and embarrassed.

I hurried to e-mail a reply:

Dear Katja,

I have read your mail! There's NOTHING to be embarrassed about, all your thoughts and feelings are very understandable!

Isabella and you are SO welcome! Let's make sure that we make this next session a wonderful experience for Isabella!

Nina

While writing this e-mail, I recalled a meeting where a social worker and a municipal psychologist spoke arrogantly and disrespectfully about "those parents who have their own problems and come from families, who for generations have been dysfunctional". The health professionals spoke as if the parents were not worthy of our deepest respect, should be looked down on, and perhaps even deserved their plight (Harrington, 2016). I found this conversation difficult to listen to and struggled to find words to express that such an attitude was unhelpful for those parents. Remembering that experience, however, helps me to understand why Katja might be terribly afraid of revealing her background (Jackson and Mannix, 2004).

As Isabella and her mum take their seats, Isabella takes the lead:

Isabella: I sat on Mum's lap all the way on the train!

I take my paper chart and begin jotting down, wanting to make as much out of this happy narrative as possible: I sat on Mum's lap all the way on the train!

Nina: Wow, what a treat! And when you sat on Mum's lap, what was good about that?
Isabella: I ate snacks, and I told Mum about school. We had the best time together.

I jot it all down.

Nina: So how did your mum make that train trip the best time together for you both, Isabella?

Tell stories that make sense and inspire 105

I could rephrase "the best time together" into "a good time" instead of repeating exactly the words Isabella said. But in narrative therapy, we take great care to repeat the exact words, to make sure the person experiences being listened to, heard and understood. If we change the words, it risks becoming an interpretation or a misunderstanding. Our focus is not on correcting grammar but helping the patient to explore how they understand their lives.

Isabella: We counted the train stations, I read all the names and the last three stations all ended in "red". You know what? We had a really good time even though Filippa was not with us.

Nina: Hold on, I can't write as fast as you can speak.

Isabella is beaming and starts to draw, while I write as fast as I can.

Nina: This is really something; you are good at reading, and you can have a good time on a train, even when Filippa is not with you.

Then Katja takes the lead:

Yes, we did have a good time, didn't we? But Isabella, we have agreed that today we need to tell Nina about how anxiety also attacks you. Can you tell Nina about that?

Isabella drawing on her paper: Nuh…

Nina: Isabella, how about you draw me a beautiful picture, and I ask your mum about that stupid anxiety? You can always interrupt. You know children are allowed to remain silent, and also, they can interrupt, and they are entitled to say exactly how they think it is, okay?

Isabella nods, continues drawing, and gives me one of her deliciously sneaky smiles.

Nina: Katja, can you tell me a bit about what you and Isabella would like to talk about today? You said something about anxiety attacking Isabella in addition to Filippa?

Katja: Yes. Anxiety attacks Isabella.

While Katja talks I write and draw a circle around this sentence: "Anxiety attacks Isabella".

Katja: I am so frustrated, I am afraid that Isabella will do what the anxiety tells her, just like Filippa. There's no way I can cope with having to fight with her too.

106   *Tell stories that make sense and inspire*

I am in a dilemma. Will I undermine Katja's authority, by allowing Isabella to disregard her mum's request of talking about anxiety? Will I make Isabella unhappy and hate being here, if her mum gets attacked by tiredness right in my consulting room? I think about Katja's e-mail. The girl's anxieties are making her feel like a piece of metal breaking, trying to turn the Titanic around, and failing. I want to give this family hope, energy, trust in the future, and in their own ability to handle anxiety. However, I am uncertain how Isabella is thinking about her anxiety and I need her to join in. I'm certain I'll fail if I try to pressure her. I'm sweating under my shirt.

Nina: Can I ask you what anxiety demands that Isabella does, that is so frustrating?
Katja: Yes, she is checking all the things that can create heat, just before we leave our home and before we go to bed. She also is beginning to do checking behaviour when she goes to the toilet, and she begs and pleads….

As Katja speaks I take a new colour and write her sentences around the circle to form a mind map. I try to use Katja's words, but also do my best to "tweak" them into externalizing language. Katja is good at externalizing anxiety by now, so this isn't difficult. I only insert the extra words, "Anxiety makes Isabella…".

I repeat Katja's words and add: This anxiety sounds like a lot of work. It must take time away from something that you, Katja, would rather be doing, is that right?

Katja doesn't get to answer, because Isabella interrupts and proclaims: We played Uno on Sunday!

I hurry on and write those words close to the nice words about the train trip, so they make a collective knowledge about good things.

Nina: You played Uno on Sunday?
Katja: Yes, but that was only because Filippa and I promised that we would do the checking instead of Isabella later.
Nina: What?
Katja: Filippa wanted to play Uno and I was tired and wanted some quality time with my daughters. Neither Filippa nor I had the energy or inclination to fight with Isabella, so Filippa had suggested that we do the checking for Isabella, so we could have some fun together.
Nina: Hang on, Isabella, does Mum follow orders from the anxiety and do the checking for you?
Isabella: Yes, Mum goes along with the anxiety!

I hurry on and write: Mum goes along with the anxiety!

Tell stories that make sense and inspire   107

Nina: Wow, how interesting! In what way does Mum go along with the anxiety? Can you tell me?

I don't want Katja to feel exposed or ridiculed, but I like the idea that Isabella can "tell on her mum". I feel compelled to pursue this thought. Isabella obviously also likes this idea because she can describe many ways her mum goes along with the anxiety. I write her sentences on the chart and Isabella is beaming.

Isabella: Mum gets angry. She says we must hurry. She says, "The anxiety just jumped on you Isabella". "We are busy, we have to go NOW". "You have to stop NOW". My mum is so impatient.

Isabella is having fun as she mimics her mother's face and voice.

Nina: Wow that's a lot! Is this how you see it too, Katja, does the anxiety make you do all these awful things?

Katja is laughing and readily admits, that yes, anxiety makes her angry. She describes how her body language changes when she feels anxiety take over the whole apartment.

Nina: What do you think happens to Isabella when you go along with the anxiety in this way?
Katja: Oh, Isabella stresses out and she gets sad. I am not being the mum I want to be.

I imagine how hard Katja is fighting to be the mum she wants to be, and how tired she is; her despair and anguish, her backbone, normally as strong as metal, slowly bending. I am reminded of a magical prompt: When the present is full of despair, imagine waving a magical wand, and visualize how you would like your life to be 30 years from now. The theory is that when despair takes up all the space in a room, and all the thoughts in the brain, it's impossible to imagine how to change actions, and it's awful being told that everything you do is wrong. We must move ourselves from that place, like magic, to a better place in the future, where we feel empowered and experience ourselves as competent, loving people. From this other place, we are better able to imagine how to change our actions (de Shazer, 1994; Epston et al., 2006; Marsten et al., 2016; Root, 2013).

Nina: Katja and Isabella, can I ask you to do an almost magical experiment with me? I want you to imagine that Isabella has grown up, and she will give a speech to her mum, thanking her for what a wonderful mother she has been. When would you like to deliver this speech, Isabella? When would you like to stand and tell

108 *Tell stories that make sense and inspire*

	your mum how grateful you are that you had such a wonderful mum when you were a little girl? At your communion or your wedding, or....?
Isabella:	Yeah! I will mum give a speech when I get married.
Nina:	Beautiful! Katja, imagine that you are preparing for your younger daughter's wedding. She has met a beautiful partner, that you really like, and Isabella has turned into this young loving, helpful and strong woman. What are the values you kept and actions you took over the years as a mum, that you would like Isabella to remember, in guiding her to become this wonderful person she is now, on the brink of her wedding?
Katja:	Oh…, this is hard, I feel emotional just thinking about you being so old, that you are getting married, Isabella.
Nina:	Yeah, it's strange, isn't it? What kind of a mum would you like Isabella to remember you being to her? Let me write: "Thank you Mum for…".
Katja:	I think she will remember that I gave good advice and that I comforted her. I would like her to remember me as a loving mum who was there when she needed me. That she will remember that I created a good structure in our daily life and that I could do all these things even when I was alone with all the responsibility of parenting. She knows it's hard, being alone with no one to help me.

Katja describes many different narratives in her answer. I hear discourses that could invite the idea of personal failure (White, 2002) and I want to stay in a de-centred but influential position as a therapist (Madigan, 2019, p. 164). Therefore, I choose to focus on the aspect I think will be most helpful in the mother–daughter relationship to keeping the metal from breaking:

Nina:	Katja, do you remember how you created such a good structure for your daughters?
Katja:	I was good at making decisions for them, so they could be the children they were supposed to be. I met them at their level. I didn't demand too much of them.

As I try to get everything on the paper chart, I tweak the words, so they become Isabella's words: made decisions for us, so we could be the children we were. Met us at our level.

Nina:	If Isabella were to choose a picture of how it was back then, when you came to me and were going through this difficult time, what kind of a picture would she use to describe her mum back then?

Tell stories that make sense and inspire 109

Katja:	Oh. I don't know. I guess she would see me as someone who stood strong in the storm, instilled faith in her, and gave her confidence, even though Filippa was attacked by anxiety, and anxiety was trying to attack our entire family.
Nina:	Let me write this down, these are strong words. Isabella, you have a very special mum, don't you?
Isabella:	Yes! My mum is a superhero!
Nina:	A superhero?
Isabella:	Yes!
Nina:	I am wondering, if either of you can remember what kind of parenting actions back then were so impressive, that Isabella began to consider her mum a superhero?
Katja:	I reassured the children, you know, I kept my cool.
Isabella:	You blew the anxiety away!
Katja (smiling):	Yes, I guess I did, didn't I? I said things like, "It's all going to be okay". I had patience and was understanding. And Isabella trusted me.

I draw a diagram of pins sticking out from a circle with "Mum is a superhero" in the centre and label the pins with these descriptions: "reassured the children", "kept my cool", "blew the anxiety away", "patience and understanding", "I trusted you, Mum".

Wondering if Katja thinks we are talking about the right thing, I ask my "catching up with you on how it is going" question:

Nina:	How is this going for you, Katja? How do you feel, talking about it this way? Is this helpful?
Katja:	I like it. I feel calmer and more relaxed. It's good when you make us talk this way, full of humour. You instil hope. You make me feel like a mum with a surplus of energy and competence. Like the best kind of pedagogues.

"Best kind of pedagogues" is an unusual choice of words in my mind. I like to hook onto words like this that stand out in the conversations. They often contain many images and stories.

Nina:	What does a mum, who is like the best kinds of pedagogues, do in her family?
Katja:	That will be a person who can turn the boat around.
Nina:	Will it be okay, if I ask you about being a pedagogue who can turn the boat around?
Katja:	Yeah…
Nina:	Let's imagine you as this mum with a surplus of energy and competence. Like the best kind of pedagogues. What makes it possible for you to turn the boat around?

110 *Tell stories that make sense and inspire*

Katja:	It's no good that the girls are hanging around the kitchen when I am trying to fix dinner and do the sandwiches for the next morning. They are tiring me. I need to be calm in the kitchen.
Isabella:	But Mum, I can make my own sandwich!
Katja:	You say that now, but I know that when we go home, you won't do it. You are not old enough.
Isabella:	Yes! I am, Noah in my class makes his own sandwich, and I can make my sandwich. I want to help you, Mum. That's why we are in the kitchen. We want to help you.
Nina:	Is this true, Isabella? Do you know how to make a sandwich? What do you think, Katja? What will that superhero pedagogue be thinking?
Katja (smiling at me):	No … the superhero-pedagogue will give the girls chores to do. Just like my Norwegian friend Britt said, "It's important for the girls to have chores".
Nina:	Chores? What kind of chores will the superhero-pedagogue mum give her daughters?
Katja:	Empty the washing machine, put out the trash, make those sandwiches and maybe even put out the clothes for the next day.

Katja is looking at Isabella who is nodding her little head. Isabella seems absorbed in a dream of helping her mum.

Nina:	Why would your daughters do chores? What's the purpose? Shouldn't you be the one helping them? Aren't you their mum?

Katja is silently laughing at me, nodding. I think Katja is onto me, because of how she answers:

> You know what? Britt was scolding me. She said that I was too much of a servant for my daughters. But I just want to make them happy and be a loving caring mum.

Nina:	Do you think you are too good for your own good? Oh, no, look at the time, it has flown! But I want to ask you Katja, can anything prevent you from carrying out these plans? It sounds like a big change, turning this boat around. What else needs to be written on the paper?
Katja:	I need a plan for Filippa and another for Isabella. Complete and detailed. It's important that the girls do some chores, so I can get the energy I need.

I want to give this new narrative substance and ask a quick witnessing question:

Nina:	Do you know anyone who can support you in doing this, someone who will not be surprised but proud of you, knowing that you went home and did all this?
Katja:	Yes, my friend Britt. Thinking of her will give me the strength to carry through with this. She knows that I can do it.
Nina:	I am wondering, do you speak or e-mail Britt?
Katja:	I e-mail her. I will love to tell her how I am giving my daughters some chores.

As we say goodbye and Isabella is happily skipping down the hallway, I give Katja a thumbs up. I am impressed by her ability to reach out for help and trust that she can use the little help I can give, only questions really. I am not going home with her; I am not going to help with the fights around dinner or bedtime; Katja is on her own the minute she leaves my office with Isabella.

However, I can write a letter and hope that it will help them to sustain their energy, trust and hope, making that metal backbone as strong as it needs to be:

Dear Isabella,

This letter is for you, but your mother and your big sister Filippa may be allowed to read it too.

We imagined that in the future when you get married, you will give a speech and thank your mother.

I imagine that your thank-you-speech to your mother might sound like this:

Dear Mother,

I want to thank you for being the lovely mother I needed. Do you remember the time when it was difficult for all three of us? You were the one who stood strong in the storm, you made the necessary decisions and gave structure to our daily lives. You were loving, gave good advice and comfort.

Do you remember that for a while I checked all the things that could give off heat? I want to thank you for not seeing me as a little girl who was attacked by anxiety, but as the girl who wanted to be big and help her mother. I thought it would be helpful if I checked all things. I didn't know any better. I was just a little girl who wanted to be big. But you saw it, Mum. You gave me chores, so I could help you. I came to feel like a big girl who could help her mother create a nice, cosy family. I didn't have any time to constantly check things out, because there were all these other, more exciting chores I could do.

I want to thank you for making schedules for me and Filippa. We both had chores we needed to do to make our family's daily life work. When

112   *Tell stories that make sense and inspire*

we were done, we could enjoy being together. You didn't treat us like little girls who could do nothing. You trusted us to be those big girls we wanted to become.

Thank you, Mum, for keeping your cool, being patient, calm, understanding, relaxed, and humorous like the best pedagogues. You were our superhero.

This is how I imagine you would like to thank your mum,

Many greetings, Nina

How did Isabella and Katja react to this letter? Katja reflected four years later, "The 'thank you speech' at the wedding made me cry like a baby. To this day I wish and hope that this will be how my lovely girls will think back and remember their childhood".

By the way, Katja insisted that her daughters do their chores, and they did!

Visual narratives help to express and endure the incomprehensible

Parents, Bertie, and Anna (see Chapters 1 and 2) could not grasp what was happening to their son Valiant's brain and wanted to find knowledge and strength to support him.

This family were avid hikers, and hiking was the one thing Valiant could still do, even when at his worst. The family had been hiking together for a week during the summer of his first admission to the psychiatric hospital before they met us. We were moved by this family's struggles and wanted to convey our respect in this letter:

As we look at the paper chart a rather wild picture emerges. Maybe this picture will make sense to you, maybe not. This is what we visualize:

It's as if two parents and their three boys have fallen off the edge of a giant canyon in a desert. A whirlwind has swept all five of you over the edge; you are whirled down to the bottom of the deep ravine, and Valiant falls hard. But suddenly you are all thrown back up on the edge.

There you are now, without any explanation. You must continue. Some of you feel dizzier than others. Should you look back, deep down, to understand what happened? Should you look ahead to find safety? Can you help each other, or do you each have to stand on your own?

Your eldest son is fast on his feet. He wants to help but doesn't want to be too close to the edge, because he fears losing his footing again. Anna is drawn to the edge in a desperate desire to investigate the depths, to understand what took you there. Bertie is breathing deeply, trying to be

Tell stories that make sense and inspire 113

rational. He asks himself, "Are we alive? Does my body still work?" It feels good with the warm air in your lungs.

Valiant falters every time he takes a few steps. One moment he appears to walk like his brothers, but then his gait becomes uncertain. Can he resist if the wind comes to catch him again?

How will you move on as a family? How can you find the right walking pace and head in the right direction? You must find an overhang or something to hide under during the storm. But since you don't know what happened, how will you know what to look for?

Being on solid ground is a relief, but also scary. You still do not understand what happened. You can only move forward, stick together, support each other, and slowly the fear loses hold on some of you, at different paces, and sometimes the fear grabs you again.

As more time passes, your course becomes more secure; you can talk together more easily, and you begin to tell each other how you experienced the terrible fall. The boys won't talk about it, however. They prefer to focus on what they are heading towards. But you, Anna, need to understand, and slowly you find ways to talk together, both about the fall and where to go and how to avoid further crevices in the ground. Maybe you will even start to enjoy the view and orient yourself to more distant horizons?

Does this narrative make any sense whatsoever? Can you use it?

Kirsten and Nina

Anna responded a year later with her own story:

You opened my eyes to the opportunity of expressing and processing Valiant's and our family's crisis through these kinds of pictorial narratives. The image with the abyss is an example, and I later wrote my own version, when we were in a bad period. Writing my own story served as a tool for expressing and enduring the incomprehensible experiences, and this helped me to cope. Here it is:

The fog came creeping as we walked. We knew we had to be careful but had no idea how great the danger was. We didn't know how close we were to the abyss. Not until Valiant, who was on my right, suddenly disappeared into it.

For a long time, we did not know if we had lost him forever. We called but got no answer. We tried to climb down after him but were unsuccessful. We tried to call for help but understood that no one else could help him. We threw a long line down, hoping that he would grab

114   *Tell stories that make sense and inspire*

it. Eventually, Valiant seemed to be grabbing the line. Slowly, infinitely slowly, and weakly, he began to rise. Our hopes grew.

At first, he was so far down in the depths and fog that we only saw him as an obscure figure, but gradually he drew closer. He eventually came so close that we could glimpse his contour and face in the fog. At one point we could almost reach out and touch him, and we thought, "He'll be safe again. Now it's all going to be okay".

But he has not yet been able to re-join us.

I see that we are now moving along the abyss. Valiant walks parallel to us a little down in the depths, along uncertain paths on the slope. We cannot see if he has attached the safety line. Maybe he doesn't know how to do it. Occasionally he disappears in the fog. Occasionally he seems to be crashing again. We cling to the line, but do not know if it is stuck. We know that we must secure ourselves and our other children as we hold onto the line and hope. We must keep walking there in the fog, on the edge of the abyss, and hold on.

Maybe there's something down there that we can't see. Something heavy that grabs Valiant by the ankles to pull him down.

Valiant's mum, Anna

I was touched by how Anna's story was attentive to other discourses, hopes, and intentions than those mentioned in my story. Her story illustrates the importance of personal wisdom in the co-creation of the narratives. Anna wrote another story, when her family was in another place in their life (see Chapter 16).

This chapter demonstrates that for narratives to be interesting they need to contain suspense and a contest between evil and good.

For a narrative therapist, the stories do not have to end happily ever after. Rather, the stories need to make sense of the lives of the families and give them purpose and agency (Bruner, 1987). Narrative therapy is about helping people to create stories that make sense, give direction, and support them in enduring and coping with life. We are our patient's appreciative co-writers.

References

Bruner, J. (1987). *Actual minds, possible worlds.* Harvard University Press.

de Shazer, S. (1994). *Words were Originally Magic.* W.W. Norton.

Epston, D., Lakusta, C., & Tomm, K. (2006). Haunting from the future: A congenial approach to parent-children conflicts. *The International Journal of Narrative Therapy and Community Work, 2,* 61–70. doi:https://search.informit.org/doi/10.3316/informit.197441631256042

Frank, A. (1995). *The wounded storyteller: body, illness, and ethics*. University of Chicago Press.

Harrington, A. (2016). Mother love and mental illness: An emotional history. *Osiris, 31*(1), 94–115. doi:10.1086/687559

Ingram, C., & Perlesz, A. (2004). The getting of wisdom. *The International Journal of Narrative Therapy and Community Work, 2*, 49–56. doi:https://search.informit.org/doi/10.3316/informit.239179486874410

Jackson, D., & Mannix, J. (2004). Giving voice to the burden of blame: a feminist study of mothers' experiences of mother blaming. *International Journal of Nursing Practice, 10*(4), 150–158. doi:10.1111/j.1440-172X.2004.00474.x

Madigan, S. (2019). *Narrative Therapy* (2nd ed.). American Psychological Association.

Marsten, D., Epston, D., & Markham, L. (2016). *Narrative Therapy in Wonderland. Connecting with children's imaginative know-how*. W. W. Norton & Co.

Root, E. M. W. C., (2013). Imagine: Bringing vision into child protective services. *Journal of Systemic Therapies, 32*(3), 74–88.

Thapar, A., Pine, D., Leckman, J. F., Scott, S., Snowling, M. J., & Taylor, E. A. (2017). *Rutter's child and adolescent psychiatry*. John Wiley & Sons.

White, M. (2002). Addressing personal failure. In *Narrative Practice and Exotic Lives: Resurrecting diversity in everyday life* (pp. 149–232), Adelaide, Australia: Dulwich Centre Publications.

9 Naming? How might a diagnosis be best for me?

When I asked my nine-year-old patient, Oscar, for advice on helping families and children like him with Attention-Deficit Hyperactivity Disorder (ADHD), he said:

> Tell them that you must talk about the same thing again and again and again and again. But that this does help. And remember to tell the parents that volcanos are also fun. I was really glad when you explained that.

"Volcano" had become a metaphor for Oscar's diagnosis of ADHD. Diagnoses are medical tools that guide a doctor's understanding of complex problems. Diagnoses for children and youth are moving targets, socially constructed, and not absolute truths (Conrad & Potter, 2014; Stein et al., 2020). Diagnoses can have hurtful consequences (Lebowitz & Ahn, 2014; Lebowitz & Appelbaum, 2019). This chapter discusses how we can talk about and use diagnoses, so that they have positive effects and make sense to children and their families.

Diagnoses are the doctor's externalization of the problem

We all have problems, somatic and mental. If our problems become bothersome, most of us will ask for help. If the helper is a medical doctor, our problem will be given a name from the International Classification of Diseases (ICD)(WHO, 1990).[1] The naming helps doctors to categorize and study the problems, give insight into characteristics, and causes of each type of problems, the prognosis, and helpful treatments. However, these reasons for using diagnoses often disappear in discussions of the economy, labelling, taboo, and stigma (Garand et al., 2009).

A diagnosis is not a label that describes a person's identity, but a way of describing the problems that are troubling the person (Mogensen & Mason, 2015). The narrative language, where we externalize problems, supports this understanding.

The specific diagnosis can be critical in determining what treatment the patient will receive. Whether we live in a country with a national health care system that provides treatment, or we access help through a private health

DOI: 10.4324/9781003171621-10

provider, all patients need a name for their illness. They need a diagnosis that entitles them to treatment. Therefore, diagnoses are also used for economic purposes.

However, we know from research, that the diagnoses are not stable entities and, for children especially, they can be fleeting in nature (O'Connor et al., 2020). Many diagnoses for children's mental health problems change over time, and many children are affected by multiple problems over time.

Discussions about which diagnosis is "correct" can deflect attention from understanding how a specific child and family is suffering, and from deciding the best help for that specific child and family (Ilgen et al., 2016). We might lose sight of what purpose the illness has, or what problem the illness is trying to communicate or help solve for the child. In short, we might lose sight of how we may best help the family.

The families that our team meet have often found the diagnostic process to be more bothersome than helpful. Usually, a family seeks a diagnosis to make sense of why their child is suffering. Unfortunately, the diagnosis itself seldom gives a helpful answer to their "Why?".

When a family refers to the specific diagnosis, we ask family members to explain what this means to them. Then we do a joint exploration of their specific problems, to understand how those problems relate to the specific diagnosis, and why this or that diagnosis might or might not be a helpful name for their situation.

We might also suggest that certain problems that have led to a particular diagnosis, seem to be shared by one or both parents. We might suggest that the parents could have received that same diagnosis, had they lived at this specific time and in the same environment as their child. Many parents enjoy this relaxed and shared approach to understanding diagnoses. It helps the family to make sense of their suffering. The story about the Braveheart family in Chapter 1 is an example of practising this principle.

Struggling with understanding diagnoses

A diagnosis can be hurtful if it becomes the identity of the person (Yanos et al., 2010). But a diagnosis is also a tool that can open the door for receiving specialized support in a school, financial help for a family, psychotherapy, medicine, and other benefits.

Brigitte, a 15-year-old girl, who had been diagnosed with anorexia came to see us. We re-evaluated her symptoms and concluded that her disordered eating was due to not being seen as a girl with autistic problems. We wanted to focus on helping Brigitte to manage her autistic challenges. I was anxious about Brigitte's reaction to receiving yet another diagnosis, since she hated and opposed her anorexia diagnosis. However, when we told her about Asperger's Syndrome, her reaction was one of relief.

"If that Asperger's diagnosis can get me into a school where I am accepted as who I am, why shouldn't I be grateful for receiving this diagnosis? And then

118 *Naming? Might a diagnosis be best for me?*

you will understand that my food intake is restricted because of my autism, NOT because I have anorexia", Brigitte said.

The last sentence was delivered with a powerful pose. Within a few weeks of starting conversations about nutritious food, the biological needs of a body, and how autism (or people with autism) loves routines, Brigitte was eating in a healthier way.

Seytan or OCD? What and how might it be most helpful to the family?

As a resident at an adolescent outpatient unit, I inherited a case from a doctor who had treated a boy with Cognitive Behavioural Therapy (CBT) for Obsessive-Compulsive Disorder (OCD) with insufficient effect. This was one of my first cases using narrative therapy.

The boy, Ahmed, and his parents had lived for a time in a refugee camp before settling in Denmark. The father had Post-Traumatic Stress Disorder (PTSD) and the municipality had supported the family in settling into their new country.

I continued the practice of individual therapy and met only with Ahmed. His mum stayed in the waiting room, gave me a polite nod, but didn't shake my hand or engage in any verbal communication.

To start with, I asked Ahmed to describe what he had done in therapy so far and how it had helped him. He spoke positively of different CBT models and home exercises that he had been told to perform, but most often he had forgotten to do. I asked what he hoped to get out of the treatment but got no real answer.

I tried to externalize the OCD: "What does the OCD demand of you?"

Ahmed: "I don't know! You guys say it's OCD, I don't know what OCD is. Aren't you supposed to know what it does to me?"

Ahmed now had my attention! This child had gone to therapy for OCD and was claiming that he had no understanding of what the diagnosis meant. I jumped into what I call my teacher role and explained OCD to him. He listened patiently and looked a little overbearingly at me; he clearly had heard all this before, and it meant nothing to him.

For many people, diagnoses are common knowledge, and they have a sense of what they mean. A diagnosis can be a short and efficient way of talking about what can be big, complex problems. But health professionals must pause and consider what words and sentences are most appropriate to use in different contexts, depending on the intentions and effects of using a diagnosis. We must step away from our professional positions and respectfully enter our patient's world, be curious about how they think, their knowledge, and what words and sentences they use to communicate about their lives. We must not

Naming? Might a diagnosis be best for me? 119

expect or demand that the patient steps into our world and uses our language, just because that's easiest for us.

Consider how often you have gone to a lawyer, a philosopher, an auto mechanic, or anybody with expertise who has their own language and terms, and heard a problem explained in a way that you did not understand.

The issue is not about learning another language as such but being aware of differences in word usage and interpretations. I find being observant about how words are used and what they mean is one of the most fascinating aspects of psychiatry. I like playing with words. Sharing this joy with the families is one of the most therapeutic techniques I know.

Remembering my narrative self, I asked Ahmed, "So how do you talk about your problems at home? What do you call it?"

Ahmed: "Seytan".
Nina: "What? What's that? A Satan?"
Ahmed: "Seytan! It means 'devil'".
Nina: "Oh … wow, tell me about that! Is Seytan in your home? How does it work?"

My thoughts ran ahead, "This is great! The family has already externalized the problem at home!" But other thoughts also ran havoc and I wondered, "Is the family superstitious? Is this good or bad? Is this part of Ahmed's culture? Something that I have no knowledge about? Oh, no…".

Both lines of thoughts tricked me into adopting the knowing-it-all-position of, "I have to know it all and I am entitled to judge whether the boy and his parents are on the right track or not". But that position was wrong. The only proper response I could give was to be curious and respectful. I decided to trust and hope that an inquiry along this path would be helpful for our collaboration and for Ahmed's healing from this ailment, which was named OCD by the hospital and Seytan by the family.

My internal dialogue was intense. I had to shove aside my eagerness to act on this new insight and remain in the curious position. Learning as much as possible was imperative. I did not want to make more wrong conclusions. I pondered how my colleagues had assumed the boy knew he had OCD and had agreed to the diagnosis and treatment. I tried to address the wrongness of these assumptions. I began from scratch, exploring Ahmed's problems with him.

I came to know Ahmed as a sweet, fun, and conscientious 14 years old. He was a talented soccer player who liked school and got good grades. His family was religious. He found his parents very strict compared with Danish parents. He loved, and was proud of, his parents' achievements and had vivid memories of the refugee camp and flight to Europe.

I learned that as Ahmed entered his teens, a very bossy Seytan invaded his home life. Seytan demanded many different rituals, starting the minute that Ahmed arrived home from school. He had to change all his clothes before

120 *Naming? Might a diagnosis be best for me?*

entering the apartment, he had to engage in long washing rituals, and his mum was required to participate in these and other weird habits around using his computer and doing homework.

So began an exciting collaboration, where Ahmed taught me about his family, their culture, and their dreams for a life in Denmark. We explored how Seytan had tried to prevent him and his mum from living life as they wanted to, and how love and respect for his parents' native culture was difficult to nurture in a Danish society.

We concluded that "OCD" was just a "doctor-name" that didn't give this family a helpful explanation in handling their problems (see Chapter 12 for a continuation of this story).

Ahmed's story is not unique. Other parents have said, "I do not understand. I thought that a diagnosis would help me understand, but I still don't know WHY my kid is suffering or how to help". Parents hope for guidance to manage problems. Diagnoses give health professionals, but not always the families, this guide. We must acknowledge and meet the needs of the family, not in a derogatory way, but with respect (Pellicano et al., 2018).

What makes sense, how is it helpful?

Do you see a boy with OCD and autism, or an autistic boy with OCD? Or OCD as a symptom of an unacknowledged autism?

I met Isaac and his parents when he was six years old. He had psychotic symptoms and many ritualistic behaviours, that were diagnosed as OCD. Isaac was on anti-psychotics, ADHD medicine and anti-depressants. He was charming and did not present with problems of autism, such as difficulties in social communication (Lord et al., 2020). OCD seemed the best explanation and had everyone's focus, even though Isaac also had an autism spectrum diagnosis. Everyone saw a child clearly suffering, but Isaac loved his school, wanted to be normal, to do things on his own, and be a good boy. He also had his own understanding of the OCD and how to combat it.

The autism spectrum diagnosis helped several years later by giving the family a nuanced understanding. By now, Isaac was 12 years old. He was placed in a new school environment with an autism-friendly structure and a more nuanced understanding. However, many different professional helpers continued to give different advice to the parents according to their private understanding of Isaac and his diagnoses.

Isaac lived in two families, changing house once a week with his older brother. His mother re-married, to a woman, and his dad also re-married and gave Isaac a younger brother when he was 12 years old. Isaac experienced great joy in the adoring physical hugs and kisses from this brother.

Early on, all four parents accompanied Isaac to his sessions. But we soon learned that meetings with only the parents also provided opportunities for

Naming? Might a diagnosis be best for me? 121

adult talk. Sometimes Isaac's biological parents came together, sometimes one of the couples came alone.

We discussed the different diagnoses. What understanding might help best? What diagnosis had the best prognosis?

I wrote this letter after a session with all four parents, when Isaac was 13 years old:

Dear Parents to Isaac,

At the end of our conversation Abigail said, "We must talk at some point, about what drives our actions. What will happen to Isaac? He asks about this himself."

Is your hope that Isaac will become an ordinary boy?
You wondered how his handicap will make itself known in adulthood. What won't he be able to do, that you have been dreaming about him doing?

What is most important for him to learn to do? Is this realistic?

I ask these questions because they also might provide good guidelines, when preparing your big family party, and when planning for other parts of his upbringing.

Must Isaac always have an escape route that he knows he can use, and enables him to feel he is a good boy, no matter what?

Consider this statement: If autism-pedagogy is used, Isaac will not learn and develop useful life competencies such as social skills. However, if a normal standard is demanded, and a higher goal is set, he will advance further.

Or the opposite statement: If applying autism-pedagogy, Isaac has optimal possibilities for growth and development; but if normal standards are demanded, he will experience failure upon failure and deteriorate.

I know you have been exposed to both statements.

How can we talk about the future, without destroying your hopes?

Does Isaac feel like a failure or a hero?

Can a person preserve hope and be realistic?

What can your hopes and dreams be about?

How do you want Isaac to think about himself?

Will you encourage him to try new things, exert himself to make an effort?

Do your thoughts align with those of Isaac on what is necessary to be a hero?

I am convinced that Isaac felt like a hero when he said, "I made it, I went to my brother's baptism!"

I also believe he needs to see the meaning and the advantages for himself, if he is to attempt anything that demands that he confronts/endures psychic pain, obsessions, or meltdowns.

What do you think about such statements?

Nina

At this point, the parents asked for Isaac to have conversations alone with me to get a better understanding of his diagnoses, and what they could mean to him.

The first e-mail after our first individual conversation:

Dear Parents,

I hope you will read this attached letter and read it together with Isaac. I suggest that reading the letter with Isaac several times during the next three weeks will be helpful. He might not like the idea of you reading it aloud to him. He might say that he will read the letter by himself. But I believe it is important that you read and talk about the letter together.

Nina

Dear Isaac,

I hope my letters help you to remember what we have talked about. I hope they help you find ways to live that give you more time to enjoy being "you", the way you see yourself: small, a tad skimpy, good at things demanding technique, light on your feet, which is a good thing when climbing trees or being a swordsman, training, and doing things you like to do.

You said that you want to be "a good boy", and that you do not want to hurt anybody. This is troublesome, because you hold back when fencing with your older brother, but he does not hold back and kicks way too hard. You believe he does not understand the word "training". You don't like him picking on you. Rather, you want the two of you to have a good time together. I wonder if Sebastian knows this is how you feel? Do you think Sebastian might be able to change a little?

You also said that you are not that good at fighting, because you have no drive for winning. Therefore, football is no good for you.

However, you are immensely knowledgeable on the Middle Age, warfare, and historical European martial arts. You can spot which webpages expose "bullshit". You can explain how to find trustworthy homepages with big truth value.

Naming? Might a diagnosis be best for me? 123

You say that the obsessions try to persuade you that people do not see you, as you see yourself. You are a boy with brown hair and brown eyes. But the obsessions insist that others see you with blonde hair and blue eyes. The obsessions say things like, "If you do not do this, then there is a big risk that…".

Together we decided the obsessions are "bullshit", just like some webpages are bullshit. But you do not have much faith that things can change. Your experience is that if one obsession disappears, another takes its place. I predicted we cannot prevent thoughts from showing up, but we agreed that they should not force you to do rituals. That is malicious. You have no energy for a fight between you and the obsessions. We considered whether other techniques might help you avoid following their demands.

I asked about your undone shoelaces. At first you did not think the laces had anything to do with obsessions. They did when you were younger, but now they were just a bad habit. However, when I suggested lacing them for you, you got worried that the obsessions might become angry at you. Since we did not want a fight, we agreed you will think about other techniques you can use, so that I can lace your shoelaces without the obsessions interfering. We might talk about this next time we meet.

You said that when doing activities you like, the obsessions seem to have more difficulty sneaking up on you. At such times, the obsessions seem to stay away and don't care. I am wondering, can you make the obsessions care more, and care less? Can you possibly lure the obsessions into not caring? Are there things you would like the obsessions to care less about? See you in three weeks,

Nina

This is my very last letter to Isaac, several months later:

Dear Isaac,

Oh my, I am going to miss you! I think back on the times we have shared together; I have learned much from you and your parents about helping families. I want to give you my biggest thanks!

When I met you for the first time, you were a small, fast-talking boy. I recall you wanting to know about OCD, and this is how you remember those early meetings too. Today we know your autism made it impossible for you to learn about OCD. Back then, you could only care about what was interesting to you, right at that minute, and when you spoke about the OCD, you were "teaching" us. I tried to follow you and to make you curious about thinking differently. But I could not. You were a little boy

124 *Naming? Might a diagnosis be best for me?*

and the autism stood tall in front of you, making it impossible for you to hear another person's perspectives. But that is not how it is for you today! At first, we all thought the OCD was your main problem. Nobody thought your autism was anything special. You were viewed as a boy who wanted to do everything in his own way. You say today, "My dad wants to do everything in his own way. That is why it is difficult for him". Maybe, initially, everyone thought, "like father like son"?

You are a charming, talkative, and bright child. These three qualities have helped you enormously. They are another part of you, the opposite to what we see when your autism challenges you. Those three qualities also make it hard for us to see that autism makes many things difficult for you, and to appreciate how much help you need.

We have learned that you need to know things in advance, and that you need to have plans, preferably a plan A and a plan B. Your autism is the kind that makes you feel insecure if there is too much unplanned or unknown. However, you have an elephant's memory, so when plans have been laid out, you don't need to look at them to know what to expect. Your autism likes to have systems and ensure that everybody sticks to certain rules. So, difficulties arise when others want to act spontaneously. Your autism tries to convince you that you prefer to do things alone. It thinks that being with other people is troublesome. It is troublesome for you if there are too many people, or if they behave unpredictably, or are opposite to you. You are a very calm person, so it's unpleasant if people are too hot-headed or worrisome.

But you have learned that although people might be troublesome, this does NOT mean that you have do things alone. You now know that asking for help is good. This is an enormous gift that you have figured that out. You are now very good at asking for and accepting help, especially from your "True Amigos".[2]

We have learned a lot about your OCD. OCD promises that "everything is in control". For a boy like you, who couldn't make sense of or understand all that was going on in your school and in your family, OCD could easily convince you that it could help you and give you control. Doing your rituals did give you a sense of control and quiet. You could stop your entire family in their tracks; you were in control and made everything quiet. But this approach created many frustrations, quarrels, and scolding. You didn't know that OCD was "lying" and that you didn't need to listen. OCD seemed like your very own thoughts.

One day, you will have enough control over your own life and feel sufficiently safe, that you won't need to do rituals anymore. But for a period, you will still need to think, "I will make a small ritual inside my brain, to make myself quiet". And those rituals are okay!

When you were younger, your parents had to learn that if they gave demands to you that your autism couldn't cope with, your OCD would appear, demand rituals, and promise to give you quietness inside your head.

Your parents had to learn how to plan and schedule a daily life for you as a boy with autism, so you didn't feel anxious. That challenge was difficult. But as you say, "My true Amigos are very clever". You have gained much faith in your parents, seeing how they have worked to understand you and how they can help you.

Isaac, you are a good boy!

Isaac, your parents are lucky to have you. They know this! And Sebastian knows he has a wonderful brother, even when you get mad at each other. I wish you and your family all kinds of happiness and joy in life. I will remember you always. You are one of those families that I will tell others about. Just like I have told you about other boys I have met. You are part of my treasure chest of wisdom about children and childhood.

Thank you for spending time with me and for being such a pleasant person to be with.

Yours sincerely, Nina

When to use, and why use, a diagnosis

The need for, and use of, diagnoses by a doctor, child, adolescent, parent, or society can differ greatly. These different perspectives contextualize how we talk about, give, and use the diagnoses.

The stigma that normally accompanies a diagnosis presents an obstacle. For example, stigma can occur when a diagnosis is used in an either-or manner instead of as a spectrum trait. We need to learn to share our thoughts about diagnoses such as autism and ADHD with a special focus on the spectrum and personality traits, not as fixed diagnoses (Adam, 2013; Aggernæs, 2018).

Two letters from parents with two very different children, who could have received a diagnosis, but didn't get it, illustrate this point. Neither of the children exhibited enough suffering or enough symptoms to meet the medical criteria for a diagnosis. But talking about the diagnosis, and gaining an understanding of their children's special needs and personalities, was helpful for the parents.

From a father:

One thing that meant a lot to me, were the conversations we had about our child; where you dared to say what we have always had in mind, about the innate personality traits that might well be contained within the light part of the autism spectrum. Our conversations on this means a lot to our approach to dealing with things, when occasionally life gets difficult.

126 *Naming? Might a diagnosis be best for me?*

I wish someone had spoken with us about this years ago. Not everyone needs diagnoses, but those around the child need the understanding in relationship to the challenges one faces as a family.

From a mother:

The real breakthrough for us came when we met with you, and you made the right diagnosis. It was certainly true that our child would not have benefited from a diagnosis at that time. But today, as things have settled down, we benefit from a more nuanced understanding and being able to put words to it. We can laugh and joke together about reaction patterns like knowing what's going on, having systems, and so on. That's helpful.

Diagnoses for children and youth are moving targets and are socially constructed, not absolute truths. Care needs to be taken to ensure psychiatric diagnoses are not either-or or are perceived as a negative label.

Ideally, our society will cater for a greater diversity of children, where the present narrow template for normality has been broadened considerably so children don't grow up feeling wrong (Pellicano et al., 2018).

Notes

1 When it's a mental health problem, both the ICD and the DSM (Diagnostic and Statistical Manual of Mental Disorders) (APA, 2013) can be used.
2 "True Amigoes" was Isaac's collective name for his three mothers.

References

Adam, D. (2013). On the spectrum. *Nature, 496*, 416–418. doi:10.1038/496416a

Aggernæs, B. (2018). Autism: A transdiagnostic, dimensional, construct of reasoning? *European Journal of Neuroscience, 47*(6), 515–533. doi:10.1111/ejn.13599

APA (2013). *DSM-5 diagnostic and statistical manual of mental disorders*. American Psychiatric Association.

Conrad, P., & Potter, D. (2014). From hyperactive children to ADHD adults: Observations on the expansion of medical categories. *Social Problems, 47*(4), 559–582. doi:10.2307/3 097135

Garand, L., Lingler, J. H., Conner, K. O., & Dew, M. A. (2009). Diagnostic labels, stigma, and participation in research related to dementia and mild cognitive impairment. *Research in Gerontological Nursing, 2*(2), 112–121. doi:10.3928/19404921-20090401-04

Ilgen, J. S., Eva, K. W., & Regehr, G. (2016). What's in a label? Is diagnosis the start or the end of clinical reasoning? *Journal of General Internal Medicine, 31*(4), 435–437. doi:10.1 007/s11606-016-3592-7

Lebowitz, M. S., & Ahn, W. K. (2014). Effects of biological explanations for mental disorders on clinicians' empathy. *Proceedings of the National Academy of Sciences of the United States of America, 111*(50), 17786–17790. doi:10.1073/pnas.1414058111

Lebowitz, M. S., & Appelbaum, P. S. (2019). Biomedical explanations of psychopathology and their implications for attitudes and beliefs about mental disorders. *Annual Review of Clinical Psychology*, *15*(1), 555–577. doi:10.1146/annurev-clinpsy-050718-095416

Lord, C., Brugha, T. S., Charman, T., Cusack, J., Dumas, G., Frazier, T., Jones, E. J. H., Jones, R. M., Pickles, A., State, M. W., Taylor, J. L., & Veenstra-VanderWeele, J. (2020). Autism spectrum disorder. *Nature Reviews Disease Primers*, *6*(1), 5. doi:10.1038/s41572-019-0138-4

Mogensen, L., & Mason, J. (2015). The meaning of a label for teenagers negotiating identity: Experiences with autism spectrum disorder. *Sociology of Health & Illness*, *37*(2), 255–269. doi:10.1111/1467-9566.12208

O'Connor, C., Downs, J., Shetty, H., & McNicholas, F. (2020). Diagnostic trajectories in child and adolescent mental health services: exploring the prevalence and patterns of diagnostic adjustments in an electronic mental health case register. *European Child & Adolescent Psychiatry*, *29*(8), 1111–1123. doi:10.1007/s00787-019-01428-z

Pellicano, L., Mandy, W., Bölte, S., Stahmer, A., Lounds Taylor, J., & Mandell, D. S. (2018). A new era for autism research, and for our journal. *Autism*, *22*(2), 82–83. doi:10.1177/1362361317748556

Stein, D. J., Szatmari, P., Gaebel, W., Berk, M., Vieta, E., Maj, M.,… Reed, G. M. (2020). Mental, behavioral and neurodevelopmental disorders in the ICD-11: an international perspective on key changes and controversies. *BMC Medicine*, *18*(1), 21. doi:10.1186/s12916-020-1495-2

WHO (1990). Mental and behavioural disorders. In *IVD-10 International Statistical Classification of Diseases and Related Health Problems*. World Health Organization.

Yanos, P. T., Roe, D., Lysaker, P. H. (2010). The impact of illness identity on recovery from severe mental illness. *American Journal of Psychiatric rehabilitation*, *13*(2), 73–93. doi:10.1080/15487761003756860

10 Me, the medicine, and my diagnosis

I am grateful that we have medicine to help our patients during times of unbearable suffering.

This chapter discusses how to collaborate with patients and their families about medication.

One of my early experiences with adolescent psychosis involved a 15-year-old girl who heard voices. A psychologist had been seeing the girl for more than a year but, possibly through ignorance, had dismissed her stories about voices. I met the girl in the psychiatric emergency room one night when the voices had tried to force her to stab her sleeping stepmother with a knife. The girl was relieved to meet someone who believed in her. This incident taught me that knowledge of psychopathology is important in developing respect for people who are experiencing painful challenges due to psychiatric illness.

When working in adult psychiatry, I read many testimonies containing a contract that the patients had made with their beloved ones. These documents had been written and signed by the patients between episodes of severe depression and filed in their medical records. When a patient fell ill with a depression, their contract was used to support them in not following the demands of their depression or stigmatizing discourses about medication but to accept a specific medicine or electroconvulsive therapy.

How does your medicine work?

> *Nina:* "Have you noticed how the medicine works?"
> *Child:* "Yes, the teachers are much nicer, and my parents yell much less!"

Children often do not know what positive effects to expect from their medicine. However, they often know what side-effects to look for. The child might have heard biomedical explanations about brain chemistry, but they and their family often say that they have not had the opportunity to discuss specific positive effects. Co-deciding with the family what symptoms they want the

DOI: 10.4324/9781003171621-11

medicine to alleviate, creates the best starting point in determining how and when to stop medicating the child.

The medicine can be explained in many ways. For example, we can use metaphors or refer to insider knowledge from other families (Epston, 2014). We find that local or lived experience knowledge is often more helpful than biomedical explanations.

When patients are hearing voices, we might say:

> Others have told me that the medicine makes it easier to negotiate with the voices. One person could mellow them during the day if she promised to talk with them in the evening. So, the medicine helped her to keep the voices quiet during the day.

> My hope is that the medicine will work a bit like a volume button. You and I might not be able to turn the voices off, but if we can turn their volume down, will this help you to ignore them?

For anxiety and Obsessive-Compulsive Disorder (OCD):

> The medicine doesn't take the aggravating thoughts away. However, sometimes it relieves physical symptoms and, when there's less sweaty hands and less palpitations making you scared of being sick, you might be able to ignore those stupid thoughts more easily. That's what we aim for. How does this sound to you?"

Let's create both the adverse and the favourable effect chart

Most doctors use a standard checking chart for registering adverse effects (Bech et al., 1986; Coleman & nPontefract, 2016). But there are no standard guidelines for creating a chart that enables us to assess specific preferred effects of the medicine.

A young girl said, "The doctor said something about the medicine entering my pores". I drew a sketch of the neurones and asked if that was what she had been told. "Yes! That's it", she said. "But what does that have to do with my anxiety?"

The girl had no understanding or expectations of how the medicine might help her. I suggested that we co-create a personal chart of favourable effects, and that she then looks out for these preferred effects. Suddenly, the medicine became more relevant, and the girl began to remember to take her medicine.

Metaphors, such as a volcano, can be depicted on a chart. Parents might experience that the volcano erupts less frequently when medication is taken and enjoy this effect, even though this outcome might not be the primary preference of their child. My colleague drew a volcano and showed how some children have lava constantly at the melting point, ready to erupt, while others

130 *Me, the medicine, and my diagnosis*

have dormant volcanoes that need a lot of heat to reach melting point and rarely erupt. She said, "Eruptions can be fun!" Everybody understood this metaphor, which provided more possibilities for thick descriptions, than if she had just said that arguments or fights can create satisfaction as well as sadness.

The volcano metaphor includes many nuances within the words. This metaphor helps parents and children to explore how they each contain lava at different temperatures, and that different contexts or challenges heat their volcanoes differently. Many types of medicine and anti-psychotics can have cooling effects on lava.

I often explain the role of medicine to adolescents and their parents this way:

> We are all different; some of us have more problems with concentration and hyperactivity than others. Some of us are more introverted, others are more extroverted. A big genetic component influences and shapes these differences. Depending on our genetic disposition, we react differently when feeling pressured. If more inclined towards autism, I will become more autistic, which could be reflected in rigidity and introversion. If more inclined to another diagnosis, I might react with more inattention, more fidgeting, or more volatility with my feelings. We have more leeway when not pressured or stressed. Medicine is a means of providing resilience in situations where we feel pressured. This might be in school, in social contexts, or when we must do new and unknown things. We can learn to perform or behave differently to our personal preferences but learning new patterns of behaviour is best done in a calm context. Medicine can help us increase our resilience towards challenges and difficulties. If I'm feeling pressured, I might react with an epileptic seizure, but I won't have a seizure if I'm calm and am feeling everything is fine. Other people with epilepsy who react with a seizure from the slightest event, like sunshine, will need more medicine than me.

I continue by suggesting that we create a list of goals for the medicine:

1 Let's look at the problems your problem (disorder, illness, or diagnosis) is giving you.
2 Let's look at what you might be able to do, if the medicine is as helpful as we hope it will be.
3 Let's make a checklist and use it every time we meet to discuss your medicine.

A 16-year-old girl, who had taken anti-depressive medicine years earlier, read this suggestion for a list of goals and said, "Fantastic! If someone had created a list like this with me, for my medicine, I think it would have been 10 million times more effective".

At the medical check-ups, we can co-assess whether the medicine is helpful according to the patient's personal list of goals. We can draw a weight scale and put the side effects in one of the bowls and the preferred effects in the other. The child's language is used. For example, instead of "Effects and side-effects", I might write "Helpful and troublesome". In this way, a decision on whether to continue, or increase or decrease the dosage, becomes more qualified.

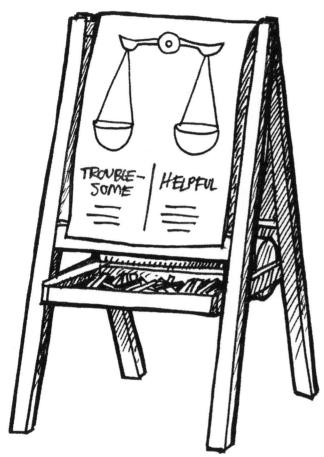

What's that medicine good for?

A child or adolescent might be more bothered by symptoms other than those we want to medicate. Our goal is to assess how different symptoms relate to each other, and what we can medicate. This task is not simple. To illustrate, I share a story and e-mail correspondence with Laura's mother, Clara, when Laura was 14 years old. Laura was diagnosed with autism when six years old and was now suffering from psychotic symptoms.

132 *Me, the medicine, and my diagnosis*

Pressure had caused Laura to experience occasional psychotic symptoms, since enrolling at school. The learning environment was too stressful for her. She had thrived before when enrolled in a more autism-friendly school.

Over the years, Clara had learned to take Laura out of school, whenever she got too burdened. Clara created a supportive structure for home schooling, and Laura thrived, often flourished, when at home. But Clara's actions were deemed wrong by schoolteachers and social workers, based on prejudices about symbiotic relationships between mothers and daughters.

This story begins at a time where Laura really wanted to stay in the new school. She was suffering badly because the school could not provide the autism-friendly structure that was necessary for her. She was sad and was experiencing anxiety and severe psychotic symptoms. Becoming psychotic was clearly related to the discrepancy between the demands the school put on her and her ability to live up to these demands. All I could do at the time to assist Laura was to medicate her.

Initially, I focused on making sure that we spoke about the same problems and agreed on what symptoms the medicine should alleviate.

We used different scales to aid our collaboration. Questions included:

- Where are you between introvert and extrovert?
- How often are you bothered by voices? Never, sometimes, or all the time? Any special time of the day?
- How tired are you? When are you tired?
- How sensitive are you to noise compared with Mum? Not at all or much more?
- How scared are you? Not at all or the most scared ever?

I created the different scales according to Laura's descriptions of her symptoms.

I wrote this letter after our first conversation on medication:

> Dear Laura and your mum,
>
> Your goal for the conversation today was to get more energy. Sometimes you really want to act, but your body doesn't respond. It's as if your body doesn't work. Do I understand this correctly?
>
> We talked about what bothers you and saps your energy.
>
> At different times in your life, you have seen or heard things that are not there, and this makes you afraid of being insane. But some people with autism respond with such symptoms when experiencing stress.
>
> You also feel lonely, and you can't find anything to be happy or excited about.
>
> You have many conflicts with your mum, and these fights and disagreements stand in the way of you enjoying that good collaboration you had when younger.

Me, the medicine, and my diagnosis 133

Therefore, until your life is on a better course, where your schooling is better for you and your everyday life is not stressing you out, it might be a good idea to take some medicine to support you during this difficult time.

You tried medicine once before, and it helped, as you felt your senses were being turned down.

Now, as you are stressed by everyday life, it is more your thoughts you want turned down. You are also feeling sad because you find that holding onto negative feelings is easier than holding onto positive feelings.

My hope is that the medication can turn down the intensity of your negative emotions. In this way, when you take the medicine, your thoughts will be easier to control, and everyday life will become less stressful.

Therefore, I have sent a prescription for medicine, and we will talk about how the medicine works after Easter. Does this sound like a good plan?

Nina

Clara's reply illustrates that untangling the complexity of problems is not easy. Directing a conversation with a distressed girl who has autism and her mum who experiences no autistic problems, is a challenge. But taking time to untangle and ensure a shared understanding of the problem is important, and I was grateful for the Clara's responding e-mail:

Dear Nina,

Thanks for a thorough conversation yesterday and for the nice letter you sent to us afterwards. An idea came to me last night.

You asked where on the Autistic Anxiety Scale Laura's anxiety was when she had to take off her clothes to be weighed, and I answered, "Eight, maybe nine". For me, the headline on that scale was, "Laura's discomfort in doing something she doesn't like". In my eyes, discomfort is part of her autism, because it is not dangerous to take off her clothes and be weighed. I think of it as something anxiety related, and I know that her thoughts and ideas are always much worse than her experience of what's going to happen. In those situations, my role is to be calm and just care for her. Typically, I quietly say something like, "You know Laura, that I know you can do it". I would have done this yesterday if it had been a blood test that was required. This kind of discomfort you saw yesterday comes at home, at school, in stores, and other places.

I don't think medicine is needed for Laura because of that kind of autistic anxiety reaction. In such cases, I know we are dealing with something that is real, because I can see that she is afraid of something she must do, which her autistic brain makes it seem worse than it really is. Yesterday I could see that Laura was sweating a lot and that is why I said, "Eight". The step

134 *Me, the medicine, and my diagnosis*

above is "Nine" where she feels she cannot breathe. "Nine" would have happened if I hadn't calmed her. At "10", her brain goes black, and she tries to get away. If I try to prevent her from doing so, she will get superpowers and hit, kick, and bite me.

I will use the Psychosis Scale to describe Laura's reactions and symptoms that prompt me to ask for medication. For me, this is a scale (or condition) for what I call "psychotic" symptoms because we are dealing with something that only happens inside Laura. The reasons come from inside Laura's head, the reactions are more protracted, and we're talking about "incomprehensible suffering" rather than an "understandable autistic anxiety". In those situations, it is as if her brain is acidified, and she describes strange sensations in her body that just sound crazy.

Yesterday on our way to you, Laura could suddenly "taste" one of the other cars. It was a bad taste, she said, so she took a sip from her soda, which she then felt tasted ugly with cucumber salad. "My senses just broke, Mum", she said. When Laura is high on the psychosis scale, she gets severe nausea and feels she must vomit. When she does vomit, it's typically at night. She has also felt that she could not endure being inside her body/skin, which she has tried to take off, and I do not want that to happen again. These are all symptoms that I do not like, and this is where I believe the medicine is relevant.

When I answered your question yesterday, I didn't consider using the psychosis scale to assess Laura's anxiety about taking off her clothes. For me, these are two different situations and therefore involve different scales, and I did not think to link the two situations. But if I must put them on the same scale, then yesterday's reaction was a "two", without anything psychotic about it, because what was going on was understandable.

Does my distinction make sense to you? Maybe we should spend five minutes talking about it next time.

Best regards, Clara

Clara's letter made good sense. I spoke with Clara on the phone, and we reached a shared understanding on how to speak about it in a way that was understandable for Laura, Clara, and me. I mailed this letter, after our next conversation:

Dear Laura and your mum,

Right now, we are investigating whether the medication can help you. Our goal is for you to be able to do more of the things you want to do.

You want the medicine to help reduce your negative thoughts and to lower your level of everyday stress. You want more peace of mind and more energy to do things and feel more joy.

Me, the medicine, and my diagnosis   135

You told us that it is working for you! You have achieved this peaceful state of mind, and your energy has been akin to pedalling the bicycle in 10th gear. But then you became exhausted. Is this right? So, when you arrived yesterday, you were exhausted.

We must remember that we can get just as tired from doing pleasant things as from doing hard things. Often the new or different things make us very tired. Therefore, it was perfectly understandable that you felt exhausted in my office yesterday.

I told you about my son, who seemed to have only one gear, 10th gear. Either he "pedalled the bicycle" at full speed or he slept. Do you feel you also have to pedal too fast, like my son? Do you want to do everything you want to do when you have the energy? And when you're tired, do you feel exhausted?

Your mother's analysis is that your medication has been helpful. But she has observed it also caused nausea during the first few days, and maybe you still feel some turmoil inside?

We must constantly consider both the benefits and the troubles the medicine gives you. Maybe you remember our list with the benefits and the troubles, side by side, and the scales on the paper chart?

We decided that you can increase your dosage. And when we meet again, we will discuss how well this is working for you.

Nina

This e-mail-writing process helped me to recall the details of Laura's initial complaints. When Laura said she was feeling exhausted and requested termination of the medicine, I could explore the pros and cons with her, on her terms. I also included a story about my son, to reassure her that others felt the same way, and to help her feel normal. Fearing insanity was a real fear for Laura.

We continued to use the weight scale to evaluate the effects of the medication. This part of the conversations was focused and concise, giving us time to explore Laura's bothersome and mournful thoughts about autism. This next letter illustrates that such conversations are a necessary element in medical check-ups, to help people manage their psychiatric problems.

Dear Laura and your mum,

For your mum, the most important aspect of this conversation was that you clearly stated:

I will not stop taking the medicine.
You said this, despite the turmoil the medicine creates in your body. We talked about how you can make that turmoil go away. We discussed decreasing or changing medicine, or you trying to do something yourself

136 *Me, the medicine, and my diagnosis*

to make the turmoil smaller. The turmoil occurs most often when you sit still, and we talked about how there is less turmoil when you move. That's why I came up with the idea that you can walk with your dog both in the mornings and in the evenings. I suggested this because other young people have said that when they exercise and make their body physically tired, the turmoil is eased at other times of the day, for example, when sitting still.

That discussion led us into a conversation about your greatest hope:
I would like to convince Mum that I can do more than she thinks.
How might you convince your mum? Will you argue with her? Do you have to show her that you can do something, for example, endure being at school even if you get tired, go walking in the morning, or ….?
I was particularly concerned that you and your mother sometimes do not see things eye to eye.

I got a feeling that you are hit with a lot of grief because you find your autism gets in the way of you doing everything you want to do. I can't take your autism away from you, but I can help you to find ways to prevent it from blocking you from doing everything you want to do.
The medicine can help you, so that the stress your autism is experiencing will not give you too many negative thoughts. The medication can provide more peace of mind, by decreasing the volume of the psychotic symptoms.

Talking about autism can also help you and your mum to find ways to organize your everyday life. Then you can do what you want and at the same time consider your autism, so it will not stand in your way. You know that. We all remember that at your old school, when you became wise about your autism, it had less negative power over you. I was so impressed by you then because you learned this at such an early age. Did you know that?

That's a path your mother would like to see you walk again. Towards a place where you know yourself and your autism, and you can ask for help and be proud of yourself because autism no longer stands in the way of everything you want to do. Rather, your autism is just a part of who you are.
Do you also dream of reaching such a place again?

The warmest greetings, Nina

Laura improved on medicine, but she experienced too many side effects, so we had to discontinue the medication. She then tried anti-depressants that improved her appetite and calmed her stress. Her mum described her being more collected. But this was still not enough to cope at school. Clara finally gave up and took Laura out of school again. Four months after choosing to home-school, Laura again thrived, still taking antidepressants, and benefiting from the effects.

I continue to challenge and address the ethical issues of medication, when services and supports are clearly underserved to people with autism (Lake et al., 2014).

Making sense of me, my diagnosis, and my medicine

A child and their doctor may not make similar sense of the same narrative, and this is a constant puzzle to be solved. Charlotte's story illustrates this:

Charlotte, who was adopted, was admitted to the intensive care unit. Her adoptive parents, Nelly and Tayler, were struggling hard to support Charlotte and collaborate with the staff. Charlotte would not accept her medicine. Her logical train of thought was that if she took medicine, this meant she was ill, and "a wrong person". How could we understand this? How could Nelly and Tyler help her to view medicine in a more helpful and healthy way?

We explored how Charlotte's parents had helped her earlier. Many stories of being unable to understand or help her began pouring out. One story was about learning to read. Her parents had tried to teach Charlotte by using her finger to point at each word as she read it, since she said she couldn't find words that were interesting to read. This strategy didn't work.

We became interested in Charlotte's exact words as the parents remembered them. Charlotte couldn't "find the words that were interesting to read". How could we understand that sentence? When did she learn to read? When she got on social media! We used our expert knowledge about autism to suggest new ways of understanding Charlotte and to eliminate the blame the parents felt. Maybe she was only interested in reading those words that she found interesting?

Just as Charlotte had difficulty in learning to read literature, we had difficulty in learning how to understand Charlotte. This gave us a new metaphor: How can we learn to "read" Charlotte?

Dear Nelly and Tyler,

As always, allowing us to explore Charlotte's life with you is touching and educational for us. You are the true supporters who have been there for a long time and can tell stories like Charlotte's story about learning to read. You do not learn to read by pointing at words with your finger. But when it makes sense to learn to read words on Facebook, you learn to read.

With Charlotte, decisions are made when they make sense to her. She learns to read when she develops an interest. She learns new things when it makes sense to learn. She does not learn when she is in the red zone and needs to be comforted and reassured.

We talked about your parenting duties, and your efforts to draw attention to Charlotte being misread. Many talented and competent people caring

138 *Me, the medicine, and my diagnosis*

for Charlotte have been wrong along the way, because "reading" her is not easy. You probably are the best translators for people she will meet in the future and for those around her now.

You already do this in your fine, respectful, and incredibly patient manner.

With our deepest respect,
Nina and Janni

We offered our medical knowledge about autism, and the parents could use this knowledge, not because we said, "Charlotte has autism", but because we said, "Charlotte takes action when it makes sense to her".

Nelly replied to our letter. Her reflections on autism are helpful to use when explaining autism to other parents:

Dear Nina and Janni,

Thank you too! "You do not read with your finger". It suddenly became obvious why that reading project had not been fruitful.

If Charlotte can see no meaning, she is not inclined to try. The unknown is too scary and awkward for her. Enduring beyond the awkwardness requires motivation to endure until the awkwardness becomes known, so it's no longer awkward but familiar. Charlotte often says, "No", because something is awkward, which for her equals physical and mental discomfort. That's why many things that are new to Charlotte have been hard for her to do.

Charlotte is also predictable. The moment the hospital told her they were allowed by law to coerce her into taking medication and then chose not to do so, Charlotte said "yes" to taking the new drug they had been encouraging her to take. Therefore, she is on medication again. We pray that this will be beneficial.

Maybe walking backwards is a good idea when trying to persuade Charlotte to do something? If we wait a little, she gets the space she needs to move forward. Maybe the solution is that simple?

Nelly

Using insider knowledge

Most doctors will at some point meet an adolescent who says, "I WON'T TAKE medicine, because as long as I do that, I am sick!" How do we cope with this? Some doctors explain the situation with Type 1 diabetes. If you do not take your insulin, then you will become very sick, but if you are good at monitoring your sugar levels and taking your insulin, you can lead a wonderful life.

I have an advantage because I can make these conversations personal and therefore more believable and credible. I have epilepsy and take medicine for epilepsy. When I talk about that, the children and their parents can ask questions. Such conversations, being upfront and candid, helps to create a bond of shared experience and trust.

I often say things like:

"By the way, do you know that I have epilepsy?" The answer is most often "NO" with a huge question mark on a big open face.

I explain that I would probably not be able to work as a doctor, if I did not take my medicine because each seizure would destroy some braincells, and I would slowly but surely become more unintelligent. I declare that I am healthy when I take my medicine. I can find it tedious and troublesome, but I am grateful that anti-epileptic medicine exists, so I can be a good mum and a good doctor.

This is often a very helpful conversation.

Charlotte's mother, Nelly, wrote to me about this "insider knowledge":

> Insider knowledge creates a special kind of equality that is felt in the stomach! I saw it the other day at the hospital in a parent group. The psychologist was halfway through presenting a slightly soulless slide show, when she told the audience that she had a son who had been home for a few years, before he was diagnosed with a mental illness and now has a good life. A father commented dryly, "Now I can listen and use what you say!" The sharing of lived experience made a big impression and the mood in the room changed noticeably. Shared experiences are a special form of communication. They are magical at times because they open up defences and reservations and encourage trust.

We aim to create dialogues about medicine a "meeting of minds" (Epston, 2014), where the child, the parents, and the health professionals contribute with expert knowledge of equal value. Trying to find if and how the medicine might work is a joint project, that can take months, and requires that we speak a shared language. As the doctor, I know about biomedical science, but my suggestions to increase or decrease of dosage, or change or cease medication, is dependent on our dialogue (Carrey, 2007; Hamkins, 2010, 2013; Thompson & McCabe, 2012).

References

Bech, P., Ahlfors, U. G., Dencker, S. J., Elgen, K., & Lingjærde, O. (1986). UKU's bi-virkningsskala: skala til registrereing af uønskede virkninger af psykofarmaka: Skandinavisk Selskab for Psykofarmakologi Udvalg for Kliniske Undersøgelser (UKU). *Nordisk psykiatrisk tidsskrift, 40*(2), 147–158.

140 *Me, the medicine, and my diagnosis*

Carrey, N. (2007). Practicing psychiatry through a narrative lens: Working with children, youth, and families. In C. Brown, Augusta-Scott, T. (Ed.), *Narrative therapy: Making meaning, making lives*. Thousand Oaks, California.

Coleman, J. J., & nPontefract, S. K. (2016). Adverse drug reactions. *Clinical Medicine, 16*(5), 481–485. doi:10.7861/clinmedicine.16-5-481

Epston, D. (2014). Ethnography, co-research and insider knowledges *Australian and New Zealand Journal of Family Therapy, 35*(1), 105–109.

Hamkins, S. (2010). Bringing narrative practices to psychopharmacology. *The International Journal of Narrative Therapy and Community Work 1*, 56–71. doi:10.3316/informit. 021018973193270

Hamkins, S. (2013). *The art of narrative psychiatry: Stories of strength and meaning* (1st ed.), Oxford University Press.

Lake, J. K., Perry, A., & Lunsky, Y. (2014). Mental health services for individuals with high functioning autism spectrum disorder. *Autism Research and Treatment, 2014*, 502420. doi:10.1155/2014/502420

Thompson, L., & McCabe, R. (2012). The effect of clinician-patient alliance and communication on treatment adherence in mental health care: A systematic review. *BMC Psychiatry, 12*, 87. doi:10.1186/1471-244X-12-87

11 Developing and co-creating shared wisdom

Family input and co-creation of new understandings and techniques enable continual improvement of treatment practices and outcomes. This chapter describes how to co-create treatment in the present moment, with families and health professionals, and explains how this collaboration benefits future families.

> Words like "illness" or "autism" do not fit me. I get stress psychoses and, for me, this is an acceptable category.
>
> Charlotte, 18 years old

Charlotte's words could be met with a "corrective speech" from a professional. Instead, we are curious. Is her truth helpful for her? Our aim is to help her make sense of her world. Let's learn from her, to improve our future work with others who might think in the same way.

Our work is founded on a broad and varied movement of change in mental health services. This movement addresses cultural and ethical issues, including shared decision-making (Slade, 2017), co-research in narrative therapy (Epston et al., 2012; Gaddis, 2004; Redstone, 2004), common factors (Hubble et al., 1999), and the empowerment and recovery-movement that uses first-person perspectives and collaborative approaches (Ness, 2013; Ness et al., 2014; Soggiu et al., 2020). It also embraces participatory action research (Cornwall & Jewkes, 1995; Khanlou & Peter, 2005; McTaggart, 1994), service user involvement (Lindow & Morris, 1995; Macaulay et al., 1999; Truman & Raine, 2002), and the "nothing-about-us-without-us" movement of people with disabilities (Charlton, 1998; Werner, 1998).

Creating and revising our guide collaboratively, with the families

We have created a guide to provide a means of evaluating the effect of our treatment (Jørring & Gjessing Jensen, 2018; Jørring & Jacobsen, 2014; Jørring & Juul, 2013, 2018). Through sharing our knowledge, other therapists can follow our process, learn from it, and make it their own. As a

DOI: 10.4324/9781003171621-12

142 *Developing and co-creating shared wisdom*

doctor, I call this guide a manual. But the word "manual" has bad connotations for many people, especially narrative therapists, who strongly resist the word, as it conveys to them that there is no leeway for improvisation (Ejbye-Ernst & Jørring, 2017; Jørring and Jacobsen, 2014; Rogers-Sirin, 2017). However, meanings of words change according to the contexts and time (Pearce, 1989). Since our manual is principle based and strives to give practical tools for empowerment, the word "guide" could be more appropriate (Davidson et al., 2008).

The guide is the foundation on which we build our treatment (Jørring & Jacobsen, 2014). Our guide demands close attention to the collaborative nature of our actions and requires that we adjust our approach to each family. We ask the same questions repeatedly:

> Are we talking about what is important to you?
>
> If we talk more about this, how might this be helpful for you?
>
> How has this conversation been for you so far?
>
> What should we do more of, less of, or change?

We co-write treatment plans and hold taking-stock sessions with families devoted to evaluations of our sessions, the treatment plan, the therapeutic e-mail letters, and the family community meetings.

We ask the families for advice on how to help new families, and we share what we learn from our work with them, especially when we say goodbye at our last conversation. These conversations are influential in developing and expanding our treatment approaches. This practice also brings energy, learning and joy into other places where we discuss our work, such as conferences.

We refer to our guide and use it as a reference, like a recipe when in doubt. We record what we learn along the way in the guide, so it gradually develops a co-created document of practices. The guide is a great way to introduce new members to the team, to teach residents and students about our work.

I strongly advocate for others to use guides and continually reflect and revise them, thereby making their own research project. Such a project adds strength and provides a framework for a team to be positively critical about their work. It also inspires team members to develop and improve continuously as new members come on board. Everyone learns as they gain ongoing experience through collaboration and co-creation.

The families have been our greatest teachers. We achieve our learnings by being in constant dialogue about what is important to the people we want to help. We know that we will learn as much as they learn, even though they are the patients, and we are the professionals.

Developing and co-creating shared wisdom   143

The families have taught us a lot about important ethical aspects and concrete details of working collaboratively, with their take-home messages including:

- Never share communication about us, before we, the family, have read and agreed to it first.
- Treat our time as equally precious, for example, planning dates for sessions together.
- Remember how vulnerable we are, so forgive us, when we forget an appointment.
- Remember to look for our good intentions, which are the hopes we have for what will happen when we perform a specific action. Do not judge us on the results of our actions.
- When you believe in us, we can also believe in ourselves.
- Thank you for telling me that I do not have to answer all the questions in your letters.
- Remember we are scared, and this is new to us. Thank you for explaining every detail to us.
- Speaking our words makes us worthy of respect, but the professional language makes us feel less worthy.
- Writing our names and dates on the paper charts helps us to see how we evolve.

How might we understand our child's problems?

Let us co-create wisdom and collaborate on the use of diagnoses.

Tim, who was seven years old, had never attended school regularly. Anxiety kept him inside the house. Tim was the younger brother to Joel, whose friendship-canoe is described in Chapter 5. Tim had been diagnosed with a pervasive developmental disorder, unspecified. However, doctors would not give him an anxiety diagnosis, as they believed his symptoms were due to the inability of his parents, school, and municipality to create the right environment for his daily life. The municipality and school wanted Tim to receive traditional treatment for anxiety, as he clearly reacted with classical symptoms of anxiety when at school. When the family was referred to us, we became curious about these different interpretations and effects of the diagnoses. We wondered how we might best help the family. How could we describe Tim's problems, so the school and municipality could provide him with the best possible help?

Before we got around to writing our e-mail to the parents after the initial session, they sent an e-mail to us. It was short and to the point:

Hi Nina and Camilla,

We are curious about what you were thinking after the conversation we had.

Thanks Andy

144 *Developing and co-creating shared wisdom*

We responded:

> Dear Mandy and Andy,
>
> Interesting that you ask this question. We really want to share our impressions of Tim with you.
>
> We see a boy who has a kind heart and manages to retain his desire for knowledge and reflection, even when in a situation with minimum outside stimulation. This must require a lot of effort and be hard work at times.
>
> We also see a powerful boy intent on being in control of the conversation. He controls us with his ability to tell stories and to talk incessantly. He seems to react violently to any adult talk he is not prepared for. It makes more sense to us now, that the caseworker called Tim a tyrant, and a tyrant at home. He has an ability to take centre stage and know his destination. This is perhaps a rare gift in relationship to the way he uses his language in such a whimsical way. For instance, he answers our questions, but in a way that he turns the content into something else. We see this ability as a force, but also as a double-edged sword, because it can easily mislead us adults.
>
> Perhaps the impression that stands out most strongly is that Tim has many potential competencies, but these also create troubles for him. Might this be why it is difficult to place his diagnosis in a traditional box?
>
> Were these some of the observations you hoped we might see, when you brought Tim to see us? Or did you hope we would have other reflections? If so, please write back to us.
> Nina and Camilla

Andy and Mandy responded right away:

> Hi
> Thank you for those good words. We have thought a lot about how you saw Tim.
>
> We are beginning to get a deeper understanding of Tim. We see his need to be in control, and what happens for him, when he loses control.
>
> We also are beginning to understand what Tim means when he says that "Things are boring". We see how Tim reacts to adult talk that he is not prepared for. It becomes frustrating for him to lose control when something happens that he is not expecting. "Boring" simply means that he is frustrated not to have control.

Developing and co-creating shared wisdom 145

What we have experienced over time when we try to "make Tim grow", also makes sense. When we get involved in what he himself is engaged in, let him feel that he has control, then he grows. Doing something he thinks is fun or telling a story (preferably one he invents himself) are examples of the kinds of things that work.

Getting Tim to school has been difficult. Training didn't work, that makes sense now, because the answer is not about getting him accustomed to the new, but rather about understanding that he only wants/can do what he himself is engaged in. If forced to do something else, Tim finds this becomes "boring", which translates to "very stressful".

We will send your letter to the school psychologist and the social worker. We think it will help them to find the right school placement for him.

We answered the parents' letter this way:

Hi again,
Wow, thank you for your thoughts and considerations. We are happy that we can go exploring together in the world of Tim, and that those discoveries we do make, might be helpful to the school psychologist and social worker.
Nina and Camilla

Some weeks later Andy and Mandy wrote to us:

Hi!
We have found it! Tim's problem.
It is called Pathological Demand Avoidance (PDA). The fit is perfect. This is the key. He is controlled by an anxiety about losing control. In everything. The prospects are terrible, and he needs help to work with that control-anxiety. Otherwise, he will shut himself down, go into his own little world. What will we do, with no school for Tim? We are so tired.

We are depressed and wondering. But also, optimistic because, when we can find words and material to read about these things, we can work with it.
Mandy and Andy

At this point, I had not heard about PDA. I googled it and was appalled at the descriptions and prognoses. I was also wondering about my "doctoral identity". Where were we going? Could I retain credibility, not knowing as much as the parents? I decided to be honest and transparent, as these practices rarely let me down.

146 *Developing and co-creating shared wisdom*

> Hi Mandy and Andy!
> I have never heard about PDA, but I just googled and skim read what I could find. It seems to be an "underdiagnosis" of autistic spectrum disorders.[1]
>
> One reason for having diagnoses is for doctors to predict a prognosis and to get an idea of what can we expect. Early descriptions of prognosis are almost always terrible because those people initially described got no help. But if Tim is placed in a school where teachers are wise enough to understand that children can have many kinds of autism that are as different as children are, then I believe this description will be helpful to you. Tim will be alright. These are my thoughts. Can you use them?
> Nina

> Hi!
> Thank you for the thoughts.
> It is all about the understanding! This is so meaningful to us. Forget the prognosis, we cannot use that as parents.
> It just makes sense to us, that anxiety arrives when Tim loses control. He uses all his talents to keep control. He is so smart. But he uses his talents wrong. Now that we have an understanding, we can help him.
> Mandy and Andy

I wrote back:

> Hi again!
> WOW! I am excited to read about your new insights. I can already see where your wisdom might help me to assist two other children. What you describe is interesting and exciting. I have an idéa: what if we interview you about these new insights that you intend to integrate into your understanding of Tim?
>
> I hope that by interviewing you about your new insights and understanding, you will not only teach us, but also become wiser yourself on how to understand and help Tim, and your communications with the school might become easier. Is this an applicable idea?
> Nina

Andy responded:

> Yes, good idea. We are still unsure about the whole thing, so your questions will help us to be more attentive and astute. If you can use it too, that's nice to know.
> See you, Andy ☺

This collaborative exploration not only helps to create new wisdom, but it also places the parents in a position of being worthy partners to a psychologist and

Developing and co-creating shared wisdom 147

a doctor. That's a powerful situation for two adults who have experienced being demeaned by disrespectful professionals instructing them on how to change their thoughts and behaviours (Charlton, 1998).

At their final family session with us, Andy and Mandy said:

> We entered your unit with some specific difficulties and diagnoses that were difficult to understand. Our conversations with you have helped us to create knowledge about diagnoses; together we have been translating this into actions in our family's everyday life. Your conversations are helping us to get to that place, where we can help our child in practice.

Consulting our consultants

We consulted with patients in a more formal co-research project, inspired by the idea of a patient being a consultant to others (Marsten et al., 2011; White & Epston, 1999). David Epston offered to interview some of the families we had in treatment about our practices, focusing specifically on the therapeutic letter-writing.

David first interviewed our team members about our values and hopes for our work, with attention to a specific family, so he could consult with that specific family afterwards about how well we were doing in adhering to our values. Among consultants that David interviewed was Agnes, a 17-year-old girl we had known for two years.

David began the interview this way:

David: This team has invited you to be their consultant. Are you okay with being their consultant?
Agnes: Yes.

David read aloud the notes he had taken from his interview with us. David then asked Agnes to comment on various aspects. Here's an edited excerpt from the transcript:

David: Okay, is there anything that you would like to tell the team about how they should go about their work?
Agnes: Keep on with their e-mails.
David: What? Everyone says this, why do you say that?
Agnes: Because I tried both without the e-mails and with the e-mails.
David: Really?
Agnes: Yes, three different psychologists have been treating me, both with and without the e-mails. And I find it best with. Because I get kind of a "red thread"[2] through our talks. They are not just, "Okay, how are you doing today? And what are we going to talk about today?" But there's a red thread through the things.
David: A thread?

148 *Developing and co-creating shared wisdom*

Agnes: Yes, through my treatment. It keeps me steady and focused on what I want to talk about. I get from the e-mails what we talked about last time, and what I need to talk more about, and what's okay.

David: Do you mind me asking you about how often do you read the e-mails?

Agnes: Well, I read them every time and I have saved all the e-mails in case I want to read them again. But otherwise, I don't read them a lot.

David: Is it reassuring they are there?

Agnes: It is. That I can read them again. But also, every time I go to a session, the first thing Kirsten and Nina do is read the e-mail aloud. So, I get to sit there for a moment and prepare myself on what we are going to talk about. It is nice the way they use the e-mails. Because, well, my father is a workaholic, so, I know for him it's a nice thing to be prepared, to have this e-mail, so he knows what we are going to talk about, or at least know where we were the last time we spoke. I can see that it's going to help me because Dad is more focused.

David: Would you say it's worthwhile?

Agnes: Yes. Because it's nice to know what the therapists thought was going on, and their thoughts about what I said. To hear it repeated from them and, when they write down things that they find interesting, then we can talk about it.

David: Have you ever received a letter that really surprised you, that what they found interesting was noteworthy? That you went, "Wow I'm surprised by that?"

Agnes: Well, I think one of the things I got most surprised by was when I had a little anger tantrum and they thought I handled it very well; that they mentioned this.

David: When you became aware that they thought you had handled it well, did you re-consider how you had handled it?

Agnes: I did! I thought, "What did I do good about it?"

David: Do you mind telling me about this?

Agnes: Well, I don't remember exactly. I was angry about something my father had said, and I said that. Kirsten or Nina wrote it on the paper chart, but Dad kept talking and I just sat there quietly until it was my turn to talk. Then I said, "Well, I am going to say it, I need to, because I am so annoyed at what he just said, because it's not true". Well, I was so angry.

David: Well, the team did mention that. I think Kirsten said that you showed dignity. I hope you do not mind me saying this, but that's not a word that's often ascribed to people your age. Do you think you showed dignity? In that situation where you were furious about something?

Agnes: I hope so. I wouldn't like to make a fool out of myself. I think I said what I needed to say without becoming upset.

David: And, as a consequence, do you think your father recognized what you had to say because you spoke in a more dignified manner?

Developing and co-creating shared wisdom 149

Agnes: Yeah, I think Dad did in the moment. But I think the main thing for me was that the adults recognized how well I handled my anger.

David: Okay. Another principle is that the therapists want to show the families they meet that they really care. By that, the team means that it is important for families to experience that they care about them, and Kirsten and Nina mentioned that they tried in their letters to represent your desire to become a person who is tolerant, open-minded, and wise. Do you think that the letters helped get that understanding across to you? Kirsten wondered when she read an e-mail aloud and mentioned the way you had handled your anger so it became useful, and made you and your father closer, if you felt the same way. She wondered if you think that, without the e-mail, you wouldn't have been able to appreciate that. Do you think that the letters helped get this across to you? Do you think that if they hadn't sent the letters that this description of you would have been lost, forgotten, or just not have mattered that much to anybody? How did the letters operate here?

Agnes: Well, the e-mails operated like kind of a reminder between my sessions, and they did tell me, "Well, you did good. This is fine". "I can see you holding on". They did write in the letters that they were proud of how I handled situations and described what I was feeling. I think my handling of the situation would have been lost, if it had not been noted in the letters, because it's hard to remember everything from time-to-time in the sessions.

David: I have asked this of quite a few people, so I hope you don't mind me asking you, too: how much do you really remember from a session? Like, if you just walked out and tried to write down everything that happened, how much would you be able to write down?

Agnes: Not much! Because when I am emotionally involved, I go blank. So, I need a few days to just think about what did happen, and what did they actually say.

David: Well, your response is similar to others who have answered this question. The others say, "I couldn't remember a thing, except a general thing, like things are going well, or things are going badly".

Agnes: Yeah, I could remember if it was a good session or a bad session. Or that one thing meant everything to me, but I couldn't say in detail what happened during the session. These e-mails, however, mention the little things and details and capture the things that are important. I can see in the letter what I actually did say and can consider if that was what I wanted to say in that session. Did the others understand what I was saying or meaning? The same as they do when they repeat and write on the paper chart what I have just said during the sessions. Then I can see on the paper chart if I have said what I wanted to say. That's also what I use the e-mails for. I can think about what

150 *Developing and co-creating shared wisdom*

we have talked about in the session. I can see what still matters to me, what I need to talk more about, what I'm okay with, and what I don't need to talk more about.

David: Yeah, I get it. Does anything else come to mind?

Agnes: Yes, there's one more thing, whether our age is eight, or 17 or 18 like I am, or an adult, and that's the way the team writes the e-mails. I think it's nice because I am not an adult yet, and I am not a child, and that's important for me, because in other ways I am being treated too much as an adult. I think those e-mails meet the needs of us all, really well.

Our team reflected afterwards on this consultation. We focused on expanding our learning from several points:

Agnes said, "It's nice to know what they thought". This speaks to the idea of neutrality, which was first described in family therapy by the Milan group (Selvini et al., 1980) and is the value that the family members should know for certain that their therapist will not align with one person against the other. It is also understood that the therapist will not bring personal values into the therapy. These ideas have been rejected as being both impossible and destructive, but nevertheless are still present (Fife & Whiting, 2007). Agnes appreciated that we shared our opinion. It was useful for her when her father heard that these professionals were proud of how she was handling her anger. This supports the narrative value of transparency and rejects the values of separating the personal from the professional (Kirkeby, 2008).

We have also heard from other families about the idea of a red thread. Families value that their conversations with us are being bound together by the e-mails, creating a process, rather than a series of separate events.

Agnes also said, "It helps me when Dad receives an e-mail, because then he is more focused, and that benefits me". Parents often have other competing problems that we must be respectful of. The e-mails become sort of a secure base for the children. They know that the professionals have done something to grasp the hold of the parent. The e-mails help the family members to focus together. The letters become a way for therapists to make it easier for people to come to therapy because they create and show the structure: "Here's what you can expect".

Agnes said, "I prepare myself for what I want to talk more about when the letter is read aloud". She said that her father would read the e-mail just before the session, and then would shut his phone and put it away.

This knowledge helped us the next time somebody said, "Oh, we don't need you to read it aloud, we have just read it". We now answer, "Reading aloud is part of the therapy. We read it to catch up on where we were. It helps us too, to remember where we were. It's a way for all of us to settle down and prepare ourselves to be here for the next hour". Reading the letter is a way of saying, "Okay, put aside school and work, and everything else, now we are here".

Developing and co-creating shared wisdom 151

Five years later, Agnes recalled that David's interview, in elevating her status to one of consulting to us, had benefited her self-esteem and belief in herself. The interview, therefore, had been helpful for us all.

Repeatedly, families have confirmed that we must practice respect, curiosity, trust and hope for collaborations to be helpful. These practices can be difficult and cannot be delivered half-heartedly or faked. However, we have learned from co-research with patients, the treatment process becomes easier when we share the burden of having the wisdom with others (Ejbye-Ernst & Jørring, 2017; Epston, 1999).

Notes

1 Today, I would call this a specific profile that we see in many children with autism. This is an example of how our language constantly changes. We must update constantly and be flexible in our understandings and communication.
2 The "red thread" is a metaphor from Greek mythology, where King Theseus found his way out of the Minotaur's labyrinth by following a red thread. It symbolizes a consistent theme or message throughout a text.

References

Charlton, J. I. (1998). *Nothing about us without us. Disability oppression and empowerment* (1 ed.). University of California Press.

Cornwall, A., & Jewkes, R. (1995). What is participatory research? *Social Science & Medicine, 41*(12), 1667–1676. doi:10.1016/0277-9536(95)00127-S

Davidson, L., Rowe, M., Tondora, J., O'Connell, M. J., & Lawless M. S. (2008). *A practical guide to recovery-oriented practice: Tools for transforming mental health care.* Oxford University Press.

Ejbye-Ernst, D., & Jørring, N. T. (2017). Doing it collaboratively! Addressing the Dilemmas of Designing quantitative effect studies on narrative family therapy in a local clinical context. *Journal of Systemic Therapies, 36*(1), 48–66. doi:10.1521/jsyt.2017.36.1.48

Epston, D. (1999). Co-research: The making of alternative knowledge in narrative therapy and community work. In P. Moss (Ed.), *Narrative therapy and community work: A conference collection.* Adelaide: Dulwich Centre Publications.

Epston, D., Stillman, J. R., & Erbes, C.R. (2012). Speaking two languages: A conversation between narrative therapy and scientific practices. *Journal of Systemic Therapies, 31*(1), 74–88. doi:10.1521/jsyt.2012.31.1.74

Fife, S. T., & Whiting, J. B. (2007). Values in Family therapy practice and research: An invitation for reflection. *Contemporary Family Therapy, 29*(1), 71–86. doi:10.1007/s105 91-007-9027-1

Gaddis, S. (2004). Re-positioning traditional research: Centring clients' accounts in the construction of professional therapy knowledges. *The International Journal of Narrative Therapy and Community Work, 2004*(2), 1–12. doi:10.3316/informit.239160853903152

Hubble, M. A., Duncan, B. L., & Miller, S. D. (Eds.). (1999). *The heart and soul of change: What works in therapy.* Washington, DC: American Psychological Association.

Jørring, N. T., & Gjessing Jensen, K. (2018). Treatment efficacy of narrative family therapy for children and adolescents with diverse psychiatric symptomatology. *Scandinavian*

152 *Developing and co-creating shared wisdom*

Journal of Child and Adolescent Psychiatry and Psychology, 6(2), 107–114. doi:10.21307/sjcapp-2018-012

Jørring, N. T., & Jacobsen, C.B. (2014). Narrative therapy in CAMHS: Creating multi-storied treatments. *Journal of Systemic Therapies, 33*(1), 89–101. doi:10.1521/jsyt.2014.33.1.89

Jørring, N. T., & Juul, J. (2013). Collaborative family therapy with psychiatric multi-stressed families. Retrieved 8 June 2021 from https://www.researchgate.net/publication/336512754_English_manual_rev_October_2013

Jørring, N. T., & Juul, J. (2018). Manual for Samarbejdende familieterapi. Retrieved June 8th 2021 from https://www.researchgate.net/publication/329269185_Manual_for_Samarbejdende_familieterapi

Khanlou, N., & Peter, E. (2005). Participatory action research: Considerations for ethical review. *Social Science & Medicine, 60*(10), 2333–2340. doi:10.1016/j.socscimed.2004.10.004

Kirkeby, O. F. (2008). *The virtue of leadership.* Frederiksberg, Denmark: Copenhagen Business School Press.

Lindow, V., & Morris, J. (1995). *Service user involvement: Synthesis of findings and experience in the field of community care.* Joseph Rowntree Foundation.

Macaulay, A. C., Commanda, L. E., Freeman, W. L., Gibson, N., McCabe, M. L., Robbins, C. M., & Twohig, P. L. (1999). Participatory research maximises community and lay involvement. North American Primary Care Research Group. *BMJ, 319*(7212), 774–778. doi:10.1136/bmj.319.7212.774

Marsten, D., Epston, D., & Johnson, L. (2011). Consulting your consultants, revisited. *The International Journal of Narrative Therapy and Community Work*(3), 57–71. doi:10.3316/informit.711700265602093

McTaggart, R. (1994). Participatory Action Research: Issues in theory and practice. *Educational Action Research, 2*(3), 313–337. doi:10.1080/0965079940020302

Ness, O. (2013). *Therapists in continuous education: A collaborative approach.* Taos Institute Publications/WorldShare Books.

Ness, O., Borg, M., & Davidson, L. (2014). Facilitators and barriers in dual recovery: A literature review of first-person perspectives. *Advances in Dual Diagnosis, 7*(3), 107–117. doi:10.1108/ADD-02-2014-0007

Pearce, B. W. (1989). *Communication and the Human Condition.* Southern Illinois University Press.

Redstone, A. (2004). Researching people's experience of narrative therapy: Acknowledging the contribution of the "Client" to what works in counselling conversations. *The International Journal of Narrative Therapy and Community Work*(2), 57–62. doi:10.3316/informit.243465070263796

Rogers-Sirin, L. (2017). Psychotherapy from the Margins: How the pressure to adopt evidence-based-treatments conflicts with social justice-oriented practice. *Journal for Social Action in Counseling & Psychology, 9*(1), 55–78. doi:10.33043/JSACP.9.1.55-78

Selvini, M. P., Boscolo, L., Cecchin, G., & Prata, G. (1980). Hypothesizing-circularity-neutrality: Three guidelines for the conductor of the session. *Family Process, 19*(1), 3–12. doi:10.1111/j.1545-5300.1980.00003.x

Slade, M. (2017). Implementing shared decision making in routine mental health care. *World Psychiatry: Official Journal of the World Psychiatric Association (WPA), 16*(2), 146–153. doi:10.1002/wps.20412

Soggiu, A. L., Klevan, T., Davidson, L., & Karlsson, B. (2020). A sort of friend: Narratives from young people and parents about collaboration with a mental health outreach team. *Social Work in Mental Health*, *18*(4), 383–397. doi:10.1080/15332985.2020.1761932

Truman, C., Raine, P. (2002). Experience and meaning of user involvement: Some explorations from a community mental health project. *Health & Social Care in the Community*, *10*(3), 136–143. doi:10.1046/j.1365-2524.2002.00351.x

Werner, D. (1998). *Nothing about us without us: Developing innovative technologies for, by, and with disabled persons*. Healthwrights.

White, M., & Epston, D. (1999). Consulting our consultants: The documentation of alternative knowledges. In *Experience, contradiction, narrative & imagination: Selected papers of David Epston & Michael White 1989-1991* (pp. 11–26).

12 Empowering the entire family

We are responsible for organizing the collaboration with the family, and the broader framework to be conducive for child development. This chapter expands the concepts described in Chapter 1, on moving away from professionalized and individualized descriptions of human identity to relational, contextual and anti-individualist understandings of people, problems, and relationships (Madigan, 2019, p. 4).

Many parents have experienced being ascribed by health professionals as either non-existing or counter-productive forces in their adolescent's life. Diagnosing only the child and prescribing individual treatment, while perhaps not intentional, supports such discourses (Strong, 2015), and can result in parents being ignored or excluded from their child's life (Bentley et al., 2016; Kopera et al., 2015; Larson & Corrigan, 2008; Schulze, 2007).

This chapter's stories illustrate the structuring of therapy and broader family collaborations to empower children, adolescents and their families, inspired by the following values (Madsen, 2009):

1. Cultural curiosity and honouring family wisdom.
2. Believing in family resourcefulness.
3. Working in partnership with families.
4. Engaging in empowering processes.

I often introduce junior colleagues and families to this way of thinking with this story:

> Imagine a child goes to therapy, comes home, and tells their parents, "I have got this new insight, so from now on I will act differently in this and that way..., and I expect that you will notice and will also change your behaviour". Such an expectation is demanding too much of a child. When I underwent therapy in order to become a therapist, learning how it is in therapy, I had difficulty sharing the content of the therapy with my husband, even though I was an adult. Expecting individual therapy with children to be effective, compared with family therapy, is in many ways unfeasible.

DOI: 10.4324/9781003171621-13

Empowering the entire family 155

When parents are not participating in tube feeding their child with anorexia, parents indirectly receive this message, "You cannot deal with this in your child's life. But we can!" (Jørring, 2009). Consider the implications this has for parental self-esteem. Professionals can learn to move from involving to fully collaborating with parents, for example, by asking, "Who has the storytelling rights of the story being told?" (Madigan, 2019, p. 9).

Naming Seytan and working collaboratively

Ahmed, whose story first appears in Chapter 9, did not know what Obsessive-Compulsive Disorder (OCD) was and called it "Seytan". I changed his treatment from cognitive behavioural therapy to narrative therapy, without changing from individual to family therapy. I was still a beginner and mostly subscribed to many of the discourses from my medical training. I met Ahmed's mum in the waiting room and did not see the father or the younger sister at all. However, as I learned more about Ahmed and his relationship with Seytan, the name the family had given the problem at home, a new line of questioning led me to explore the family's struggles to help their son.

Ahmed said that his parents, in utter despair, had written to a wise man in their homeland and asked for help, because things had become steadily worse. The parents had received a letter that they read to him every evening. Sometimes, they posted the letter on the bathroom wall for him to look at.

Nina: What did the wise man write to you?
Ahmed: I don't know....
Nina: How can you not know? Don't you hear his words every evening? Can't you read?
Ahmed: No! It's in Farsi. I don't understand Farsi, I only speak and read Danish.
Nina: Okay! Do you think your parents might be able to translate the letter?
Ahmed: I don't know if that's allowed.
Nina: Could you ask them?
Ahmed: Could you ask my mum?
Nina: Yes, I could! Yeah, why don't I ask your mum? I have an idea. What do you think about your mum coming along and joining us next time?

Thereafter, Ahmed's mum attended all our sessions. Her involvement enabled descriptions of how awful the OCD also was to the mum, who had been enlisted by the OCD to behave like a servant for her son. For example, she was expected to provide Ahmed with a clean cloth as he stepped into the apartment upon coming home from school. She was expected to wash him from top to toe in the door entrance. She was expected to allow Ahmed to use her computer-mouse, when his own was touched by his younger sister, and

156　*Empowering the entire family*

therefore was considered contaminated. Ahmed was unable to tell how many rules Seytan had put on him; much like many children are unable to tell what OCD demands of them. Coming to therapy alone was not helpful for Ahmed. His mum was necessary as his witness and ally in their mutual fight for freedom from Seytan.

We were fortunate that Ahmed and I were able to include his mum in the treatment.

I felt overwhelmed because I knew nothing about the family's culture. Our therapy taught me how to be curious because I could not pretend to understand. I asked many questions, often beginning with, "Remember, I am a Dane. I have grown up in this Danish culture and have no idea about your culture, your rules, values, dreams and hopes, but I am wondering, if what you are telling me now is in accordance with what you would do, if this Seytan was not in your home?" Ahmed and his mum often laughed loudly because of my ignorant questions. Obviously, their behaviour was not in accordance with their values when Seytan was in their home.

We discussed what Seytan would demand of Ahmed, his mum and other family members. I asked them how they responded to these demands, and I learned a lot.

As we proceeded, Ahmed and his mum teamed up against Seytan and threw it out of their home. The fight was vicious. Mother and son suffered during these trials, but Ahmed's knowledge about soccer and being on a team was helpful as was the mother-son humour. Humour was something Ahmed's dad also used to manage his own mental health challenge, post-traumatic stress disorder (PTSD).

Eventually, Seytan left Ahmed's family, and the time came for us to say goodbye. I asked them to attend an extra session, not only to say goodbye, but also to give me an opportunity to invite their advice on helping other families. I felt overwhelmed when the entire family showed up. They all wanted to thank me. I had not only helped Ahmed; I had helped every family member to break free from Seytan's vicious grip.

Ahmed's family described being met with respect for their culture. They were impressed that I respected their culture as equal to mine. In return, they had gained respect for my culture. They had loved my questions and had spoken about them at home, acknowledging that the process of providing responses to increase my understanding, also had led to them becoming wiser about themselves. They said this was one of the best "tricks" I had used. They liked that I was convinced that they would be able to manage life in Denmark and that I did not look down on the dad because of his PTSD. They loved my humour and humility.

The family had two requests during our final meeting. The mum and dad wanted me to tell Ahmed that Danish children also must respect their parents. Ahmed wanted me to tell his parents to be more like Danish parents who were more lenient and allowed their children more freedom. I was puzzled by these requests.

Nina:	Why do you ask me to tell you this? Haven't we agreed that you should live your life according to your values, not mine?
Ahmed's mum:	Yes, but we want to become part of the Danish society, so we often discuss how we can stay true to our old culture and become part of the new one. We deeply respect you, and we think you give real advice; you don't take sides or demand undue sacrifices from us.
Nina:	Wow! How do you expect or want me to answer?

This made them laugh. We laughed together for a while, and I enjoyed watching the camaraderie of the family. Ahmed's mum answered:

> You just gave us the best advice. Whenever we are in doubt, we will ask each other: What might Nina think about this? And we will know that she thinks it is possible to acknowledge both sides and find middle ground.

As we came to say our goodbyes, the family stopped me from rising from my chair and the father spoke. He said that in his culture the touching of other people's hands, out of respect, was improper, as one's own hand might be dirty, so one did not shake hands but would nod and smile. But as they knew I would like to shake hands, they had decided that today, if I would like to, they would shake hands with me. Their intention for this action was to express their deep gratitude. I still feel warm inside thinking about that moment.

Don't forget the siblings!

As Ahmed's story shows, the siblings are often forgotten, and rarely seen in therapy or in research. They only receive help if they have identified problems of their own (Bågenholm & Gillberg, 1991; Ma, 2014; Ma et al., 2015). Finding appropriate ways to include siblings is a challenge. Shall they participate all the time as in traditional family therapy or be excused, with the risk of feeling left out?

We believe in being open and flexible. We often suggest conversations for the siblings, where they can come alone with their parents, so they can have their own space. A father's reflection on how his son Oliver coped while daughter Trudy was in treatment, validates our approach.

> Dear Nina,
> I remember Oliver attending family conversations before we met you. It was not a success, and we continued the conversations alone with Trudy (or tried, Trudy was very unstable at the time). I remember the conversations were very fierce and were burdensome for Oliver to witness. They were about Trudy and did no good for Oliver.

158 *Empowering the entire family*

I also remember him being far too small, trying to take on responsibility and paying more attention to how Trudy was than to his own situation and that worried us.

Then we met you, and we had one conversation with only Oliver, focusing on him, his situation, and a more direct description of Trudy's challenges. I remember the conversation as very positive and necessary for Oliver. It helped him through a difficult period.
Based on our family's situation, I do not believe that siblings can, or should be, involved in the treatment of another sibling. It's not their responsibility.

On the other hand, I think it is important that a support program is initiated simultaneously for the siblings, because they can be squeezed out or forgotten in the therapy process. I am grateful for the conversation you had with Oliver. In retrospect, he might have benefited from more focus and professional support around his own situation, but he managed. He wasn't the one who was "hospitalized" or undergoing treatment, and I know the resource problems in the health sector.

Oliver's father

All members of the family must be acknowledged as experiencing suffering, for siblings to receive appropriate help.

Next-of-kin involvement

Some children with mental illness live in residential treatment centres where staff sometimes become "extended-family". Nelly and Tyler, Charlotte's parents, came to us when Charlotte was 15 years old and had experienced several admissions in an intensive care ward at our Child and Adolescent Mental Health Centre. The parents had endured many struggles, such as described in Chapter 10, when Charlotte refused to take her prescribed medication. Eventually, Charlotte was admitted into a residential treatment centre.

Nelly and Tyler wanted help to collaborate with the staff, both in the intensive care ward and the residential treatment centre. They understood a lot about Charlotte but were often stupefied by her behaviours. They desperately wanted someone who could be their curious sparring partner in exploring these confusing experiences. However, when they tried to speak with the staff at the treatment centre or the hospital, they usually felt dismissed or excluded. I wrote to Nelly and Tyler after a parent session on the dilemmas of being a parent to an adolescent and wanting to collaborate with the staff:

Dear Nelly and Tyler,
I think you should know that the conversation with you really got me thinking:

Empowering the entire family 159

What are good ways of next-of-kin involvement?

Your overarching goal is to support Charlotte, just as other parents wish to do for their child.
You want to be available for Charlotte as parents, even though she has a psychiatric illness.

You considered these questions:

- Can you help the professionals with the expert knowledge you have about your child?
- Can you as parents, be the ones to help Charlotte remember her full story, and help her when she needs to place her illness experience in the context of her life as a whole?
- Are you, as parents the only constant presence providing continuity in Charlotte's life, and the only people who know what her life is, and has been?
- Can you be available to Charlotte as a parent, even if she has a mental illness?

We discussed different interpretations of meaningful collaboration, and how parents might support a child like Charlotte.
We agreed that all relatives probably want to be helpful and courteous to their loved one and will have wisdom and knowledge that can be useful for others.

However, on numerous occasions, your offers of help have been refused. This could be because professionals in general do not appreciate and understand the resources parents have. Much wisdom and support are lost when parent's help is declined or dismissed. Perhaps parents and other relatives need to stand back, shrug their shoulders, and accept that some professionals have difficulty in accepting their support, and hope that this situation will change soon?

We spoke about how parents can learn a lot from the treatment staff, and we wondered if the staff know that one of their duties could be to pass on their knowledge, so the parents can use that knowledge at home. Can the staff make time for this? You cited examples of this happening. Early on, there were rules about who could visit Charlotte when she was hospitalized, and you would hear about what was supportive for her. But staff members no longer have time to communicate with you. You were told, *"Collaboration with families has been on our staff meeting agenda, and we need to be better about this"*. I wonder if the staff know that a five-minute conversation or a text message with you, can shorten Charlotte's suffering?

Then we focused on what you want to do as parents, things that the psychiatric illness prevents you from doing.

160 *Empowering the entire family*

You want to help your daughter to remember her whole story.

You want to be there to help Charlotte to create an overview and a meaningful understanding of her experience. This will require you to have ongoing and up-to-date information from the treatment team, so that you know whether Charlotte has good or bad days. You will need to know whether she is on a hunger strike, whether she is hospitalized, whether she is at her residential housing, when she is capable of doing homework, when she self-harms, when she has good experiences, who her friends are, and so on.

Tyler explained that to achieve daily contact and obtain this knowledge, daily contact with Charlotte's treatment staff will be necessary. You show great understanding in appreciating that the staff are busy. But I wonder how would the staff react, if they knew this kind of collaboration could enable you to become an "external memory" for Charlotte? I wonder if the staff could set aside time, if they reminded themselves that patients recovering from psychiatric illness need somebody to talk with about the hard times. It can be frustrating for the patient when family members have not been present and do not understand what they need to talk about. As parents, you need to follow Charlotte's developments while she is growing up, so that you can continue to meet her and be there for her wherever she is in her life.

You spoke about providing continuity for Charlotte, by being accessible as parents through her life, for as long as you live. But how can you be accessible, when she is hospitalized or at the residential centre, and is incapable of calling you, herself? It's not enough that she calls only when there's a crisis and needs you to come immediately and collect her.

You wish that a treatment goal could be that Charlotte learns to contact you, her parents, and tell you about small and big things. That you will not only hear about things when she is totally out of it, but over time can hear by the tone of her voice, on the phone, that something is underway, making your early intervention and support possible, so issues can be attended to before they boil over or explode. You already have experienced several times that Tyler has been able to "talk Charlotte down", when she calls. But you also would like to have conversations on those days when she is feeling good, and on those days that are ordinary. You have thought about the knowledge you can gain through experiencing the good days and understanding how Charlotte feels on such days. Knowledge you can share with Charlotte to support her. You can provide the continuity that is hard for her to generate herself.

We wondered with you that maybe Charlottes' staff can start this process by calling you once a day, at a set time.

As a first step, can the staff speak with Charlotte before deciding what to tell you, with Charlotte listening to the conversation? A next step can be that the staff talks with Charlotte about what to say and suggests that she speak with you. In time, it can become a habit for Charlotte to call and share a little with you. Or maybe send a text message ☺. I do not propose that you form an "unhealthy symbiosis" with your child, but I proposed this form of communication because she probably always will need you support. You are the only people who can be a constant in her life. Charlotte will lose contact with the professionals eventually; they will change jobs or Charlotte will move.

You can probably read between the lines, this is a subject close to my heart, and I have felt inspired by the topics that you raised, and the ideas we have created together.

I look forward to seeing you,
Nina

Nelly wrote back. Her mail to me and my response can be read "in one go" because my responses are inserted in italicized sentences between the lines of her letter.[1] I began my response with a brief introduction:

Dear Nelly,
You write so wonderfully. This metaphor:

The contact with psychiatry feels like hanging onto a thin thread behind a truck driving at full speed. Holding on is difficult on the long stretches. This description illustrates for me how much better I feel in the driver's seat, or at least being inside the truck while it is speeding. It's an amazing picture of the difference between feeling impotent or in power.

I wonder if this picture might be helpful when we talk about involving the patients and their relatives? Can we invite the relatives inside the truck? Can we take turns sitting at the wheel, reading the map, setting the coordinates on the GPS[2] and deciding the destination?

I have an idea that I think will work. I will try to reply between the lines inside your mail, *in italics*, so you can see where I have added something to your mail. I'll be excited to hear if you think it will work.

Sorry if this seems cumbersome!

You don't have to reply if you do not think my suggestion will be helpful for you!

Dear Nina,
Many, many thanks for your long epistle. It has been helpful to read about

162 *Empowering the entire family*

the many good points on this huge question about what constitutes our role in providing next-of-kin-involvement.

You said clearly:

We are Charlotte's external memory, to fill her story and avoid a huge hole during the period of hospitalization and institutionalization. Our role is to also provide a security-line for Charlotte in her adult life, when issues are boiling or burning for her.

We discussed the good idea of helping Charlotte to develop a habit of calling us at our meeting with the staff.

How impressive! I would love to know how you prepared yourself for such a conversation, what you said word by word, how the staff reacted, and how you ensured that it became a positive result. The experience you describe is very interesting, as parents' good intentions are not always heard. Do you think, you have some knowledge to share here, that I might share with other parents?

But calling is difficult, it seems, as sometimes when Charlotte gets poorly, it is not safe for a staff member to leave her in order to make a telephone call to us. So that is a dilemma. It makes it difficult to decide whether to call us and risk a disturbance.

But why do staff have to leave Charlotte when making the call to you? Is there something here I do not know? Can Charlotte benefit from listening to the staff speak with you, so they can be her role model on how to collaborate?

All in all, both parties clearly try to reach out and meet each other and we need to focus on this.

This is wonderful to hear. It's much easier when you know and feel that you are working towards the same goal, even when there are structural and other barriers.

Here is an example: Charlotte and her support worker came on a joint home visit on Saturday and we enjoyed a shared afternoon coffee. The togetherness connected dots in Charlotte's world in the best way.

After that, our dear child sent a text message saying, "Thanks for all you do for me". I take this as a sign that there are many conversations about family and this is heart-warming.

This is heart-warming! What do you think these new experiences will mean for your collaboration with staff in coming days? I think about what Tyler is reminded of, that you have had good collaboration with them early on, and that this gives him energy and a belief that communication can become good again. Is this what you refer to with your comment about it being heart-warming?

You also write that we should step back, shrug our shoulders and accept that this next-of-kin-collaboration is difficult. Believe me – we practice this! We fall off the path now and again, when there are obstacles in the communication, and logic seems impossible.

I don't know if it's "logic". I think my response, "If the staff don't understand what they're missing, they don't deserve our wisdom", was childish, because I didn't have Charlotte's best interests in mind when I wrote it. But when you write that you practice all the time, does this mean you have another thought that can be good for Charlotte? What thought is that? What experience guides you here?

Empowerment feels SO much better than the grief experienced when feeling powerless.

That I can believe!

Such grief is hard to endure and Charlotte's impending adulthood at 18 years of age is constantly appearing to us as a chute that leads directly to hell. We must prepare for it, and this is a great worry for us.

Yes, that's what we hear a lot. But I believe stories reveal the chute doesn't only lead to hell. Exits on the chute also lead to fresh air, to new and scary, but better worlds. I wonder how often these stories are told? What will it mean if I can find some of them for you? What will you want such stories to include for you?

I am SO scared that the municipality will make Charlotte move out of the residential centre, that it will all go wrong, that she will run away and end up in the intensive care ward with young criminals and in a security cell.

Yes, that fear must be overwhelming, and paralyzing?

If she can just be stopped from behaving in such a way....

Will knowledge like this be good to share with the staff? What do they know, and what do you know, about how to help Charlotte learn to stop that behaviour? Can it be helpful to write down some knowledge that can be good for Charlotte to read?

The contact with psychiatry feels like hanging onto a thin thread behind a truck driving at full speed. Holding on is difficult on the long stretches.

I think this picture, comparing communication with psychiatry to trying to hold onto a speeding truck, will stay in my mind. I like the way it can illustrate how parents can hold on and fight their way back into the driver's seat. ☺

Best wishes, Nelly
Best wishes, Nina

Nelly went on to become a parent mentor at our hospital. In a letter five years later, she wrote:

164 *Empowering the entire family*

I often use the metaphor with the truck; it has a lot of vitality. I also refer to our conversation when I speak with others. I describe what you did to help empower us to overcome the task. The metaphor, where you drew the truck and put me inside that truck was magic, because I noticed the difference, being part of something and not being thrown off. We were involved together in an alliance. I once heard a former patient drily saying, "You can certainly also have that experience as a patient!" Everyone in the room understood that, too.

Now, you may use this metaphor too.

I asked Nelly, "With all the knowledge you have today, what is your main message for helpers in psychiatry? What story can I tell to describe your point?"

Nelly answered:

Dear Nina,

The basic essence of what is effective is found through awakening a sense of equality and sharing a discovery of what creates empowerment. Then the seeds are planted, and they grow with the tasks. When you drew me as a co-driver, a process began. I noticed that this was SO much better (the body gave full response), and I was provided a direction on which to focus my powers and agency.

Hope gives motivation and agency. But each one of us must be able to notice and discover where our hopes lie.

I know that shame can be relieved only by gentle eyes and a loving look. And shame is something you cannot avoid when your child is in total disruption.

Psychiatry… so very non-understandable. The bio-psycho-social, all three are entwined.
Nelly

This chapter emphasizes the importance of families standing together and having allies, and an audience, for their struggles. Cultural curiosity and powerful metaphors help to deconstruct negative dominant narratives and create openings for a family's personal agency and power. Asking for and using advice, for example, on how to bring siblings into the therapy, means taking patient and family involvement in mental health services seriously (Grundy et al., 2016). This is how we can co-create alternative narratives that support development and empowerment.

Health professionals who practice according to the narrative ethics in empowering conversations give families the re-authoring right to their stories (Bruner, 1993; Madigan, 2019, pp. 43–49; White & Epston, 1990).

Notes

1 This is a technique I learned from David Epston.
2 Global Positioning System.

References

Bentley, K. J., Cohen-Filipic, K., & Cummings, C. R. (2016). Approaching parental guilt, shame, and blame in a helping relationship: Multiple methods for teaching and learning. *Journal of Teaching in Social Work, 36*(5), 490–502. doi:10.1080/08841233.2016.1238024

Bruner, J. (1993). *Acts of meaning*. Harvard University Press.

Bågenholm, A., & Gillberg, C. (1991). Psychosocial effects on siblings of children with autism and mental retardation: A population-based study. *Journal of Intellectual Disability Research, 35*(4), 291–307. doi:j.1365-2788.1991.tb00403.x

Grundy, A. C., Bee, P., Meade, O., Callaghan, P., Beatty, S., Olleveant, N., & Lovell, K. (2016). Bringing meaning to user involvement in mental health care planning: A qualitative exploration of service user perspectives. *Journal of Psychiatric and Mental Health Nursing, 23*(1), 12–21. doi:10.1111/jpm.12275

Jorring, N. T. (2009). Forst tog Anoreksien magten, så tog hospitalet den – Gennem narrativ terapi kan behandlere og familie sammen skabe en alliance og tage magten tilbage til familien. [First Anorexia Nervosa took power -Then the hospital did the same. But narrative therapy can help therapists and families co-create an alliance against Anorexia and the families can regain their personal power]. *Fokus på familien, 37*(4), 286-283.

Kopera, M., Suszek, H., Bonar, E., Myszka, M., Gmaj, B., Ilgen, M., & Wojnar, M. (2015). Evaluating Explicit and Implicit Stigma of Mental Illness in Mental Health Professionals and Medical Students. *Community Mental Health Journal, 51*(5), 628–634. doi:10.1007/s10597-014-9796-6

Larson, J. E., & Corrigan, Patrick. (2008). The stigma of families with mental illness. *Academic Psychiatry, 32*(2), 87–91. doi:10.1176/appi.ap.32.2.87

Ma, N. L. T. (2014). *The mental health and wellbeing of siblings of children with mental health problems: Two decades of research*. University of Adelaide, Retrieved 23 January 2021 from http://hdl.handle.net/2440/88695

Ma, N. L. T., Roberts, R., Winefield, H., & Furber, G. (2015). The prevalence of psychopathology in siblings of children with mental health problems: A 20-year systematic review. *Child Psychiatry & Human Development, 46*(1), 130–149. doi:10.1007/s10578-014-0459-1

Madigan, S. (2019). *Narrative Therapy* (2nd ed.). American Psychological Association.

Madsen, W. C. (2009). Collaborative helping: A practice framework for family-centered services. *Family Process, 48*(1), 103–116. doi:10.1111/j.1545-5300.2009.01270.x

Schulze, B. (2007). Stigma and mental health professionals: A review of the evidence on an intricate relationship. *International Review of Psychiatry, 19*(2), 137–155. doi:10.1080/0954 0260701278929

Strong, T. (2015). Diagnoses, Relational processes and resourceful dialogs: Tensions for families and family therapy. *Family Process, 54*(3), 518–532. doi:10.1111/famp.12140

White, M., & Epston, D. (1990). *Narrative means to therapeutic ends*. Norton.

13 Family community meetings that matter

Extending collaborative ethics to all aspects of our interactions with families, including in our community, is possible and desirable but requires more development. This chapter explores the benefits of holding meetings with families in municipalities and schools. Whether we conduct the meetings, or attend in a guest-position, potential exists for influencing the ambience, process and outcome.

We call these gatherings "family community meetings". Sometimes next-of-kin or friends attend too, so some participants might not be there in a professional role. Other people might attend in roles that focus on legalities or economics rather than on helping the family. "Helpers" (Madsen et al., 2021) or "stakeholders" can therefore be appropriate collective terms for all participants.

In the same way we have extended the family-focused, collaborative, and respectful stance from family conversations to clinical conferences and paperwork, we can extend this stance to family community meetings. This work is inspired by the use of Collaborative Helping Maps (Madsen, 2007, 2009, 2011, 2014), Coordinated Management of Meaning (CMM) (Pearce, 1989, 2007) and Open Dialogue (Galbusera & Kyselo, 2018; Seikkula, 2011).

About 10 years ago, my team worked with a family comprising divorced parents and three children. Two of the children had been referred to us, individually. Advice from health professionals was pulling the parents in opposite directions. For example, they were advised that the older child who had psychotic symptoms, should live with the father, but without her siblings, to meet a need for a structured and quiet environment. Another agency recommended that the two other children be moved back and forth between the parents' two homes.

To encourage collaboration, I recommended a meeting with all professionals involved with helping this family. I envisaged that we could find a shared understanding, create a mutual plan, and cooperate for the good of the family. At the time, the family was receiving help in different contexts, but nothing was coordinated.

Collaboration did not happen. Instead, the different professionals (including social workers, school counsellors, teachers and school leaders) began

DOI: 10.4324/9781003171621-14

discussing economic and legal issues regarding who should be responsible for helping who and with what. The joint meeting seemed to give these "helpers" ideas about getting out of their responsibilities and saving money for their department. The parents were left at the end of the table, positioned as listeners, without a voice. Eventually, the mother left the meeting. She was crying and desperate. As host of this meeting, I felt deeply embarrassed and vowed to find ways to provide better support for parents.

Boardroom psychology and seating etiquette

In most meetings with other professionals during my training, the doctor began with a summary and status of the case. Such a format gives the professionals a high level of power, because those who speak first set the agenda (Pearce, 1989). Exerting such power though can be contra-therapeutic, putting the families in a lesser position, and making them less powerful (Ness et al., 2014).

Many of us have experienced feelings of being pushed into positions where there is pressure to choose whose side to be on. As a young resident in adult psychiatry, I was taught to be the patients' advocate against the family. I have often experienced being pulled into being the parents' allies against the municipality. Psychiatric illness can lead us to think in terms of allies and enemies (Corrigan et al., 2014; Pearce, 1989), and there's a high risk of this positioning also happening in meetings with different stakeholders. The hospital, municipality, school, and parents can become contestants in a vicious game instead of working together as collaborators seeking the best outcome for the patient.

Family community meetings can create more hurt than help (Root & Madsen, 2013). To avoid inflicting hurt, we must aim for a collaborative setting, where nobody has the sole right to define the truth. There should be no contest over who owns the truth. Our aim must be to create meetings, where everybody can be present and treated as knowledgeable and worthy of respect.

Another detail requiring attention and respect is that parents have not attended this kind of meeting before or have only experienced being relegated to the lower end of the table as a listener. They have no or minimal knowledge about interventions or help that might be possible, so they cannot request specifics. They are in a disadvantaged position.

This situation presents therapists with the important task of preparing parents to assume their rightful role in these meetings. When we host meetings, we are inspired by the theories behind Coordinated Management of Meaning (Imran et al., 2019; Pearce, 1989):

- Whoever speaks first decides the topic and direction.
- Whoever speaks the language best has the most power.
- The person who feels most secure has the greatest power.

168 *Family community meetings that matter*

In contrast, traditional meetings are conducted where:

- The professionals present the case and decide the conclusions.
- The professionals know the procedure and know the terminology.

We apply this knowledge when designing our community meetings.

Before the meeting, we use our helping map to structure a conversation with the parents. We prepare the parents for stepping into the meeting with enough knowledge about the roles and agendas of such meetings, to be familiar with the procedures. We start by imagining the conclusion of the upcoming meeting, and we ask the parents about their visions and hopes for this event (Madsen, 2009):

- If you were to decide and I had the magic wand, what would you like to get out of this meeting about your child?
- What would you like to be the outcome of the meeting?
- What would you like us to talk about? What results do you want from such a conversation?
- Where will this lead you as a family?

Then we discuss what might support and obstruct the desired outcome. We often use the helping map (see Chapter 6 for a description of this map) as a template for the notes on the easel during this preparation.

We want the parents to be heard first and support them in preparing to set the agenda, the purpose, and the vision for the meeting. We aim to use the parents' language and way of speaking during the meeting.

Since the parents have often been ascribed a lesser position in earlier dealings with the hospital, school, municipality, and so on, supporting their credibility among attendees at the meeting can be helpful. We can begin the meeting by asking each person to introduce themselves, share how long they have known the child, and how they have acquired their knowledge of this child. We might also ask each person what they appreciate most about the child. At such times the room's ambience can change dramatically. The parents' status as knowledgeable participants, for example, can be elevated when those high in the classic hierarchy admit to never having met the child.

We take notes publicly during this meeting using the helping map as a template and create a meeting format that is familiar to the parents. As a result, the meeting often becomes more relaxed and less formal. There's less focus on regulations and economy and more focus on how to help the child and the family, in line with the main theme stated at the meeting's outset.

Parents at the head of the table

Traditionally, meetings at the hospital with the municipalities involve delivering a diagnostic assessment. After that, the municipality assumes responsibility for

Family community meetings that matter 169

the case and delivers support to the family. These meetings are often loaded with professional language and medical and legal terms that are unfamiliar to the family. The parents are often relegated to a position of being necessary, but somewhat bothersome guests. There is a much better way. Creating a shared understanding and vision for collaboration, together with conveying a diagnosis with the child and family, requires more preparation time with the parents but is very worthwhile.

I want to tell you about Jack. Now 19-years-old, Jack is a happy, energetic and ambitious young man. He has a girlfriend, is self-confident and is studying at a prestigious university in England. Jack's father has provided updates on his progress since we parted more than six years ago. When asked what we did that was most helpful for the family, the dad said, "The meeting with the school and social worker".

Jack was 12-years-old when he suddenly and unexpectedly was expelled from school. He had developed "hysterical seizures" and had begun fleeing from school when things became unbearable for him. No one understood what was happening to Jack and his teachers became afraid.

Jack came to us for assessment and received an autism diagnosis. My colleagues conveyed the diagnosis to his parents in a way that was non-blaming and non-stigmatizing. This approach enabled the parents to be curious of this "autism-thing" and they became eager to explore it. The parents learned about the problems this developmental disorder can create, and about the fascinating, wonderful competences that autism can give people.

My colleagues met with the Jack's teachers, school counsellor, social worker, and parents. They acknowledged the school's predicament before explaining the boy's diagnosis and what autism-friendly pedagogy looks like. Both the obstacles and the benefits of the autism-specific traits were explained. The use of knowledge from my colleagues' examination of Jack's problems, and their conversations with the parents ensured that the parents had opportunity to contribute to the meeting as true specialists on their child.

My colleagues drew on their narrative therapy knowledge to make everybody present at the meeting feel respected and in positions of honour. Their own stance of offering knowledge enabled everyone present to be curious, respectful, and open to new ideas. The meeting inspired the teachers to re-admit Jack to the school.

Our conversations with the family focused on the challenges of living with autism in two different homes. We continued in this way for about six months, until the parents felt secure enough to say goodbye.

The father sometimes asks questions. He helps Jack, and steps back at times, like any good dad. As well, he behaves like an autism wizard, embracing both the problems and wonders of Jack's autism.

The co-examination of the child's problems and the collaborative nature of that early meeting with the other "helpers" provided a foundation for the father's curiosity and pride in his son's autism.

170 *Family community meetings that matter*

Let's co-create new knowledge by digging into the messy business

The collaborative stance we take towards the parents enables them to voice problems for which they may fear ridicule. These problems are often related to issues that can lead to the professionals developing disrespect for the parents. The parents can be incorrectly described as being resistant instead of being seen as parents with obstacles they are struggling with and would rather be without.

A mother had been trying to hide her anxiety and economic problems from the municipality out of fear of losing her child. When we were able to communicate to this mother, our respect for her and her dreams of being the perfect mum, we gained her trust. We wanted to ask the municipality to provide help to the mother. However, this municipality had the practice of separating the help to adults from the help to the children, and the case became complicated. We invited the stakeholders, including the child's social worker and the professionals attending to the grown up's issues, to a family community meeting, using the helping map. We then co-created a vision of helping the child by helping the mother to become the best possible mum for this child.

The successful outcome of the meeting was ensured, because we made time to call the municipality and speak with relevant social workers in different departments and authorities. Holding onto the mother's vision of being the best possible mum and explaining her actions through this narrative was instrumental in creating a shared understanding of what needed to be done.

Meet me by understanding and respecting my handicap

The structure of a meeting is important when making space for creative and collaborative thinking. After the initial welcoming of everyone at the meeting, and after a short opportunity for everyone to present themselves (maybe inviting them to tell a story about their relationship with the family/ the child), we explain that a paper chart or white board will be used to record the meeting.

The agenda is produced by asking the parents about their hopes for the outcome of this meeting. The parents usually repeat what they arranged at our preparatory conversation. This is written at the top of the board, under the headings "Vision" and "Hopes". Everyone is drawn to the parents' agenda and speak to this vision for the remainder of the meeting.

Before using this method, I had a long and difficult therapy course with the parents of a girl who refused to attend school. The girl had autism and reacted with anxiety to any unplanned activity. I believe the outcome would have been different if I had used the helping map method at the family community meetings. This story illustrates that respect and collaboration can vary in appearance in different situations, and in helping families.

We had several unsuccessful meetings with the school and social worker that always ended with harsh demands on the parents and an inference that the parents were troublesome. The parents and I analyzed the meetings using the helping map. As we looked at the obstacles, we explored what had gone wrong at the previous meetings. We concluded that one problem was responsible for preventing a shared understanding at the meetings. This problem was that the parents experienced that they had the same problems as their daughter. They needed time to digest the information, to reflect, prepare, plan, and execute. They felt overwhelmed with the need to wait for the school to decide on a plan, and when the school and municipality decided on the plan, to quickly act on it.

The parents needed time to think through new information, ask clarifying questions, then accept the changes in their own minds, before planning how to tell and prepare their daughter. As we mapped these obstacles out, the dad said, "Can you explain to the school and municipality, that we have the same genes and autism as our daughter, and we need to be treated with the same respect as if we had that diagnosis?"

I asked the parents if they were afraid of being ridiculed if the school and the municipality knew how they felt. Their answer was astonishing. No, they were not scared. In their experience, nobody from the school or the municipality had ridiculed their daughter or refused to help her. The parents also said that when I discussed autism, everyone became respectful of that handicap, not condescending. They felt safe in their knowledge that the municipality had great respect for people with autism.

The parents asked me to attend the meeting without them. They believed the professionals would listen to me more easily if they did not have to consider how to phrase their responses in front of the parents. I was impressed by the parents' insightfulness. They were right in their assessment. I was asked many relevant questions that were not formulated in the most respectful manner, but nevertheless were respectfully thought out. I met this family only once more after that meeting, but later the parents sent letters with positive updates. Their daughter gained admission into the parents' choice of school, formerly deemed unsuitable by the school psychologist and municipality. The daughter thrived in this school, and the family began living a life much closer to the life they had dreamed about.

Dialogic communications and the production of knowledge

Both positive and negative effects can flow from our verbal and written statements. The impact is illustrated in this story about the Braveheart family comprising Flora, who has autism, her younger sister Gloria, and parents Em and Dave (see Chapters 1 and 3).

When we received the referral for Flora, her diagnosis was reactive attachment disorder (RAD). The school and municipality had received an

172 *Family community meetings that matter*

official statement with this diagnosis and were expected to help the family according to this understanding of Flora and her family. RAD and autism spectrum disorder (ASD) are often difficult to separate in a clinical assessment (Davidson et al., 2015). Em had described her bipolar disorder during Flora's assessment, and Em's own diagnosis was a contributing factor for choosing RAD instead of ASD.

Em's story demonstrates that the effects of a diagnosis can be detrimental to respectful collaborations. Consider what each of the family's diagnoses address. Since the International Statistical Classification of Diseases and Related Health Problems (ICD-10) and Diagnostic and Statistical Manual 5th Edition (DSM-5) classifies reactive attachment disorder as a trauma and stressor-related condition of early childhood caused by social neglect and maltreatment, discourses about RAD can lead to compassion for a neglected child and contempt or anger towards the parent (Pedersen et al., 2017). Teachers try to give the child extra love and care. An autism diagnosis, on the other hand, often leads to respect for the need for predictability, letting the child decide how physically close and what kind of physical contact they can handle, as well as exhibiting respect and curiosity towards the parents (Pedersen et al., 2017). The reactions are very different.

As a schoolteacher, Em had hoped for a diagnosis within the autism spectrum. Em understood what would be helpful for her daughter at school. But after the school received the RAD diagnosis, Em's ideas and pleas for help were ignored. She did not believe that Flora had been neglected in early childhood, and she became burdened by the diagnosis of RAD. Em had read widely in an effort to understand her child, so by the time Flora was diagnosed, Em knew a lot about autism and other diagnoses. In Em's view, the collaboration with the school and municipality had deteriorated after Flora's diagnostic assessment at the hospital.

When we met Flora, we saw a clingy daughter, who could easily be considered as insecure, having an anxious-ambivalent attachment style. However, viewed through autism-spectrum lenses, Flora was insecure about the unknown, relying heavily on her mother to translate, explain and direct her.

We re-read the assessment and diagnostic evaluation, made extra observations of Flora, and re-evaluated the anamnestic history. We noted that Em's and Flora's relationship had suffered as a result of the advice Em had received about her mothering practices. Clearly, the diagnosis had to be altered. We also had to meet with the decision-makers who had used the diagnosis to understand Flora's behaviour, and to decide the most appropriate help for her.

We met at the school, at the headmaster's office, with Flora's teachers, school psychologist and social worker. We presented a new medical statement and explained why, although the first diagnosis seemed right, that it was wrong. We explained the new diagnosis, and how we hoped this would change the way the school and the parents could collaborate and create the best possible contexts for Flora at school and at home. The teachers and headmaster asked many good questions. Clearly, this change in understanding

Family community meetings that matter   173

and stance towards the parents was difficult. Importantly, as the health professionals, we took full responsibility and blame for initially providing the wrong information. Being able to apologize for unintentionally misleading the school staff, in addition to explaining why the initial diagnosis made sense in the beginning, was instrumental for the school staff to begin changing their understanding.

Everyone seemed to understand the situation, and I returned to my office. Before the day was over, an e-mail arrived from Em:

> Dear Nina and Kirsten,
>
> I just wanted to send a thank you note.
> You have no idea how relieved we were to have you with us today. We felt that Flora got described so well and not least because you made sure her interests were heard.
>
> Tears have been running down my face all day in relief because I can finally dare to believe that my beautiful girl will get the help she needs. When I got home from the meeting, I got a call from the social worker who suddenly has a lot of offers for Flora. We will talk more about it on Monday.
>
> The social worker will bring our case to the team meeting on Thursday, and she might have a need for more information from you. Perhaps you've already heard from her.
>
> Em

I met with the school at three-to-six-month intervals over the next two years. A preparatory conversation took place with Em and Dave before each meeting, exploring what they hoped to achieve, noting which supportive interventions were in place, and what obstacles were hampering Flora's well-being. The headmaster sat at the head of the table, and my role was that of consultant.

As I was not leading the meetings, I did not have the power to run them. However, I could bring my expert knowledge about group processes to the table and could spot when people of different positions and authority might start going down roads that could lead to conflict. This often occurred when the goal was unclear, when narratives of accusations or blame were aired, or when a person felt insecure of their own competencies and position.

I would sit back and take notes at the meetings, carefully listening for openings to make the best possible contributions. I was aware of the discourses attached to my position as a chief consultant from the psychiatric hospital and the animosity or awe this could awake. I knew, in these cases, the importance of not appearing as the one holding the truth and nothing but the truth. Therefore, I would often start with opening statements aimed at channelling the knowledge into ideas, suggestions, praise, or questions,

174 *Family community meetings that matter*

depending on what I heard. In commenting, I tried to downplay my role as chief consultant to avoid alienating anyone by using hierarchical powers, but at the same time be clear that I had child and family psychiatry expert knowledge. For example:

- Your explanation makes a lot of sense but being a child psychiatrist and thinking about and looking at Flora through those autism glasses, I get different ideas as how to understand her. Are you interested in hearing about them?
- I am impressed by your interventions and how Flora has responded to them. Would you like me to explain how and why I appreciate what you do as an autism-pedagogy in those situations? I'm wondering if you realize how brilliant it is!
- In this case, I am impressed by the stories I have heard from Em and Dave about how they tackle situations like the one you have just described; I think Em has some insider knowledge on how Flora's brain works that we can all benefit from; is it okay if I invite the parents to tell you what they have told us?
- I'm not that good at laws and regulations, but I think I've heard in other municipalities, that you can.... Does anybody here have experience on how to handle this situation in your municipality?
- This reminds me of another case, where we had similar troubles. Is it okay to share this with you?

Since I was not the "owner" of the meeting, I was mindful of speaking only from my own perspective. I explained my position and took care to avoid impinging on others' responsibilities or tasks.

About a year later, I sent this e-mail to the colleague who had diagnosed Flora initially and had referred the family to us:

> We just had a taking stock conversation with Flora's parents, and I want to share with you how well they are.
>
> As you know, we've changed Flora's diagnosis to Asperger's, and that has completely changed the school's approach to her. The parents' understanding and approach to her also has changed!
>
> It has really paid off. Clearly, Flora has a social developmental disability that they now see and can train(!), also in school.
>
> The parents use preparation and structure, and the mother no longer feels so burdened by blame or shame.
>
> Flora has become much happier at home, and no longer has "meltdowns".
>
> You can see our revised treatment plan, if you are interested.

Family community meetings that matter 175

A reply was swift:

> How good to hear from you. It makes great sense to follow the children over time, especially in cases like this, where differential diagnostic considerations of autism or attachment disorder are at play.

Flora's story illustrates the effects of family community meetings and official documents on helpers and stakeholders in understanding a child's needs. Once we create a specific narrative about a family and the parents, much work is required to change that narrative. Therefore, we must be attentive to the power of our verbal and written medical statements and be aware that besides being helpful, they also may be harmful.

This chapter has described the importance of broader collaborations for families. Being curious about what meaning and significance others ascribe to a diagnosis or a statement is as important as the right medical and therapeutic knowledge.

Dialogue is preferable to monologue, discussion, or debate. Dialogue is not like delivering a message that we expect another person to receive like a parcel sent by mail. Ideal dialogue is mutual, curious, respectful of everybody's perspective, and seeks to co-create new ideas and knowledge. In the absence of the ideal dominance-free communication, we must maintain constant dialogue, talk about how the communication is experienced, what hierarchical powers are at play, and what effects are achieved (Bevington et al., 2017; Fuggle et al., 2016; Phillips, 2011).

Our team's communication practices are based on the conviction that people with disabilities know what is best for them, as described in theories from Participatory Action Research (Macaulay et al., 1999) and Nothing About Us Without Us (Charlton, 1998). When this conviction is combined with the question, "Who and what might my statements speak to?" the following basic rules about communication with patients and families become imperative:

- We do not engage in meetings without the parents, except with the parents' specific requests.
- We do not issue statements without the patient or parents having read and accepted them first.
- We share the power, responsibility and the expert status with the parents.

References

Bevington, D., Fuggle, P., Cracknell, L., & Fonagy, P. (2017). *Adaptive mentalization-based integrative treatment: A guide for teams to develop systems of care.* Oxford University Press.

Charlton, J. I. (1998). *Nothing about us without us. Disability oppression and empowerment* (1 ed.). University of California Press.

176 *Family community meetings that matter*

Corrigan, P. W., Druss, B. G., & Perlick, D. A. (2014). The impact of mental illness stigma on seeking and participating in mental health care. *Psychol Sci Public Interest*, *15*(2), 37–70. doi:10.1177/1529100614531398

Davidson, C., O'Hare, A., Mactaggart, F., Green, J., Young, D., Gillberg, C., & Minnis, H. (2015). Social relationship difficulties in autism and reactive attachment disorder: Improving diagnostic validity through structured assessment. *Research In Developmental Disabilities*, *40*, 63–72. doi:10.1016/j.ridd.2015.01.007

Fuggle, P., Bevington, D., Duffy, F., & Cracknell, L. (2016). The AMBIT approach: Working with hard to reach youth. *Mental Health Review Journal*, *21*(1), 61–72. doi:10.1108/MHRJ-04-2015-0012

Galbusera, L., & Kyselo, M. (2018). The difference that makes the difference: A conceptual analysis of the open dialogue approach. *Psychosis*, *10*(1), 47–54. doi:10.1080/17522439.2 017.1397734

Imran, M. C. Y., Wei, X. M., & Akhtar, S. (2019). A critical study of coordinated management of meaning theory: A theory in practitioners' hands. *International Journal of English Linguistics*, *9*(5), 301–306. Retrieved 9 February 2021 from https://pdfs. semanticscholar.org/62a7/91ab913376e3130c8cc3b63cf60c02f053dc.pdf

Macaulay, A. C., Commanda, L. E., Freeman, W. L., Gibson, N., McCabe, M. L., Robbins, C. M., & Twohig, P. L. (1999). Participatory research maximises community and lay involvement. North American Primary Care Research Group. *BMJ*, *319*(7212), 774–778. doi:10.1136/bmj.319.7212.774

Madsen, W. C. (2007). Working with traditional structures to support a collaborative clinical practice. *The International Journal of Narrative Therapy and Community Work*(2), 51–61. doi:10.3316/informit.060824685990920

Madsen, W. C. (2009). Collaborative helping: a practice framework for family-centered services. *Family Process*, *48*(1), 103–116. doi:10.1111/j.1545-5300.2009.01270.x

Madsen, W. C. (2011). Collaborative helping maps: a tool to guide thinking and action in family-centered services. *Family Process*, *50*(4), 529–543. doi:10.1111/j.1545-5300. 2011.01369.x

Madsen, W. C. (2014). Taking it to the streets: Family therapy and family-centered services. *Family Process*, *53*(3), 380–400.

Madsen, W. C., Roth, E., & Jørring, N. T. (2021). Mattering as the heart of health and human services. *Journal of Contemporary Narrative Therapy*, *1*, 19–31. Retrieved 9 February 2021 from https://www.paperturn-view.com/?pid=MTY161367&p=21

Ness, O., Borg, M., & Davidson, L. (2014). Facilitators and barriers in dual recovery: A literature review of first-person perspectives. *Advances in Dual Diagnosis*, *7*(3), 107–117. doi:10.1108/ADD-02-2014-0007

Pearce, B. W. (1989). *Communication and the Human Condition*. Southern Illinois University Press.

Pearce, B. W. (2007). *Kommunikation og skabelsen af sociale verdener* (T. Bøgeskov, Trans.). Dansk psykologisk Forlag.

Pedersen, L., Mølgård, B., & Rothenborg, J. R. (2017). *Autisme & Tilknytning*. Dansk Psykologisk Forlag.

Phillips, L. (2011). *The Promise of Dialogue*: John Benjamins Publishing Company.

Root, E. A., & Madsen, W. (2013). Imagine: Bringing vision into child protective services. *Journal of Systemic Therapies*, *32*, 74–88. doi:10.1521/JSYT.2013.32.3.74

Seikkula, J. (2011). Becoming dialogical: Psychotherapy or a way of life? *Australian and New Zealand Journal of Family Therapy*, *32*(3), 179–193. doi:10.1375/anft.32.3.179

14 Weaving the collaborative spirit through all our practices

The cultures and structures of mental health services shape a clinician's interaction with patients (Sfantou et al., 2017). Sometimes collaborative approaches can seem counterintuitive to dominant organizational assumptions (Madsen, 2007a, p. 323). Stigma, taboo, demands, and pressures influence the decisions of clinicians and can create disrespectful attitudes that counteract their ethics and collaborative practices (Assing Hvidt et al., 2020; Lauber et al., 2004; Madsen, 2007b; Paro et al., 2014; Shapiro, 2008). This can lead clinicians, who are embracing collaborative ideas, to believe they are breaking unspoken rules and to question themselves (Madsen, 2007a, p. 323), to the point that they feel a failure (White, 2002). Stories in this chapter describe my experience in managing these issues.

The dangerous or the scared dad?

As a young, inexperienced leader of the eating disorder outpatient unit, I was standing in a small staff kitchen, listening as colleagues talked about the families that we had seen that day. We were sharing our experiences over cups of tea and coffee.

Ad hoc and relaxed conversations can provide opportunities for health professionals to support each other by engaging in helpful, collegial supervision. But if we are careless, these everyday discussions can also be detrimental, both for the team members and for the families we aim to help. When we share in supportive, creative, and positive ways, we improve the quality of our work. When we share in derogative, competitive, and negative ways, we risk engaging in degrading ways of treating people (White & Epston, 1990, p. 2).

We had worked and struggled a long time with a family whose daughter, Lisa, had developed anorexia. Lisa was nine years old when we met her for the first time. Her parents had divorced several months before the arrival of anorexia. The parents lived near each other and shared custody of Lisa and her younger brother. The children moved back and forth between the two homes. This case was special, because Lisa was so young, and she seemed as scared as we were that she would die from

DOI: 10.4324/9781003171621-15

178 *Weave collaboration into all our practices*

starvation. She did not ascribe to any classic anorexic ideals about thinness, perfectionism and empty stomachs. She was unaware of calories and could not explain what was happening to her, having no words for her experience.

As time went by and Lisa's parents, teachers, and health professionals could not find a way to combat this illness, the adults around her became increasingly frustrated. That's when our kitchen conversation took place. Two therapists observed that Lisa's father, John, had been more upset than usual from the minute he arrived at the hospital. The therapists talked about feeling scared and threatened by this big, strong man. He didn't need to use his physique to intimidate; he was so articulate with his words that he could make the therapists feel small, just by talking.

My colleagues did their best to soothe and support each other, "He has to learn to show respect for you", and "I think it's time for you to call him out on his behaviour and ask him to leave, if he cannot behave".

So, here I am, standing in the kitchen, feeling the ambience growing increasingly hostile and aggressive. I begin to wonder:

- How might our frustrations be experienced by the father?
- This dad must feel so scared when professionals, who clearly have not healed his daughter, meet him with an aggressive and hostile demeanour.
- What kind of narrative are we creating about this father?
- A team leader is responsible for the therapists' behaviour towards patients and families.
- I am responsible for the quality of our treatment, and clearly, we are not doing a good job.
- Are we about to make the situation worse?
- Alienating the dad cannot be helpful for Lisa. What can I do?

By now, my mind is racing:

- We are speaking disrespectfully about this father, yet respect is one of our values.
- We are qualified in descaling conflicts; we know these techniques, but clearly, we are not using them in this case.
- We have shared our feelings of helplessness and disempowerment at conferences. We know we are supposed to portray hope when parents are unable to feel hopeful. But we cannot see any hope in this case either.
- Our frustrations come from feeling that we are failing the child. Our feelings are probably similar to what the dad is feeling, but is anorexia making us enemies?
- Why is this happening? Whose fault is it? The dad's fault, our fault, or should we blame anorexia?

Weave collaboration into all our practices 179

- What techniques is anorexia using that I have to expose in order to reconnect us with the dad?
- Anorexia is using blame! The illness makes us think that in blaming the dad, we can find the reason for anorexia's presence, and then we can acquit ourselves of any failing.

I remain standing in the staff kitchen, feeling frustrated and drawn into these shared conclusions about who to blame, but also annoyed with myself and my colleagues for not seeing that we are about to alienate a daughter and her dad. What right do we have to do this? We know they love each other! But now Lisa's affection for her dad is interpreted as an unhealthy attachment.

Animosity grows as the minutes pass, and our next family appointment is almost due. This is not the right frame of mind when greeting parents and children. I have to do something! But what?

I don't like scolding and have never seen any benefit from it, so I disregard that possibility. I imagine my colleagues will think I am daft if I disagree with their conclusion that is now cemented in collaborative contempt for the father.

I interrupt the conversation by stepping into a curious position:

I am wondering, do you think John is aware of the effects of his behaviour? What might John think if he knew how we talk about what he does to us? I am wondering what he might have been hoping to achieve with his behaviour today. What good outcome might he have hoped for at today's session for him and Lisa?

These questions change the tone of conversation in the kitchen. Our discussion becomes a time for reflection, and compassion for John:

He must feel really scared.

But why is he so aggressive?

That's how men behave when they are scared!

Ha ha...

But really, if we feel scared, think about how scared he must feel, too.

Yeah, he is supposed to be the breadwinner, the one protecting his family. Remember the time when John talked about the failure of his marriage? He wasn't the one to walk away! He talked about that lost dream, feeling incompetent, a lesser man.

Oh, he must feel scared, and I treated him with contempt and hostility. Not good!

180 *Weave collaboration into all our practices*

The exchange in the kitchen that day, together with my colleagues' actions that emerged in subsequent weeks, became fundamental in my development as a leader. The conversation inspired me to look for, and attend to, parental feelings that include anxiety, sorrow, dread, frustration, and incompetence. Being mindful of such feelings helps us to meet the parents with more compassion, and we become better at shouldering these difficult feelings with them.

I met Lisa's dad in the parking lot several weeks later. As he approached, he took my hand and said, "I want to tell you, that I appreciate what your colleagues are doing for us. I know you are as frustrated and scared as we are. But I also know that you are doing your best, and I have a lot of confidence in what we are doing together. Your colleagues are good people, and they are expertly skilled".

How did my colleagues turn this situation around? They thought that John had changed his behaviour. However, I am certain they effected that change by changing their narrative about him. Whereas a behaviour occurs at a specific time, the meaning ascribed to the behaviour remains over time (White & Epston, 1990).

This is just one of the stories I share when younger colleagues seek guidance on how to meet difficult or "bad" parents with respect. My answer is that there are no bad parents, only bad circumstances and bad effects of ill-conceived behaviours. In my view, all parents want to be good parents.

When we behave respectfully, our respect for the person we meet increases, and we are met with respect. If we act patronizingly, our contempt for them increases, and we are met with hostility. We must always attempt to become a family's appreciative allies (Madsen, 2007a).

A narrative therapist trusts in their patient and I believe what I hear from my patients and their families. I don't "call them out on what they are saying". I know they are telling me the truth as they see it.

Mutual trust and respect in psychiatry, is this possible?

Psychiatric illnesses are different from physical illnesses. Psychiatric illnesses try to make us distrust each other (Jackson & Mannix, 2004; Larson & Corrigan, 2008; Maisel et al., 2004).

Anorexia is a good example of this. The illness continues to promise that things will be better, but never keeps the promises. Anorexia is a lying cheat. To combat it, we, as health professionals, have to be the opposite; we have to be totally trustworthy. If we are not, then anorexia has easier access to the child.

The situation becomes more complicated when the social stigma of having a psychiatric illness makes patients feel unworthy of other peoples' trust (Gumber & Stein, 2013). This might be one of the most devastating problems for mental health services (Eriksen et al., 2014). This was illustrated at a meeting with leaders of mental health services early this century,

Weave collaboration into all our practices 181

when we were working on co-creating a vision for the culture of our mental health organization.

One of the sentences proposed to describe our culture was, "We meet our patients with respect". The leader's response was, "How can you have respect for someone who is mentally ill? I mean, they are insane, right?"

I stood and asserted that I could not work in an organization that spoke about our patients with such disdain. This went against everything I believed in. But I did not leave this organization. With like-minded others, I stayed and fought for a more respectful, worthy, and trustful approach to people who suffer from psychiatric illnesses. Today most mental health centres have written values from the empowerment and recovery movement into their mission statements, but explicit models of mental health services leadership based on these values are still lacking (Happell & Scholz, 2018; O'Hagan, 2009; Stewart et al., 2019).

I share this story to address the narratives and discourses in our society that indicate that having a psychiatric illness makes a person untrustworthy (Carrey, 2007). When the therapist interprets what the patient says and calls them out on what they say, they are telling the patient that they cannot trust their own thoughts or feelings. The impact of this attitude is devastating on our patients and their families. They lose trust in their own self. The effect is devastating on relationships because the parents, siblings, partners, and friends are taught that they cannot trust each other either (William Madsen, personal communication, 2013).

The belief that those with a psychiatric illness are "insane" or that being affected by psychiatric illness makes someone a lesser person, makes it difficult to create meetings where mutual respect is indeed mutual. These matters stand in the way of the patients and parents being respected and feeling sufficiently trusted to be able to voice their own thoughts and to be taken seriously. Collaboration requires the experiencing of mutual respect and trust.

This is a necessary but long, tedious, difficult, and exhausting process. Let me tell you a story about one of my pitfalls.

How do we speak about the patients and their families?

Valiant and his parents wanted assistance to understand and help their child (see Chapters 1, 2, and 8). I received the referral for Valiant by phone late one afternoon from a colleague at an inpatient unit for adolescents. She and her team had diagnosed and treated this 15-year-old boy. My colleague was worried for Valiant, who had been in a schizophrenic stupor, drooling, standing around doing nothing, approaching people seemingly unaware about the effects of his own behaviours and of the feelings of others. My colleague feared for his prognosis.

Valiant had been discharged and had improved for a period but had deteriorated again and was re-admitted. My colleague wanted to try medication, but the boy refused. My colleague's understanding was that the parents refused to acknowledge that their son was developing schizophrenia. Since we know

182 *Weave collaboration into all our practices*

that the duration of untreated psychosis (DUP) is often prognostic (Jeppesen et al., 2008; Souaiby et al., 2016), the shorter the time before medication, the better the prognosis, she was worried by the parents' apparent lack in accepting the diagnosis. She also felt that she had lost the alliance with the parents. She hoped that together we could encourage the parents to accept the diagnosis, to give the boy a chance of getting the right treatment and accept the poor prognosis. I readily agreed to help, saying, "Maybe one of us can be the bad cop and the other can be the good cop?"

"The good cop and the bad cop!" Think about the messages hidden in this metaphor and "the presumptuous arrogance of professional representations and descriptions of the other" (Epston, 2018) inherent in this sentence.

I knew this approach would create a bond between two doctors, providing an "us against them" feeling. I have learned and practiced "speaking the professional lingo" for many years. It comes naturally to me. I feel ashamed admitting that this was how I spoke, but I want to share it, so you might be aware when something similar happens to you.

Even though I was supposed to be the good cop, the metaphor implied that I would be acting only in a good, but not the genuine way. In terms of externalized language, I became an ally to psychiatric illnesses. Psychiatric illnesses lie to not only those who are affected by psychiatric illness, but also family members. Psychiatric illnesses command that people obey and believe them. Psychiatric illnesses tell people that they are no good, and command people to perform embarrassing or tedious compulsions, and sometimes even kill themselves (Freeman et al., 1997; Maisel et al., 2004). To handle psychiatric illnesses, we have to behave in ways opposite to this. We have to be trustworthy. We can never lie or pretend.

I needed to put the arrogant discourses from the "good-cop-bad-cop"-conversation aside before meeting Valiant's parents, so they would not taint my relationship with his parents. We have several ways to do this. It helps me that we always start our first conversations with respectful inquiries and wonderfulness interviewing. It helps when I can joke and admit the advantages I have with my doctoral title and power. Another source of help comes from my colleagues, who ask curious questions about my intentions and the effects of my actions. It works the same way as with any other problem; when we speak about the problem loudly and clearly, they lose a lot of their negative power.

We ask ourselves how the family might feel if listening to what we are saying right now. We commit ourselves to this practice:

Always speak as if the family is listening to what you are saying.

Do I have autism, or am I autistic? Yes, but does it bother you?

Here's another story about personal discourses leading me to speak about diagnoses in ways that are unhelpful for a family.

Deciding how to speak of diagnoses, that some days are terrible illnesses and other days helpful diagnoses, is a challenge. How do we speak of autism, Attention-Deficit Hyperactivity Disorder (ADHD) and schizophrenia as entities that can give terrible symptoms that might destroy lives, but when treated correctly can make them only minor handicaps?

Speaking about diagnoses so they are not considered negative labels or in any way stigmatizing, can be difficult. Mental health problems remain taboo in many places (Jackson & Mannix, 2004; Larson & Corrigan, 2008), and deciding how to explain that a patient might have a diagnosis but might not suffer from the illness all the time can be challenging.

I am still searching for the right approach. One way is to tell my patients that I have epilepsy. This illness would make it impossible for me to study medicine, had I not taken medicine for it. But since I do take medicine, I am healthy. I can deconstruct stigma by asking my patients questions such as: Am I sick or am I healthy? Or am I insane? Do I have an illness or just a diagnosis?

My work with Laura on how to use medication is described in Chapter 10. I got to know her and her family over many years. When Laura was in fourth grade, she attended a school for children with autism, where she learned a lot about her autism. Her teachers once explained that Laura would tell other children to ask the teachers for help. They recollected how she would speak, "We all have different kinds of autism, and we do not grasp that the grown-ups can help us. But they can, so when you are unhappy, you must tell them, and they can help you".

I had a series of individual conversations with Laura, when she was in fourth grade, and in one session I spoke with her about how clever she was at reflecting on her own and others' thoughts and feelings. I said that had I not met her before but was meeting her for the first time right then, I would have been unable to diagnose her autism. This was because she was adept at understanding the difficulties her illness gave her, she knew how to cope with it, and at present, it was not causing her any sufferings.

When Laura proudly told her parents about my evaluation, they felt scared and angry. They feared I would take the diagnosis away, and thereby cause Laura to lose support from the municipality, school, and hospital. I had no intention of taking the diagnosis away, but I wanted to give Laura and her parents the hope and the knowledge, that if we find ways to establish a good daily life with the right contexts, then she would have many possibilities for completing her education, holding a job, creating a family, and building a purposeful life. I was so governed by discourses about people hoping to get rid of diagnoses, that I forgot to look at the situation from the parents' perspective.

Later, this special school changed to become a school also for children with ADHD and could no longer provide Laura with the environment she required. Her symptoms recurred, and she had to leave the school. It became obvious that when Laura was in a context where the autism received too

184   *Weave collaboration into all our practices*

little respect and care, it began making trouble again, more trouble than any family could handle.

When the school had provided the right environment, Laura did not suffer from her autism and did not experience symptoms from it. Therefore, her parents were understandably worried about her losing her diagnosis.

Take on wonderfulness, when blame and shame tries to get in the way

The Braveheart family, with daughters Flora and Gloria, appear in Chapters 1, 3, and 13. Flora is the elder sister with autism, and Em and Dave are their parents.

Em grew up with a mother who had bipolar disorder. She experienced both manic and depressive episodes several times during her youth but was only diagnosed with bipolar after giving birth to her daughters. The bipolar disorder led to a lot of mother blame. Em wanted to protect her daughters by hiding her problems. But the results, as with many other parents in the same situation, were often the opposite of her intentions. We did not want blame and shame occupying our conversations, so we externalized the bipolar disorder and the discourses around psychiatric illness and parenthood with Em and Dave. We wrote a letter and hoped that this, besides showing Em how wonderful we saw her, would help to expel her mother blame, and would help to empower her and Dave:

> Dear Em and Dave,
> I'm sitting here in my office looking at the picture of the paper chart[1] from our last conversation and thinking, "What a tough conversation". But then I got the most beautiful e-mail from you, Em. You wrote that you are going to apply for 15 hours less work per week and for compensation for lost earnings. Wow!
>
> So, in a way, you've already acted on the conversation and maybe you think it's been a long time since we spoke. But I still want to share some reflections on the conversation, from our side.
>
> In our view, you used courage when we met that day. You said, "This is about me refusing to accept the fact that I have that bipolar illness and, also, I realise that I thought I was to blame when Mum was ill with bipolar during my childhood".
>
> Perhaps "trust" is a better word than "courage"? Trusting in other people, trusting that we will not use these stories against you?
>
> Courage is required to dare to reflect on one's own actions. You are daring to reflect on how you try to behave in the opposite way to your mother. You are daring to believe that we will not "use your dreams against you" when you consider whether you will act the same way as

Weave collaboration into all our practices 185

your mother, or in the opposite way. You are brave to look "Mr Bipolar" in the eyes, accept he is there, and to step out and be open about "Mr Bipolar".

This is a beautiful conversation to reflect on, and I'm deeply touched. I am moved to be allowed to bear witness when a mother contemplates and dreams about how to be the best possible parent with the challenges one has been given in this life.

You told us about your considerations of whether you fail if you talk about your illness or fail if you don't talk about it. You spoke about your dreams, and what you hope your two girls will remember you for and how these dreams contrast with your memories about your own childhood and mother.

What stories do you want in your family? (Note that stories are in plural, because no one story can accommodate all, most stories have only a single or a few messages. Isn't that true?)

I once learned that no stories are exciting if all is easy and good. There has to be a challenge, because only then the outcome becomes impressive.

I imagine how Gloria and Flora will tell many loving stories about their mother. I imagine them describing a mother and a father who saw their daughters' different needs and adapted their upbringing according to their uniqueness.

I imagine they will remember a mother who had her own "Mr Bipolar" that sometimes made her say, "My illness is teasing me right now, but I'll get Dad for you", or "My illness is teasing me, so I can't help you right now, but fortunately, I know you can do it yourself".

I imagine that one day your daughters will tell their own lovely children, your grandchildren, about their upbringing. They might say:

We were lucky we had a mother who clearly stated how she was coping, what she could do and what she couldn't do. As children we did not need to "scan her" when we came home from school, as many other children had to do with their parents. We knew and felt totally safe. Mum knew how much she could handle, and she took responsibility for getting us what we needed, either from her or from our dad.

We could "go wild" because it was always clear whether a day was a "be quiet-day" or an "make noise-day". We could easily accommodate the changes. We could clearly see and understand what the rules were, and that Mum had control. She also made sure there were other adults we could go to, when she wasn't able to be there for us.

186 *Weave collaboration into all our practices*

Most of all, she made sure we never thought it was our fault. We knew if we were naughty or if it was Mum's "Mr Bipolar" who was troublesome. Mum was so clear, we were never in doubt whether she was upset because we were naughty, or she was upset because "Mr Bipolar" was after her. We felt safe and secure, growing up with such a lovely mother.

We wonder if you can use this small tale. We sincerely hope we are not off track. If we are, please delete this letter.
Sincerely, Kirsten and Nina

Stories in this chapter illustrate how our clinical practices and organizational culture are shaped by our language and governed by discourses that we rarely question. We can question these discourses, deconstruct and evaluate them according to how they support or suppress us from adhering to our values in our daily practices. Being mindful in this way supports us in creating better treatments and a better work environment (Madsen, 2007c).

Doctors learn to do quick evaluations, diagnose, and act to save lives. But an ideal of making fast solid judgments in psychiatry can cause havoc. In psychiatry, the ideals of co-research and sharing responsibility and power among patients and health professionals provide our best guiding light (Madsen, 2006; Winslade, 2002). I like the metaphor of "walking alongside" people to describe this collaborative practice (Ness et al., 2014).

Note

1 We take a digital picture of the paper chart after each session and use this to help our memory when writing the e- mail. See more in Chapter 5.

References

Assing Hvidt, E., Søndergaard, J., Hvidt, N. C., Wehberg, S., Büssing, A., & Andersen, C. M. (2020). Development in Danish medical students' empathy: Study protocol of a cross-sectional and longitudinal mixed-methods study. *BMC Medical Education, 20*(1), 54. doi:10.1186/s12909-020-1967-2

Carrey, N. (2007). Practicing psychiatry through a narrative lens: Working with children, youth, and families. In C. Brown, Augusta-Scott, T. (Ed.), *Narrative Therapy: Making Meaning, Making Lives.*Thousand Oaks, CA: SAGE Publications, Inc.

Epston, D. (2018). In pursuit of goodness: Dignity and moral character in narrative therapy. *Journal of Narrative Family Therapy, 3*, 2–26.

Eriksen, K. A., Arman, M., Davidson, L., Sundfør, B., & Karlsson, B. (2014). Challenges in relating to mental health professionals: Perspectives of persons with severe mental illness. *International Journal of Mental Health Nursing, 23*(2), 110–117. doi:10.1111/inm.12024

Freeman, J., Epston, D., & Lobovits, D. (1997). *Playful Approaches to Serious Problems.* W. W. Norton.

Gumber, S., & Stein, C. H. (2013). Consumer perspectives and mental health reform movements in the United States: 30 years of first-person accounts. *Psychiatric Rehabilitation Journal*, *36*(3), 187–194. doi:10.1037/prj0000003

Happell, B., & Scholz, B. (2018). Doing what we can, but knowing our place: Being an ally to promote consumer leadership in mental health. *International Journal of Mental Health Nursing*, *27*(1), 440–447. doi:10.1111/inm.12404

Jackson, D., & Mannix, J. (2004). Giving voice to the burden of blame: A feminist study of mothers' experiences of mother blaming. *International Journal of Nursing Practice*, *10*(4), 150–158. doi:10.1111/j.1440-172X.2004.00474.x

Jeppesen, P., Petersen, L., Thorup, A., Abel, M. B., Ohlenschlaeger, J., Christensen, TO, Krarup, G., Jorgensen, P., & Nordentoft, M. (2008). The association between premorbid adjustment, duration of untreated psychosis and outcome in first-episode psychosis. *Psychological Medicine*, *38*(8), 1157–1166. doi:10.1017/s0033291708003449

Larson, J. E., & Corrigan, Patrick. (2008). The stigma of families with mental illness. *Academic Psychiatry*, *32*(2), 87–91. doi:10.1176/appi.ap.32.2.87

Lauber, C., Anthony, M., Ajdacic-Gross, V., & Rössler, W. (2004). What about psychiatrists' attitude to mentally ill people? *European Psychiatry*, *19*(7), 423–427. doi:10.1016/j.eurpsy.2004.06.019

Madsen, W. C. (2006). Teaching across discourses to sustain collaborative clinical practice. *Journal of Systemic Therapies*, *25*(4), 44–58. doi:10.1521/jsyt.2006.25.4.44

Madsen, W. C. (2007a). *Collaborative therapy with multi-stressed families* (2nd ed.). The Guilford Press.

Madsen, W. C. (2007b). Sustaining a Collaborative Practice in the "Real" World. In *Collaborative Therapy with Multi-stressed Families*. (2nd ed., pp. 323–353): Guilford Press.

Madsen, W. C. (2007c). Working with traditional structures to support a collaborative clinical practice. *The International Journal of Narrative Therapy and Community Work*(2), 51–61. doi:10.3316/informit.060824685990920

Maisel, R., Epston, D., Borden, A. (2004). *Biting the hand that starves you: Inspiring resistance to Anorexia/Bulimia*. New York, NY: W.W. Norton & Co.

Ness, O., Borg, M., Semb, R., & Karlsson, B. (2014). "Walking alongside": Collaborative practices in mental health and substance use care. *International Journal of Mental Health Systems*, *8*(1), 55. doi:10.1186/1752-4458-8-55

O'Hagan, M. (2009). Leadership for empowerment and equality: A proposed model for mental health user/survivor leadership. *International Journal of Leadership in Public Services*, *5*(4), 34–43. doi:10.5042/IJLPS.2010.0110

Paro, H. B. M. S., Silveira, P. S. P., Perotta, B., Gannam, S., Enns, S. C., Giaxa, R. R. B., Bonito, R. F., Martins, M. A., & Tempski, P. Z. (2014). Empathy among medical students: Is there a relation with quality of life and burnout? *PLOS ONE*, *9*(4), e94133. doi:10.1371/journal.pone.0094133

Sfantou, D. F., Laliotis, A., Patelarou, A. E., Sifaki-Pistolla, D., Matalliotakis, M., & Patelarou, E. (2017). Importance of leadership style towards quality of care measures in healthcare settings: A systematic review. *Healthcare*, *5*(4), 73.

Shapiro, J. (2008). Walking a mile in their patients' shoes: empathy and othering in medical students' education. *Philosophy, Ethics, and Humanities in Medicine*, *3*, 10. doi:10.1186/1747-5341-3-10

Souaiby, L., Gaillard, R., & Krebs, M. O. (2016). Duration of untreated psychosis: A state-of-the-art review and critical analysis. *Encephale*, *42*(4), 361–366. doi:10.1016/j.encep.2015.09.007

188 *Weave collaboration into all our practices*

Stewart, S., Scholz, B., Gordon, S., & Happell, B. (2019). 'It depends what you mean by leadership': An analysis of stakeholder perspectives on consumer leadership. *International Journal of Mental Health Nursing, 28*(1), 339–350. doi:10.1111/inm.12542

White, M. (2002). Addressing personal failure. *The International Journal of Narrative Therapy & Community Work, 3*(3), 33–76.

White, M., & Epston, D. (1990). *Narrative means to therapeutic ends.* W.W. Norton & Company.

Winslade, J. (2002). Storying professional identity. *The International Journal of Narrative Therapy and Community Work*, (4), 33–38. doi:10.3316/informit.662762822487071

15 A continuously curious learning team

A mental health service's organization and alignment of values, visions, and practices affects the culture and the ability of clinicians to provide patients with the best possible treatment (Glisson & Hemmelgarn, 1998, 2008). This chapter describes how we can understand and work with discourses and team practices to support collaboration and empowerment.

Discourses and their implicit values

Part of the foundation for our practices stems from our understanding of discourses (Jørring & Jacobsen, 2014; Madsen, 2006; Strong & Sesma-Vazquez, 2015, 2011).

Discourses are statements, thoughts or practices that share common values and interpretations, and lead us to believe in certain taken-for-granted truths. They are truths that we do not question, and we are often unaware of their power. When we try to make sense of something, we only remember those stories that support these discourses or taken-for-granted truths, and we ignore many stories that don't fit with these truths (Madsen, 2007b).

The discourses we tell (or "just know") have a monitoring and corrective effect on us. We monitor others and ourselves and evaluate whether we adhere to these taken-for-granted truths. These inside-our-head practices have a corrective influence on our thoughts.

Discourses can be explained in several ways (Madsen, 2007a):

Universal truths

- Ideas or rules we agree on, but don't talk about, investigate or wonder about.
- Those things that stand between the lines.
- What is implied, but not spoken about.
- The absent but implicit.

The etiquette

- Rules for how we should behave.

DOI: 10.4324/9781003171621-16

190   *A continuously curious learning team*

- The expectations we demand to have about ourselves, others, the system, and society.

Society's thinking and behaviour

- Ways of being together, our interactions at home, work, and in society.

In the hospital system, clinicians have three taken-for-granted truths:

1. Our job is to identify symptoms, discover their causes, and then intervene to cure or ameliorate these symptoms.
2. We are experts who assess patients, develop a treatment plan, implement the treatment designed to bring the patient relief and closer to our definition of healthy functioning.
3. Patients are vulnerable and in vulnerable positions; we must use our responsibility and power to ensure patient safety.

These three discourses can be juxtaposed with three other discourses (Madsen, 2007b) that support our patient's empowerment:

1. Focus on possibilities. We ask questions to co-create new knowledge about new possibilities for the patient's and the family's preferred actions, thoughts, and feelings.
2. We collaborate. We imagine and believe that patients and families have knowledge that we need to include to provide the best help; we trust the patient's and the family's wisdom; we hope and expect to learn from them.
3. The patients and their families are the best judges of the effects of the treatment. Our work benefits from receiving patient and family feedback. We are transparent and remain accountable for our actions, allowing patients and families to evaluate and judge us.

These discourses can be expressed in this way:

- Discourses of deficits and discourses of possibilities.
- Discourses of professional expertise and discourses of collaboration.
- Discourses of protection and discourses of transparency.

When trying to oppose the six discourses, some might seem more valuable than others. But there are good reasons for all six discourses, and we can just as easily fail if we adhere only to the last three, as if we adhere only to the first three.

Being attentive to all six discourses provides the best outcomes. This is the foundation on which I meet patients and families, lead clinical conferences, teach trainees, hold professional meetings and meetings with stakeholders, and in all other contexts as a child and adolescent psychiatrist.

Constantly paying attention to which discourses are speaking to me, my team, and in the hospital, helps me to find ways to be a leader and build a good team. The ethics of the treatment I deliver must be aligned with the ethics of the entire organization.

We all have unique knowledge and are worthy of being in the room

Our local context influences our work so therefore, any guide, manual or treatment method must be adjusted to local contexts. For example, in our hospital's context, the organization's leaders are measured according to production and effectiveness. Our ongoing training and supervision, traditionally the "spiritual food" for mental health professionals, is continuously being reduced. This adds to the challenges for a leader and their colleagues. We all must look for new ways to care for each other (Glisson et al., 2008; Kirkeby, 2008). Conferences and staff meetings are also opportunities for giving and receiving mental and emotional nutrition, and the leader has the responsibility to ensure colleagues continually grow as professionals and personally (Madsen, 2014; McCormack et al., 2018).

Our team shares lunch together and engages in staff meetings, conferences, and supervision. Each of these domains nurtures us differently, but all are important for our mental health. At lunch, we do not discuss cases; we talk about ourselves, personal things, like how many children we have and what we like to do with our family, our hobbies, and so on. We share difficulties and "expose" ourselves as ordinary people with ordinary problems. We share how our work affects our thinking about society and our family. There is a healing effect of growing together through sharing joys and struggles (Madsen et al., 2021; White & Hales, 1997).

We aim to incorporate this mattering culture (see Chapter 4) in all contexts, so that researchers, clinicians, secretaries, and interns feel welcome and acknowledged. Research, clinical and secretarial work must be of equal value and interesting to all. Staff meetings allow people to share their work with others. When researchers share their work and ask clinicians for questions and advice, the clinicians become fascinated by both the research questions and the interim research results (Ejbye-Ernst & Jørring, 2017). Some medical and psychology interns undertake research in our setting and share the findings with us (Ejbye-Ernst et al., 2015).

Secretaries welcome the families into the reception rooms of most organizations. One family told us that they knew from the first minute they entered the waiting area that this would be a good place for them because of the way our secretary had greeted them. The secretary had treated them as long-lost friends, as people she had looked forward to meet, and expected to like. The parents said, "If Jette (the secretary) acted that way, we knew that other people in this workplace also would be good people" (Madsen et al., 2021, p. 29).

Secretaries get to know the families and their unique knowledge makes them worthy of being in the conference room, so they can share their knowledge. Secretaries, and interns too, have life experiences that are valuable to reflect on. They deserve to be included at our conferences and staff meetings so their knowledge can be utilized.

Hierarchical languages and conferences cultures

For the best outcome, health professionals need to communicate difficult messages to families in respectful and honouring ways.

When stigmatizing or derogatory discourses arise, for example at conferences, we might say, "You have an interesting and probably valid point. How would you formulate this message if the parents were present right now?" If we cannot share this view with the parents in a respectful and honest way, it will not be useful for any of us.

Importantly, we don't fabricate stories or avoid saying what we think and believe in. We ask ourselves:

- How would the parents perceive what we just said?
- How can we present information so parents can hear that we are in awe of the enormity of their problems, that we respect their efforts, and that we hope this information will be helpful for them to consider? So much so, that they feel inspired to consider this?

A traditional clinical conference has a clear purpose, where the team leader shoulders the responsibility for the actions of other team members. Traditional conference culture is based on hierarchical discourses that the leader has power and responsibility. Medical science and hospital cultures are still largely governed by these hierarchical values and discourses, and the language reflects these discourses.

This is how it was when, as a junior doctor, I reported back to my superior on my cases. She would decide if I was handling the case correctly; she had the power to make decisions on diagnoses, treatments, and other aspects of the case. My superior needed information to fulfil her responsibility. If time permitted while reporting to her, she would also provide guidance.

Questioning the effects of language and discourses that support hierarchy can be enlightening, especially when we study the effects on our relationship with patients and on treatments (Gergen & Davis, 1990; Larson & Corrigan, 2008; Strong & Sesma-Vazquez, 2015). We have found, for example, that presenting our knowledge as ideas instead of stating them as "doctor's orders" has profoundly different effects on how our knowledge is received and used by our patients.

A continuously curious learning team 193

For example, the following sentences have similar messages but can affect feelings of personal agency differently:

"Your statement shows that you have a depression"

or

"I am wondering if your statements could be signs that you are being affected by a depression?"

"That is the Anorexia speaking!"

or

"Do you think your best girlfriend, or the Anorexia, would like you to think this way?"

We use the helping map (see Chapter 6) for case reviews at our clinical conferences, with the family's visions as our guiding lights. One team member leads the conversation and takes notes according to the helping map. We ask questions as we would at a therapeutic conversation.

We ask each other questions about what we like and respect about the parents and the children. We also discuss the family's intentions and the parents' hopes and expectations, rather than focusing on the effects of their actions. We focus on helpful questions.

Examples of questions presented during a case review:

- What would you like to understand more clearly, for this conference to be helpful for you?
- If the parents were here, what would they like us to figure out?
- What might the parents say they want to achieve?
- What do you like most about this family/dad/mum/child?
- What might be the intentions behind that? (When an act by a family member, or their own action, is described).
- What supports have you heard about in the conversations would be helpful to be reminded of now?
- What obstacles are there for the family?
- What supports and obstacles would the family tell us about?
- Are we talking about the right thing here or am I going out on a tangent?
- Is this conversation helpful for you?
- Is it okay if I ask the others about their thoughts now?
- What about personal experiences?
- Did I remember to ask about the secretary's and the interns' views?
- What have you heard that has inspired you most?
- What did you become most concerned about while listening?
- What ideas or values did you hear about that you think are important for this family?

- Are there questions you would like to ask that I did not address?
- Do you have advice for me on what direction to take now?
- As you listened to the others, what did you especially get inspired by?
- As you listened to this, what would you be keen to try right now, if you were their therapist? Why? What would you hope to attain?
- Did these reflections help you to develop new perspectives?
- What would you like to do now?

Power issues are addressed, with the purpose of lessening their negative effects and increasing their positive effects.

Many hospital wards share their conferences with patients and parents. This inclusiveness is an example of respecting and empowering patients and parents.

Co-therapists as dancing partners

Families referred to our team have complex problems, for which usual forms of treatment have been insufficient. This fact inspired us to develop a collaborative treatment approach (Jørring & Jacobsen, 2014) that includes the participation of two therapists in all sessions (Hendrix et al., 2001; Hoffman & Gafni, 1984). However, the use of this collaborative practice appears to be dwindling due to economic pressure, and a focus on short term cost-effectiveness. This is despite evidence showing that shared decision-making, working in teams, and involvement of the patient's caregivers is cost-effective (Cosgrove et al., 2013; Elwyn et al., 2016).

When two therapists are in the room, more attention can be given to everybody. We especially look for and point out that there's always more than one truth, and more than one perspective.

Sufficient professional expertise is required in these complex cases to enable effectiveness and to prevent burn out (Ben-Zur & Michael, 2007). We often use a metaphor, that the burden of psychopathology must be met by an equal amount of professional support. An advantage of co-therapy is that the burdens can be shared, and each therapist can be the other's supervisor. The learning curve is steeper with co-therapists.

We aim to create an ambience in our sessions that is conducive to talking about difficult emotions, including those that are taboo, and those loaded with shame and guilt. This is possible in an environment where mutual trust and kindness outbalance shame and blame. When with a family, our trust in the family and each other must counterbalance the distrust, arrogance, and stigma that psychiatric illness pours into the room.

We have another metaphor for this teamwork: just as parental love is the soil that children grow in, the mutual respect and kindness we feel for each other is the soil that family therapy grows in.

Many families tell us that they greatly appreciate the fact that there are two therapists. Some of the more mundane, but important feedback from the families, is that they are happy because this approach provides continuity even if one of us falls ill or moves on.

The parents also appreciate that we can disagree respectful of each other in front of them during the session. We demonstrate that we can see things from different sides, and we can speak about the different ideas in respectful and curious ways. We exemplify or role model how to work together as parents.

We have rules that we call "The partner's dance". We are inspired by all kinds of couples' dancing, the idea of lead and follow, mutual inspiration, changing the leader, and the graceful patterns this makes on the dancefloor. These are our rules for our co-therapy partner's dance:

* We take time to prepare together before the conversation.
* We are punctual with session times in respect of both the family and ourselves.
* We use the paper chart for notetaking, and usually the interviewer is also the note-keeper.
* No extra questions are put while writing on the paper chart.
* We allow our co-therapist to finish their questioning without interruption.
* If moving in two directions, we point this out openly and invite the family to choose which route to follow.
* For transparency, we use a "time-out" hand signal and explain why we are asking a question.
* We ask each other and the family for help when we feel stuck or are in doubt.
* We ask the family if we are talking about the right thing several times during a session.
* The therapists' "after-talk" is for positive reflection, with a focus on content for the post-session therapeutic e-mail.

Therapists are required to learn to meet each other with the same level of respect, curiosity, trust, and hope that they exhibit when meeting with a family. In my experience, this requires ongoing training within the team. Mutual respect must be present even when therapists do not know each other well.

Preparation involves sharing our thoughts on different themes to explore during the conversation. We use the metaphor, that our hypotheses and curiosities are like melodies, both polyphonic and harmonized.

The practice of "after-talks" has proven worthwhile. At first, our "after-talks" explored only "the case", how the collaboration went, and whether something could be improved next time, often leading the therapists to criticize each other. Now, we start each "after-talk" by sharing something that we were inspired by or liked about our co-therapist's questions. This leads to honouring each other with respect and curious reflections. The letter writing practice also generates respect and curiosity.

196 *A continuously curious learning team*

Our clinical conferences and other interactions transcend the same ethics. We practice transparency and tell each other and the families why we act and ask questions as we do. We ask each other in the middle of a session how to direct the conversation further, why a specific question is important, or what ideas are behind it. This creates opportunities for family members to get involved in designing the therapeutic process. These interactions are fun, and the effect is therapeutic.

When we have challenges, for example understanding the problems that burden the family, or how our "dance partner" thinks or conducts their "dance", we bring them to the clinical conferences or supervisory meetings, where we use the same practice of questioning as in the therapies.

First and foremost, effective therapist and team collaborations are about wanting, talking about, and practising collaboration, repeatedly. Just like learning to dance, or learning anything else we want to master, we are dedicated to giving our best effort.

Being humble and asking for help

No therapist will ever have the permanent right answer for the best approach. Our society, the contexts and our problems will continue to evolve, so we must keep learning.

To learn from the families, we must position them and ourselves in a respectful relationship that allows the families to feel confident that we are seriously considering their perspectives (Epston, 1999; Guilfoyle, 2015; Redstone, 2004).

The practice of humility is effective in gaining respect from families and achieving a therapeutic relationship with patients. I have experienced that collaboration can be hampered by arrogance and can be nurtured by humility. To practice humility, we use the narrative technique called witnessing (White, 2007):

1. The expression (what caught your attention?)
2. Images (what does the image say about what's important to the person?)
3. Resonance (what in your experiences of life explains why this caught your attention?)
4. Transport (where has this experience taken you and what is different for you now?)

Let me expand on this practice of humility when working with a family:

1. I mention what the family has said, which made me realize that they are teaching me something.
2. I speak to those ethics the family has made me aware of, and I value, and the related behaviour.
3. I explain why I am struggling with this, and what I am realizing. I might share a story or a metaphor about myself.

4. I convey what I will try to do more of, less of, or differently, in the future.
5. Lastly, I thank the family for helping me become a better doctor.

We can easily forget the many ways we can misuse our own implicit professional power to bully or scare others. After meeting with parents, Olga and Oluf, I wrote a document for them to present to their municipality, requesting better assistance from the school for their daughter. This was a standard procedure from my perspective. I e-mailed the document to the parents and asked for any comments or corrections and their permission to send it to the school.

The parents answered by e-mail and had no corrections. But Olga also wrote:

> I feared you would decide that the best solution for Mary would be to take her from us, and you would say that it would be better for her to live with another family.

> That's what the municipality had said to us about Mary long before we met you, so that's why I was so scared at our last meeting.
> Olga

I shared Olga's comment with my team, and we thought about parents who experience situations that make them scared of losing their children, or of being subjected to criticism.

That got me thinking and I wrote a short letter to Olga:

> Dear Olga and Oluf,
> I want to thank you for writing about what you heard the municipality had said in the beginning about Mary.

> It strikes me that professionals can be arrogant and thoughtless; such behaviour borders on being malicious. But I too act arrogantly, when I forget that what I say or write can elicit such memories and thoughts, and I forget to ask people if they have such experiences or thoughts.

> You have reminded me that I always must consider what I say and write to families and wonder what experiences and traumas they may have, that I do not yet know of. I must be mindful of this, otherwise I can do much harm. I hope that, with your help, I will become better at expressing myself and asking the right questions, so my conversations, e-mails and documents can be used well and not cause hurt.

> Do you remember what I said in our conversation that triggered your fear that the best solution for Mary would be for her to be placed with another family? If you remember, this might help me to be a better doctor.
> Thank you for your help,
> Nina

198 *A continuously curious learning team*

May we have a lifeline into the hospital?

We can continue our learning by maintaining communication with our patients and their families, after treatment is completed, because they can teach us a different kind of knowledge about prognosis than that found in books (Slade & Longden, 2015).

When we maintain contact with the families, they teach us a lot about the long-term prognoses. However, opportunities for gathering this kind of knowledge are rare, if we meet only those patients who return with recurring problems. If we don't see those families who fare well, we do not learn from them. Investing in maintaining contact with families who do well, has huge potential for teaching us about what empowers families (Schrank & Slade, 2007).

Classic research uses a specific number of sessions as a golden standard, and management and economic paradigms also support discharging patients after a certain amount of time (Guidi et al., 2018). This prevents the patients and their families from participating in shared decision-making about how they want to be helped. The practice of not discharging families after a certain number of sessions, but letting the families decide the length of the course, has proved to be a very helpful aspect when we begin a collaboration (Jørring & Gjessing Jensen, 2018; Madsen & Javed, 2018). This approach lessens the anxiety that families experience, wondering when they will be discharged.

Our experience from "taking stock" meetings is that when the families begin to believe in themselves and do not need us anymore, they sometimes remain afraid of the future. They want to be independent of our help as soon as possible but are fearful of doing this too soon. When they know that they can always come back and meet the same therapists, who they have found helpful, they become more confident and eager to try coping in the community on their own. We try to give families this opportunity for independence.

Several families have called this approach a lifeline. A mother provided this metaphor: Going to therapy is like learning how to rock-climb. You start with indoor climbing with a trainer providing rope set-ups and ensuring that you get to know safe techniques. Later, you and your friends learn to belay the rope for each other and, when you are very experienced, you can do solo-climbing.

We aim to create a sense of optimism and self-agency when we tell the families that they can stop coming for sessions and become "sleeping members", until they feel ready to leave treatment.

This chapter explores how we are changing our discourses about our practices, from professional-led treatments and research only, to collaborative patient-professional-led-treatments and research (Baum et al., 2006; Ejbye-Ernst & Jørring, 2017; Gaddis, 2004; Hoffman & Gafni, 1984; Lake & Turner, 2017; Ness, 2013; Pellicano et al., 2018).

In summary, this could be our set of narrative psychiatric discourses:

- We co-create knowledge about competence, dreams, and hope before we inquire about difficulties.
- We use family wisdom to co-create solutions to difficulties in the family's lives.
- We always consider how our language shapes our thinking about our patients, and how it will be experienced by the families.
- We always ask for patient feedback about their hopes for our collaboration and the effects of our actions on them (Epston, 2018; Madsen, 2006).

References

Baum, F., MacDougall, C., & Smith, D. (2006). Participatory action research. *J Epidemiol Community Health, 60*(10), 854–857. doi:10.1136/jech.2004.028662

Ben-Zur, H., & Michael, K. (2007). Burnout, social support, and coping at work among social workers, psychologists, and nurses: The role of challenge/control appraisals. *Social Work in Health Care, 45*(4), 63–82. doi:10.1300/J010v45n04_04

Cosgrove, D. M., Fisher, M., Gabow, P., Gottlieb, G., Halvorson, G. C., James, B. C., Kaplan, G. S., Perlin, J. B., Petzel, R., Steele, G. D., & Toussaint, J. S. (2013). Ten strategies to lower costs, improve quality, and engage patients: The view from leading health system CEOs. *Health Affairs, 32*(2), 321–327. doi:10.1377/hlthaff. 2012.1074

Ejbye-Ernst, D., & Jørring, N.T. (2017). Doing it collaboratively! Addressing the dilemmas of designing quantitative effect studies on narrative family therapy in a local clinical context. *Journal of Systemic Therapies, 36*(1), 48–66.

Ejbye-Ernst, D., Jørring, N. T., & Jacobsen, C. B. (2015). Klientperspektiver på anvendelsen af sporgeskemaer i opstartsfasen af et psykoterapeutisk behandlingsforlob. *Fokus på familien, 43*(2), 109-101.

Elwyn, G., Frosch, D. L., & Kobrin, S. (2016). Implementing shared decision-making: consider all the consequences. *Implementation Science, 11*(1), 114. doi:10.1186/s13012-01 6-0480-9

Epston, D. (1999). Co-research: the making of alternative knowledge in narrative therapy and community work. In P. Moss (Ed.), *Narrative Therapy and Community Work: A conference collection*. Adelaide: Dulwich Centre Publications.

Epston, D. (2018). In pursuit of goodness: Dignity and moral character in narrative therapy. *Journal of Narrative Family Therapy, 3*, 2–26.

Gaddis, S. (2004). Re-positioning traditional research: Centring clients' accounts in the construction of professional therapy knowledges. *The International Journal of Narrative Therapy and Community Work, 2004*(2), 1–12. doi:10.3316/informit.2391 60853903152

Gergen, K. J., & Davis, K. M. (1990). Therapeutic professions and the diffusion of deficit. *Journal of Mind and Behavior, 11*(3-4), 353–368.

Glisson, C., & Hemmelgarn, A. (1998). The effects of organizational climate and interorganizational coordination on the quality and outcomes of children's service systems. *Child Abuse & Neglect, 22*(5), 401–421. doi:10.1016/s0145-2134(98) 00005-2

200   *A continuously curious learning team*

Glisson, C., Schoenwald, S. K., Kelleher, K., Landsverk, J., Hoagwood, K. E., Mayberg, S., & Green, P. (2008). Therapist turnover and new program sustainability in mental health clinics as a function of organizational culture, climate, and service structure. *Administration and Policy in Mental Health, 35*(1-2), 124–133. doi:10.1007/s10488-007-0152-9

Guidi, J., Brakemeier, E. L., Bockting, C. L. H., Cosci, F., Cuijpers, P., Jarrett, R. B., … Fava, G. A. (2018). Methodological recommendations for trials of psychological interventions. *Psychotherapy and Psychosomatics, 87*(5), 276–284. doi:10.1159/000490574

Guilfoyle, M. (2015). Listening in narrative therapy: Double listening and empathic positioning. *South African Journal of Psychology, 45*(1), 36–49. doi:10.1177/008124 6314556711

Hendrix, C. C., Fournier, D. G., & Briggs, K. (2001). Impact of co-therapy teams on client outcomes and therapist training in marriage and family therapy. *Contemporary Family Therapy, 23*(1), 63–82. doi:10.1023/A:1007824216363

Hendrix, C. C., Fournier, D. G., & Briggs, K. (2001). Impact of co-therapy teams on client outcomes and therapist training in marriage and family therapy. *Contemporary Family Therapy, 23*(1), 63–82. doi:10.1023/A:1007824216363

Hoffman, S., & Gafni, S. (1984). Active-interactional cotherapy. *International Journal of Family Therapy, 6*(1), 53–58. doi:10.1007/BF00924365

Jørring, N. T., & Gjessing Jensen, K. (2018). Treatment efficacy of narrative family therapy for children and adolescents with diverse psychiatric symptomatology. *Scandinavian Journal of Child and Adolescent Psychiatry and Psychology, 6*(2), 107–114. doi:10.21307/sjcapp-2018-012

Jørring, N. T., & Jacobsen, C. B. (2014). Narrative therapy in CAMHS: Creating multi-storied treatments. *Journal of Systemic Therapies, 33*(1), 89–101.

Kirkeby, O. F. (2008). *The virtue of leadership*. Copenhagen Business School Press.

Lake, J., & Turner, M. S. (2017). Urgent need for improved mental health care and a more collaborative model of care. *The Permanente Journal, 21*, 17–024. doi:10.7812/tpp/17-024

Larson, J. E., & Corrigan, Patrick. (2008). The stigma of families with mental illness. *Academic Psychiatry, 32*(2), 87–91. doi:10.1176/appi.ap.32.2.87

Madsen, S., Javed. M. (2018). Give anerkendelse og blive anerkendt i narrativ familieterapi. Reserach assignment. *Børne- og Ungdomspsykiatrisk Center, Region H.* Copenhagen, Denmark.

Madsen, W. C. (2006). Teaching across discourses to sustain collaborative clinical practice. *Journal of Systemic Therapies, 25*(4), 44–58. doi:10.1521/jsyt.2006.25.4.44

Madsen, W. C. (2007a). *Collaborative therapy with multi-stressed families* (2nd ed.). The Guilford Press.

Madsen, W. C. (2007b). Sustaining a collaborative practice in the "Real" World. In *Collaborative therapy with multi-stressed families*. (2nd ed., pp. 323–353): Guilford Press.

Madsen, W. C. (2014). Applications of collaborative helping maps: Supporting professional development, supervision and work teams in family-centered practice. *Family Process, 53*(1), 3–21. doi:10.1111/famp.12048

Madsen, W. C., Roth, E., & Jørring, N. T. (2021). Mattering as the heart of health and human services. *Journal of Contemporary Narrative Therapy, 1*, 19–31. Retrieved 16 February 2021 from https://www.paperturn-view.com/?pid=MTY161367&p=21

McCormack, H. M., MacIntyre, T. E., O'Shea, D., Herring, M. P., & Campbell, M. J. (2018). The prevalence and cause(s) of burnout among applied psychologists: A systematic review. *Frontiers in Psychology*, *9*, 1897. doi:10.3389/fpsyg.2018.01897

Ness, O. (2013). *Therapists in continuous education: A collaborative approach*. Taos Institute Publications/WorldShare Books.

Pellicano, L., Mandy, W., Bölte, S., Stahmer, A., Lounds Taylor, J., & Mandell, D. S. (2018). A new era for autism research, and for our journal. *Autism*, *22*(2), 82–83. doi:10.1177/1362361317748556

Redstone, A. (2004). Researching people's experience of narrative therapy: Acknowledging the contribution of the "Client" to what works in counselling conversations. *The International Journal of Narrative Therapy and Community Work* (2), 57–62. doi:10.3316/informit.243465070263796

Schrank, B., & Slade, M. (2007). Recovery in psychiatry. *Psychiatric Bulletin*, *31*(9), 321–325. doi:10.1192/pb.bp.106.013425

Slade, M., & Longden, E. (2015). Empirical evidence about recovery and mental health. *BMC Psychiatry*, *15*(1), 285. doi:10.1186/s12888-015-0678-4

Strong, T., & Sesma-Vazquez, M. (2015). Discourses on children's mental health: A critical review. In M. O'Reilly, Lester, J. (Ed.), *The Palgrave Handbook of Child Mental Health* (pp. 99–116): Palgrave Macmillan, London.

Strong, T., Sutherland, O., & Ness, O. (2011). Considerations for a discourse of Collaboration and Psychotherapy. *Asia Pacific Journal of Counselling and Psychotherapy*, *2*(1), 25–40. doi:10.1080/21507686.2010.546865

White, C., & Hales, J. (1997). *The personal is the professional: therapists reflect on their families, lives and work*. Dulwich Centre Publications.

White, M. (2007). Definitional ceremonies. In *Maps of narrative practice* (pp. 165–218). W.W. Norton.

16 The art of true helping: dare to care

The never-ending journey to become a better narrative family psychiatrist fills me with joy. My practice of narrative family psychiatry progressively evolves from a foundation of collaborative values comprising respect, curiosity, trust, and hope.

Each health professional begins their journey to become a professional with a dream. These dreams are different, they evolve and change, and they need to be nurtured to keep growing. I embrace the fact that personal narratives greatly influence professional narratives and actions (Duncan, 2014; Graff et al., 2003). For many years, I have taught child and adolescent trainees about storying one's identity as a therapist and as a doctor (Winslade, 2002) to sustain collaborative clinical practices (Madsen, 2006). This chapter draws on storytelling and reflection to explore ethics and practices that can nurture the dreams and practices of a narrative family psychiatrist.

We each find inspiration for our values in different places, and two Danish philosophers, Søren Kierkegaard and Knud Ejler Løgstrup, nurture my dreams and practices.

Løgstrup, a Danish philosopher and theologian, writes metaphorically of having something of the other person's life "in our hands" (Løgstrup et al., 1997, p. 25). I cherish this metaphor of the ethical demand, and find help in his writings to my calling as a doctor:

> In its basic sense trust is essential to every conversation. In conversation as such we deliver ourselves into the hands of another (Løgstrup et al., 1997, p. 14).

> A person never has something to do with another person without also having some degree of control over him or her. It may be a very small matter, involving only a passing mood, a dampening or quickening of spirit, a deepening or removal of some dislike. But it may also be a matter of tremendous scope, such as can determine if the life of the other flourishes or not (Løgstrup et al., 1997, pp. 15–16).

> Unconsciously, we nonetheless have the strange notion that the rest of us are not part of another person's world.... The fact is, however, that it is

DOI: 10.4324/9781003171621-17

completely wrong, because we do indeed constitute one another's world and destiny (Løgstrup et al., 1997, p. 17).

Herein lies the unarticulated and one might say anonymous demand that we take care of the life which trust has placed in our hands (Løgstrup et al., 1997, p. 18).

However, no one has the right to make him or herself the master of another person's individuality or will. Neither good intentions, insight into what is best for him or her, nor even the possibility of saving him or her from great calamities which would otherwise strike him or her can justify intrusion upon his or her individuality and will (Løgstrup et al., 1997, p. 27).

Kierkegaard, an existentialist philosopher who lived in the 19th century has inspired existentialist therapies (Cooper, 2003). In *The Point of View* (Kierkegaard, 1998), he explores the art of helping and describes helping as leading a person to a new place:

If one is truly to succeed in leading a person to a specific place, one must first and foremost take care to find him where he is and begin there. This is the secret in the entire art of helping. Anyone who cannot do this is himself under a delusion if he thinks he is able to help someone else. In order truly to help someone else, I must understand more than he - but certainly first and foremost understand what he understands. If I do not do that, then my greater understanding does not help him at all. If I nevertheless want to assert my greater understanding, then it is because I am vain or proud, then basically instead of benefiting him I really want to be admired by him. But all true helping begins with a humbling. The helper must first humble himself under the person he wants to help and thereby understand that to help is not to dominate but to serve, that to help is not to be the most dominating but the most patient, that to help is a willingness for the time being to put up with being in the wrong and not understanding what the other understands.

(Kierkegaard, 1998, p. 45)

True helping is not the opposite of untrue helping. True helping can be viewed as an art, as opposed to only practicing specific techniques. Imagine two scenarios for a patient and family who, having received successful treatment, now have the following knowledge:

1. The doctor has cured me and if I get ill again, I will seek her help.
2. The doctor has helped us to develop ways to deal with life, and the next time we run into problems, we will know how to cope.

204   *The art of true helping: dare to care*

Neither of these perspectives is wrong or excludes the other. However, the second outcome is my vision for helping, because it provides for personal and family empowerment.

When I share stories or discuss cases in my teachings, the stories become descriptions of my values and identity as a professional. The story plots become metaphors for the values that guide my practice as a narrative family psy-chiatrist. When patients and their families share stories of their experience and relationship with me, I become witnessed and co-authored as a doctor (Walther & Fox, 2012; Winslade, 2002).

I hope the stories that I share will inspire your professional journey, by inspiring you to remember, tell and re-tell many stories about who you want to be, both as a person and as a professional, and what stories you want to be told about you.

If I don't like the parents, there's something I don't understand

"What do you do, if you do not like one of the parents?"

In response to this frequent question, I tell a story about a father, Don, who taught me about being respectful, curious, and trusting. This story gives hope and I share it when colleagues seek guidance on addressing parents who appear aggressive or scary.

This story began years ago when Don's daughter, Danielle, was admitted to the hospital with anorexia. Against medical advice, Don withdrew his daughter from the inpatient unit. The parents were divorced, but Don's ex-wife persuaded him to later bring Danielle back for outpatient help. At this point, I was the doctor to meet Don and his family.

Don introduced himself by announcing that he had no problems being recognized as a violent or aggressive man. He made me feel afraid, so I asked if he wanted to sit next to my consulting room door. My work doing acute psychiatric assessments in the emergency department had taught me that, to help minimize the risk of violence, patients should have an easy exit from the room. I explained this reason for my suggestion to Don, and he gave a thumbs up.

After introducing myself, I asked what kind of help Don hoped for from me and my team. He answered by speaking proudly about being the father who confronted doctors and that he had no expectations that I would be helpful. He had only showed up so his ex-wife would get off his back.

I responded, "Being a father is clearly something you are proud of. Is it okay if we spend some time with you describing what kind of father you want to be?"

Don described his values of being a father, a husband, and a man, in ways that differed greatly from my personal values. To resist the temptation to interrupt and try to convince him of his "wrongdoings", I busied myself with documenting everything he said on my paper chart. Don spoke of being the

The art of true helping: dare to care 205

strong man who protects his women and children, being the responsible breadwinner, setting the rules and putting his family in their place, and making them feel safe from other men in a dangerous world.

This led me to ask what experiences had led him to adhere to these values and dreams of being a father. I said, "You seem to have strong feelings about fatherhood. I wonder how you came to develop these values, and why they are important to you?"

Don said he had been raised in different orphanages. He had been a scrawny boy, bullied and beaten up. He had been extremely scared and learned in his pre-teens that the only way to combat anxiety was to get drunk. As a grown up, he was so courageous when drunk, that he was not scared of law enforcement. But when sober, he was overcome by anxiety and would often hide in his bed under the duvet. This "weakness" was deeply shameful to him, and he tried to hide this behaviour, even from his girlfriends. Owning a bar had allowed him to stay drunk most of the time.

I decided to share with Don how his story affected me, trying to be open with my thoughts. In my eyes, he was living an impossible life, wanting to be the fearless protector of his loved ones while living under anxiety's cruel dictatorship. I was amazed at what Don tried to do. I found it unjust that a traumatic childhood, anxiety, and alcohol continued to rule over him and now his family.

As we explored this further, we realized the vastness between the intentions of Don's actions and the effects of his actions. Nobody had done these explorations with him before. That's how far we progressed at our initial meeting.

Don later decided to participate in a programme for alcoholics and in group therapy for anxiety. He met me for follow up talks that were supposed to focus on how to support Danielle in her fight against her anorexia. But we seldom spoke about eating disorders; rather, we spoke more about how Don's history should not become his, or his children's, destiny.

As time went on, Danielle's mother told me about the development of a parental collaboration. As Don found ways to stay sober and combat anxiety, he began to keep more appointments, listen to Danielle's mother, and compromise on many issues about their children.

Don said that I had taught him not to be ashamed, to hold his values in front of his nose and evaluate the effects of his actions.

Today, when an argument arises over concerns a parent is intentionally harming their child, I remember Don. Every parent can become a good parent, when given the right help. Nobody's history should become their destiny.

At a supervisory meeting a colleague, Janni described what she does when she doesn't like what the parents are saying or doing. She said, "I tell myself that there must be something I have not understood, otherwise I would not be experiencing these feelings. I must 'get closer to them' and ask more curious questions until I find that I do understand enough to respect their choice and can find my compassion for them".

206 *The art of true helping: dare to care*

I find "getting closer to them" a helpful metaphor for Kierkegaard's description that all true helping begins with a humbling of one self (Kierkegaard, 1998).

Literate means to therapeutic ends[1]

Anna and Bertie, the parents of Valiant (Chapters 1, 2, 8, and 14) envisaged creating a story that could be helpful for their entire family. This vision kept emerging in our conversations. What would a meaningful narrative about their son and family comprise? Anna first created a story that describes hiking along an abyss, to understand the incomprehensible as a response to one of my e-mails in Chapter 8. I wrote another letter to this family, containing another story, a year later.

> Dear Anna and Bertie,
>
> When we look at the paper chart from our conversation, a particular phrase stands out: *Never forget how strong you are.* We imagine you, Anna, sitting at your computer writing a book about Valiant. We imagine Valiant reading the book and being inspired to begin a transformation of his own tale of himself and his struggle for a dignified life.
>
> You are both intent on Valiant knowing how proud you are of him. Your book oozes with this pride.
>
> Your book title might be: *Never Forget How Strong You Are.*
>
> Maybe, Anna, you will write something along these lines:
>
> Once upon a time a charming, strong, boy went swimming against a tidal wave, a tidal wave that grew stronger and stronger. This boy had powerful swimming strokes and fought through the masses of water. Wave after wave rushed over him. Time after time his head re-appeared above the water, and he shook the water from his hair. He coughed and spat the saltwater out of his mouth and fought the next wave. The tidal waves steadfastly sucked energy and life out of him.
>
> I now know that my strong wise boy made the hardest decision a stubborn fighter can make, to let go and to allow himself to flow. That decision saved his life. It takes wisdom and courage to know when to stop fighting and let yourself be taken by a tidal wave. My son was propelled onto a beach where he lay lifeless, fighting for his life.
>
> I see my son still struggling. He has battle scars from the tidal wave, and I am about to burst with pride over his stubbornness to keep moving forward. Every day I see him fight.
>
> I marvel at how a person can survive a strong tidal wave and tsunami. How did my son survive the harsh treatment he was subjected to? It's impossible to imagine how he survived and how deeply the

The art of true helping: dare to care   207

struggle hurt him. All that time he fought, all that time he was propelled around inside the tidal wave, turned over, hitting the seabed. What rocks on the sea floor did he hit? What branches, rafts, large and small fish, sharks, or other monsters attacked him in the wave? Did he roll himself into a ball, so the monsters couldn't catch him? Did he pretend to be lifeless, so they didn't see him? What tremendous intuition and survivor's instinct does my son possess? Who gave him the strength to survive and land on the shore, where he now searches for his home?

Do these pictures make sense to you?

Do they provide inspiration, or are we intruding on something you should be allowed to write yourself?

You have our greatest respect for the great care, love, and support you give your son.

Many greetings,
Kirsten and Nina

Anna wrote her own story and shares it for this book:

Dear Nina,

Here is my story of the tidal wave, which was strangely healing for me to write.

Sincerely, Anna

Imagine a big blue sea, where the sun beams on a lovely summer day.

I imagine it was such a lovely, peaceful ocean you were swimming in, on a sunny summer morning. You were swimming out with your friends, and you were swimming far and wide, far from the coast, for you were all good swimmers.

But you were swimming over an undercurrent that nobody knew about. And while swimming, the undercurrent became unnoticeably stronger. You had to use more force. At first you did not notice it, but simply swam on with strong strokes. In the meantime, your friends got tired and cold, and one by one they swam in. None of them had any idea you could be in trouble.

The undercurrent slowed you down, and you began to feel it. You knew you could overcome the current, you knew it was something you had to do, to get back in, so you fought stubbornly. But the current kept growing stronger.

Your head started to sink under the surface and even though you re-emerged, the effort weakened your strength. You kept swimming, focused and persistent, while everything but the water and your own strokes disappeared around you. Maybe you felt the exhaustion entering your body, but you kept going. You didn't yell for help, because you had to spend all your energy on staying afloat and swimming. You swam for your life. People saw you from ashore, but no one saw how much the struggling with the undercurrent had sucked and pulled you. They just saw a strong, young boy who was good at swimming. I looked at you from ashore and didn't see your fight.

Then it came. The tsunami. It swelled behind you, high as a mountain. As it washed over you, you realized in a split second, sensing more than deciding, that you had to let go and let the tidal wave take you. From ashore we saw the tidal wave, and only then realized that something was wrong. We stood, helpless, and watched you disappear.

The tidal wave swirled you around, so you didn't know what was up and down. Lumber and debris swirled around you, and you were thrown against sharp rocks. But you did not fight, you did not become stiff with fear; instead, you let yourself be led and you were not crushed. You let go of everything you had learned so far and instead became like the water, without resistance, without will. For minutes at a time, you were underwater without air, but occasionally your head surfaced long enough to breathe. Were you scared? Were you numb? Did you know that you would make it? Did you know how strong you were?

We tried to save you. A rescue helicopter arrived and flew back and forth across the sea, which was now in turmoil, trying to help you. But the waves were too wild, or the rescuers were not skilled enough, because they couldn't find you. To us, they appeared to be constantly risking hitting you with the swinging steel hook they lowered down to the sea, hoping you could grab it.

For a long time, you were thrown around in the waves. For a long time, you were led without fighting, like water. You suffered deep wounds and injuries, you hit the bottom, you were hit by debris, and became unconscious by air deficiency and fatigue. But you didn't drown.

Finally, you were washed up on the shore somewhere, far, far away from the beach where you had been swimming. Bleeding, beaten, exhausted and alone. But alive.

You got your breath back. You sat up and looked around.

Now, I see you get up. You appear dizzy and your legs are insecure. But you straighten your body and begin to walk.

I had to respond to this letter. By putting into words, the feelings and thoughts that Anna's letter evoked in me, my narrative about myself as a health

The art of true helping: dare to care 209

professional evolved and became stronger. Hopefully, Anna's story about herself as a wonderful mum was enhanced too.

> Dear Anna
> Thank you!
> There are many nuances in your narrative that an outsider may not understand. Nuances that are hard to describe in words, but that in the narrative, make me humble and full of respect for your parenting, love, and struggle you have been in and remain in.
>
> Phrases like, "I saw you from land and did not see your fight".
>
> You write: "But the waves were too wild, or the rescuers were not skilled enough, because they couldn't find you". This might be one of the best descriptions of how it is to be a parent to a child struggling like Valiant has struggled.
>
> I understand that you had to write that story. I am captivated by the positive power of storytelling and grateful that you could use my clumsy and sketchy draft as inspiration.
>
> Warmest, Nina

Daring to be in the not-knowing position

Great courage is required to admit my not-knowing and to be openly curious and critical about the science that I subscribe to as a health professional. This story about a young boy, Tim, and his friendship canoe (described in Chapter 5) illustrates the effects of this kind of daring:

Early in our collaboration, when we were becoming acquainted with each other, Tim's father, Andy, asked as he was leaving for home, if he could e-mail and ask about diagnoses.

> Hi Nina,
> Thank you for letting me ask about understanding the diagnosis of reactive attachment disorder and the connection to other diagnoses such as autism and ADHD.[2]
>
> I have been told that autism can be a "differential diagnosis" for reactive attachment disorder. I have a hard time understanding that. I have googled the symptoms of an attachment disorder and can see some similarities to autism; you can probably have autism while also having an attachment disorder. But does one exclude the other?
>
> I have come across a case where a psychiatrist examined a child and the parents. The psychiatrist changed the child's diagnosis from autism spectrum to attachment disorder.

I guess theoretically something can be overlooked but it's nevertheless striking, for I understand that attachment disorders develop due to serious neglect of care in early childhood. From my knowledge of this child, this is not the case.

This child's mother is diagnosed with schizophrenia and the new psychiatrist may think that the child's illness has developed as a result of a form of neglect.

The new psychiatrist uses the word "differential diagnosis" as an argument that one diagnosis must exclude the other, and I wonder about the professional argument for this.

In my understanding, developmental disorders are something that a person is genetically predisposed to and develops in the environment: the exposure to vulnerability is there from birth, the environment is crucial to whether it develops, and how it develops.

What do you think?
Andy

Dear Andy,
Psychiatric diagnoses are not absolute. If you have a high fever, you can have a blood test and sometimes see bacteria in the blood. We call this phenomenon sepsis. Such a diagnosis is either true or false. This is NOT the case with psychiatric diagnoses.

Psychiatric diagnoses are an attempt to provide words to systematize what people are experiencing, put phenomena in boxes, make generalizations, and investigate if one treatment is better than another.

Initially, diagnoses were clusters of symptoms put together with causal explanations. Later, the focus was descriptive, symptoms or behaviours that the patient can describe and that others can see (Dalal & Sivakumar, 2009; Surís et al., 2016).

Both WHO's ICD-10[3] and the DSM-4[4] have been created as compromises between describing what is observed, and causal explanations. This makes diagnosing complicated, and we can often give a child several diagnoses, depending on which theory we ascribe to.

The purpose of a diagnosis is to help doctors to treat people who are suffering. The diagnosis intends to provide knowledge about prognosis and appropriate treatments.

In my experience, the reactive attachment disorder can potentially create blame and contempt. This is less so with autism. I am always reluctant and sad about giving diagnoses that can cause people to feel guilt or blame. There are many children born to

The art of true helping: dare to care   211

mothers with schizophrenia that don't get a reactive attachment disorder, and we can always only guess about the causes of the child's symptoms.

Is this helpful?
Nina

Much later, I learned that Andy and his wife Mandy had been exposed to a lot of blaming for their children's problems. They had acquired the blame from misinformed people who wrongfully thought they were being helpful, and by reading outdated literature which claimed that children's psychiatric diagnoses were due to parental neglect.

Self-blame and parent-blame can be the most devastating problems we encounter when helping people who access mental health services. We must be mindful that our diagnoses and actions dissipate rather than add more blame.

At a meeting with Andy and Mandy several years after concluding their treatment, we reflected on their therapy course. Mandy appeared much healthier, with more energy and laughter in her eyes. She recalled her experiences of diagnoses in relationship to the parenting role and parent-blame. The parents' experience was that in the early years when their children were not thriving, helpful support could not be accessed, even from a psychologist or doctor, due to the discourses of parent blame from a society that, as parents, they were at fault.

I asked Andy and Mandy about the aforementioned e-mail communication on the two diagnoses and what that had meant to them. That communication had been a significant moment in my development as a doctor. But how had it been for them?

Andy recalled that my answer had articulated the fact that the parents might be blamed in one of the diagnoses. I had not ignored but had seriously considered his question about whether the parental role was dysfunctional, or the child was ill. He appreciated that I dared to speak openly about those societal discourses on parent blame.

Mandy: When you are in midst of chaos with children who are unhappy, it is incredibly nice to have someone to share things with; to be acknowledged as a competent parent while mulling over our problems; to not be seen as an incompetent parent.
Nina: But what's the difference here?
Andy: Nina, you come with a different passion to what we have experienced previously. Your passion is heart-warming, and sometimes we have wondered if you were hurting as much as us, when you sat there.
Mandy: I feel you were empathetic and that you felt the hurt with us.
Andy: Yes, but you have to be comfortable in what you yourself stand for,

212 *The art of true helping: dare to care*

	so that you can do it, right? That you dare to go into our narrative fully, that's how we experienced it anyway.
Mandy:	Yes, that's how we felt it.
Andy:	But you stepped out again and let our narrative remain our story. That's what you did! In every conversation, you entered fully into it and symbolized it by writing down exactly what it was, that was being talked about, on the paper chart, thus both witnessing and acknowledging. You would step out again and close our conversation with the e-mail. It was like this: "Yes, yes, this is your story; it is not mine; it is yours. I won't take my own values and project them into your world, I pass your narrative onto you".
Mandy:	Therapy with you became very human. We felt like we were equal. I have a particular memory of those meetings. We had brought Tim's WISC[5] test, and after looking at it you said something like, "That shows a big difference between the verbal and performance", and you were quite shocked. I was a little startled because you expressed that Tim had to work with a big challenge, and you were the first therapist to acknowledge this in an empathetic way. You acknowledged how difficult it must be for Tim and us. Everyone else had said, "It's just a piece of paper. He is in the middle range and it's nothing really". But you were there with your feelings, and you expressed your emotions to us.
Andy:	You were not dramatic, but you were there with us. You drew on your professionalism and stood by our side, to help us find that path. A path that was our path.
Mandy:	Yes, being helped back onto the right path, my path. That was a turning point, realizing how to get back to my path.

As they continued talking, I imagined how hard Mandy must have worked to find her way back to who she wanted to be over the years, and my respect and awe for her deepened.

I was also struck by Andy's picture of me stepping wholeheartedly into their story. Being there with them, and stepping out again, like reading a fascinating book. That this was possible because I used therapeutic letter writing, sending letters, describing how I had experienced being in their story. In this way, I was giving their story back to them. I always take care to give narratives back to families in ways that convey my deepest respect. I want their best intentions to star in the narrative. I am a witness to their plight and quest.

With this conversation, Andy and Mandy had provided a new metaphor for my practice.

This final chapter is about daring to weave personal and professional values into a patchwork of narratives about who we want to be. When witnessing people as the best possible versions of themselves, we experience the transformations that occur within their lives. (Carlson et al., 2016; Greenhalgh & Heath, 2010; Hastrup, 1992; Sælør et al., 2014; White, 2002).

Notes

1 This sub-heading is drawn from Michael White and David Epston's first book *Literate means to therapeutic ends* (White & Epston, 1989).
2 Attention-Deficit Hyperactivity Disorder.
3 WHO: World Health Organization ICD: International Statistical Classification of Diseases and Related Health Problems.
4 DSM: American Diagnostic and Statistical Manual of Mental Disorders.
5 WISC: Wechsler Intelligence Scale for Children.

References

Carlson, T. S., Corturillo, E. M., & Freedman, J. (2016). There's always a puppy (and Sometimes a Bunny): A story about a story about a story. *Journal of Systemic Therapies*, *35*(3), 73–82. doi:10.1521/jsyt.2016.35.3.73

Cooper, M. (2003). *Existential therapies*. Sage Publications Ltd.

Dalal, P. K., Sivakumar, T. (2009). Moving towards ICD-11 and DSM-V: Concept and evolution of psychiatric classification. *Indian J Psychiatry*, *51*(4), 310–319. doi:10.4103/0019-5545.58302

Duncan, B. L. (2014). The person of the therapist: One therapist's journey to relationship. In K. J. Schneider, Pierson, J. F., Bugental, J. F. T. (Ed.), *The handbook of humanistic psychology: leading edges in theory, practice, and research* (2nd ed.). Sage.

Graff, J., Lund-Jacobsen, D., Wermer, A (2003). X-Files: The Power of personal stories in private-professional consultation human systems. *The journal of Therapy, Consultation and Training*, *14*(1), 17–32.

Greenhalgh, T., Heath, I. (2010). Measuring quality in the therapeutic relationship. part 1: Objective approaches. *Quality & Safety in Health Care*, *19*(6), 475–478. doi:10.1136/qshc.2010.043364

Hastrup, K. (1992). Out of anthropology: The anthropologist as an object of dramatic re-presentation. *Cultural Anthropology*, *7*(3), 327–345. doi:10.1525/can.1992.7.3.02a00030

Kierkegaard, S. (1998). *The point of view* (H. V. Hong & E. H. Hong, Trans.). Princeton, NJ: Princeton University Press.

Logstrup, K. E., Fink, H., Macintyre, A. (1997). *The ethical demand* (H. Fink, Macintyre, A., Trans.). University Of Notre Dame Press.

Madsen, W. C. (2006). Teaching across discourses to sustain collaborative clinical practice. *Journal of Systemic Therapies*, *25*(4), 44–58. doi:10.1521/jsyt.2006.25.4.44

Surís, A., Holliday, R., & North, C. S. (2016). The evolution of the classification of psychiatric disorders. *Behavioral Sciences*, *6*(1). doi:10.3390/bs6010005

Sælor, K. T., Ness, O., Holgersen, H., Davidson, L. (2014). Hope and recovery: A scoping review. *Advances in Dual Diagnosis*, *7*(2), 63–72. doi:10.1108/ADD-10-2013-0024

Walther, S., Fox, H. (2012). Narrative therapy and outsider witness practice: Teachers as a community of acknowledgement. *Educational & Child Psychology*, *29*(2), 8–17.

White, M. (2002). Journey metaphors. *The International Journal of Narrative Therapy and Community Work*, *4*(4), 12–18. doi:10.3316/informit.662334264148132

White, M., & Epston, D. (1989). *Literate means to therapeutic ends*. Dulwich Centre Publications.

Winslade, J. (2002). Storying professional identity. *The International Journal of Narrative Therapy and Community Work*, (4), 33–38. doi:10.3316/informit.662762822487071

Afterword

The five tales shared in the Foreword and here in the Afterword have been brought to mind by reading the manuscript of this book you hold. Each story, as I now recall them, inaugurated periods of reflection: reflection-in-action as I would experiment time and time again and then reflection-on-action where I would read relevant literatures. As well, each story was prophetic and provided me with what might be described as the "heart and soul" of my practice. What so intrigues me about Nina's book is to consider her doing something almost identical in establishing the 'heart and soul' of her practice and that of her team.

Read on.

Tale Three

In 1976, I travelled from New Zealand to England to do my Master's degree in Social Work at the University of Warwick in Coventry, United Kingdom. After six months of classroom teaching, I wildly anticipated my placement at Coventry Child Guidance Service where I was to practice as a family therapist. Because the rural campus was miles from the city, I had bought a one-speed bicycle. I arrived at my placement at the 19th century building in the grounds of a public hospital, raring to go, to find a referral waiting on my desk. From the emergency department, it read:

> "15-year-old young woman…suicide attempt. Lacerated arms with razor slashes. No sutures. Discharged. Please follow up immediately".

Whatever doubts I had about travelling so far from New Zealand for post-graduate studies were dispelled. I knew that in a matter of hours, I would save this damsel from her distress. After speaking with my supervisor, I rang and spoke to the girl's mother who said the girl's father, who worked in an automobile factory, would not be home until 5:30 pm. Since I was a family therapist in-the-making, I agreed to arrive at their home around then. While cycling to their home in a working-class area of the city, my zeal was such that I wondered if I could win a stage of the Tour de France, so fast was I pedalling

Afterword 215

my one-speed bicycle. I was cycling towards what I considered to be my destiny. In ways other than I expected, that is perhaps how it turned out.

I boldly knocked on the front door. Sheila, the 15 year old, opened it, exposing bleeding razor slashes on her arm, and loudly accused me, "You made me do this!"

I faint at the sight of blood, mine, or anyone else's. I had never considered this failing to be pertinent to practice as a social worker. The next thing I recall was dreaming that I was seeking entrance to heaven and I could hear serious voices, standing over me, what I took to be adjudicating the matter. I listened carefully to see how I was doing but heard comments I couldn't immediately fathom, "Do you think we should call an ambulance?"

I wasn't dreaming; instead, I realized I was sitting in a chair with my head bowed between my legs, staring at the carpet. I concluded this was somewhat unprofessional. Summoning up what remained of my zeal, I leapt to my feet, much to the family's surprise, and said authoritatively, "Let the family therapy begin". I directed them into their own living room and ordered each person where to sit. I had no trouble knowing what to do next. I had read every book. With a veneer of my new professional mantle, I asked:

"Who would like to tell me what the problem is?"

I soon wished I hadn't, as Sheila jumped to her feet, ran upstairs, and started jumping up and down right above us while screaming blue murder. This led to the chandelier swinging wildly and plaster flakes started to fall like a snowstorm on a film set. The parents looked at me perhaps hoping that I might have some way to save the day. Events such as this had not been included in any text I had read. I was bewildered, and they must have realized this as they ignored the ructions from above and kindly asked, "What are you studying at Warwick University?"

I described my Family Therapy studies and they seemed interested in what I had to say. We continued over a cup of tea and amazingly, the noise from above abated and the plaster flakes no longer floated upon us. The parents insisted that because I looked so pale that they would put my bicycle in the trunk of their car and drive me home. This was one more humiliation I would have to bear. Arriving at the campus, I was wondering how to say goodbye when they asked, "What are you doing next Monday?"

"Why?" I asked.

"Why don't you come over at the same time next week and tell us more about Family Therapy?"

I did so for several months at their insistence. As I slowly recovered my dignity, I began to look forward to our meetings. As weeks passed, Sheila joined in our conversations which always began by the family asking, "What have you been learning since we last talked together?"

I would explain Family Therapy and by way of exchange, they would tell me about their family.

216   *Afterword*

By now, I cycled home unassisted. After one such meeting, the parents handed me a sealed card as I left. It was an invitation to their 25th wedding anniversary at a nearby community centre.

How could I repay my debt to this family? I virtually starved myself between then and the date of their anniversary to save and buy an expensive bottle of French wine. I arrived late, to avoid observation. However, my Afro hair style identified me as a stranger, and I heard murmurs of, "Who the hell is that?"

The parents rushed to my rescue, embracing, and proudly introducing me, "Everybody…meet David. He's our social worker! He's been helping our family. He has come all the way from New Zealand".

With that welcome, everyone wanted to have my ear and tell me that, "The daughter is a little bitch", "They're too soft", "She needs a good smacking", and so on. I realized I should go home early. With this in mind, I asked to speak to the parents alone. I reached into my backpack for the bottle of wine with card which read, "Thanks for your help with my studies".

To my surprise, they had a bottle of French wine of similar vintage and later, when I read their thank you card, it read, "Thanks for your help with our family".

This made me realize that these meetings with those who consult us can be considered what the French anthropologist, Marcel Mauss, writing in 1925 in his "essay on the gift", called a "gift exchange" (Mauss, 2002). In 1985, Michael and I began the first paper we wrote to represent narrative therapy, with a quote from an essay by Mauss (Mauss, 2002, p. 63):

> To accept without returning or repaying more is to face subordination, to become a client and subservient, to become a minister…while to receive something is to receive a part of someone's spiritual essence. To keep this thing is dangerous, not only because it is illicit to do so, but also because it comes morally, physically, and spiritually from a person. The thing is not inert. It is alive and often personified and strives to bring its original clan and homeland some equivalent to take its place.

Tale Four

In Boston, 1995, I was invited to participate in a day-long consultation with the South Shore Educational Collaborative (known as Beal Street). Tim Nichols, who had issued the invitation, had studied narrative therapy training and was Director at Beal Street. His agency provided residential care and treatment for secondary school students who could not be contained for various reasons within their classrooms or schools.

We corresponded ahead of time and I asked Tim what he would wish for us to address together. He considered that a primary concern was that families didn't respect the service or staff at Beal Street. I mulled this over and asked if we might reconsider this by consulting with selected families and instead ask them if Beal Street respected them. Remember (see Foreword) Michael pondering this very matter in 1984. Tim wholeheartedly agreed to my proposal. Accordingly, I asked if he might invite two families to consult with Beal Street, who in his opinion did not respect the agency. To indicate that we would all treat the consultation seriously, the invited families would be offered payment of an honorarium equivalent to 50 per cent of my hourly rate. They were also informed that the consultation would take about three hours and would culminate in a shared meal with staff members, all of whom would also participate.

Tim dutifully sent me a clinical summary of, in this case, the Brown Family. Their 14-year-old eldest son had recently graduated from Beal Street; his 12-year-old brother followed in his footsteps and was currently in residence. I started counting the diagnoses of the parents and their two sons and reached nine.

Prior to the family's arrival for the consultation, I interviewed the entire staff except for a few who had to remain on duty. I asked them about their "best intentions" as to their agency practices and the ideas, beliefs, or experiences on which these "best intentions" were grounded. The purpose of this first round was to make connections between ideas and intentions, transparent to staff and later to client families so they could be readily available for review and revision. This produced a document that we scrupulously constructed, and I wrote down and finally read aloud for the assembled staff to ratify. The agency did not make any claims aside from stating their "best intentions" and how they hoped these had been expressed in their relationships with the family members. This took about an hour.

In the second round, I became the agency's consultant who engaged the client families as co-consultants on my behalf and that of the agency. Family members were interviewed with their consent in the presence of residential staff. I read aloud the agency's "best intentions", and "the ideas, beliefs or experiences" behind them, to Mrs Brown and her two sons. They were authorized to adjudicate whether they considered that the "best intentions" of the agency staff were realized in practice. Or, as I proposed, could the staff's "best intentions" resemble good talk but no action. And if so, could the family assist the Beal Street staff to put their "best intentions" into practice? As well, family members were invited to indicate which of the agency's staff members had shown they embodied the "best intentions" of the agency's practice and in their opinions, how such designated staff or the agency went about it.

The form, content, and manner of speaking of each query intended to elevate the family members to the status as "knowledgeable" persons who were "knowledged" with their own knowledges of life. I emphasized that they had a privileged position because they were and remained the recipients of the agency's services.

In the third round, the staff were interviewed in the presence of the family members about any discoveries, or further questions that were forming in their

218   *Afterword*

mind. They also were invited to share any clues or leads meriting consideration for co-research with all the families they served.

In the fourth round, the family members were given the "final word" for this sequence of conversations. The family, after sharing coffee and cake, was then farewelled, which culminated with me clearly stating the debt we now owed them and a promise to keep them in the loop of any consequential co-research that their consultancy had initiated.

In the first round, I had been told of an incident in which 14-year-old Adam had climbed onto the roof of this three-storied building, threatening to jump to his death. Out of desperation and wishing to forewarn his parents of such a prospect, the staff contacted his mother. She informed them she was familiar with such threats and provided advice how to have him safely come down from the roof.

When I asked about their thinking behind this approach, some staff disapproved, describing such action as unprofessional. I left the matter there, intending to take it up with the Brown family.

The family made quite an entrance. Adam and Jerome, aged 12, were hiding behind ski masks and mimicking the cartoon characters, Beavis, and Butthead. Their mother and I persisted over their banter. Soon the boys took off their masks and assumed their own character.

Deborah:	This place is willing to listen to you...the staff listen to the parents and even the children.
David:	(turning to Jerome and seemingly catching him off guard): Did you like being listened to or did you find that too much of a burden for you? (no comment) Did you find that hard work to be listened to? Or would you rather have people telling you what to do?
Jerome:	What are you talking about?
David:	Well, your mum said what was different here was that these people listened to you and listened to her. You don't think they do? Sorry, I thought I saw you nodding your head. Maybe you haven't had a chance to get listened to yet. Adam, do you feel you were listened to?
Adam:	Yah.
David:	Who do you think here has the best way of listening to you? Do you want to identify them? But if you don't feel like doing that, don't.
Adam:	Everyone listened to me in the same way but not at the same time.
David:	Of course not. Were you surprised, like your mum, who said she didn't feel listened to where you sought help before?
Adam:	Yah.
David:	What happened when you started getting listened to? Was it unusual? Was this okay with you?
Adam:	Yah.
David:	Did you like it or not like it?

Adam:	It didn't bother me.
David:	Deborah, what's your preference – to be listened to or to be told what to do?
Deborah:	Definitely, to be listened to. As well, it's important that the boys and all the residents are listened to, as well as the parents.
David:	Is there anyone here that you would be comfortable to identify as good at listening from your point of view?
Deborah:	Those I know; I don't know everyone. But I could turn to any of them…Chip, Jeff, Kimberley, and I know Don now, plus Susan, Karl, and Tim.
David:	Do they have different listening ways than some of the other people?
Deborah:	They are all themselves but it's the consistency of what they say.
David:	What did you feel on the inside when Karl rang you up about Adam being on the roof and threatening to jump off?
Deborah:	I first felt concerned…but no one knows these boys better than me and their dad. I took the call as a sign of respect for me instead of saying "these are the rules" and that's how it's going to be.
David:	If these people wanted to show respect to other parents, do you have any ideas how they might go about that differently than how Karl went about it?
Deborah:	I don't know how…. I guess do it before anything happens, and touch base with each other.
David:	Let me summarize your ideas for showing respect to parents so far: that parents know a lot of things staff couldn't know, keeping in touch on a regular basis…keeping all the bases in touch with the agency. Can you think of other ways they have shown respect for you as Deborah…a person, a woman, and a mother? Or other ways they could show respect?
Deborah:	I'm not sure…. but see me as a person who might have some knowledge.
David:	Have they given you the impression that you are a knowledgeable person?
Deborah:	(nods head and speaks with assurance) Yes.
David:	How do you think they go about indicating to you that you are a knowledgeable person, knowledgeable woman, and knowledgeable mother?
Deborah:	I shared a few ideas with Chip, and he discussed them with the staff, and they implemented them.

In the subsequent and lengthy discussion, Deborah's tentative suggestion was unfolded over agency practice with her and her sons as witnesses. A co-research agency-wide project was initiated where henceforth the staff member who most identified with a resident would phone the family every day to touch base and discuss matters of mutual concern, especially

220   *Afterword*

seeking their advice, regarding the agency's residents and the family's sons and daughters.

I was to return annually over the following two years. I was to learn after the first year that the Mother's Group had gone on strike until Beal Street agreed that a mother/father and young person of their choosing would precede any admission and represent the agency and transport and welcome the family to Beal Street. This became one of the Beal Street's most enduring rituals. When I returned the next year, the Mother's Group had made another non-negotiable demand that every day of the week, a nominated mother or parents of a resident would plan and oversee the preparation of home cooking for the residents. As well, I was met by a menacing trio of young men outside a distant toilet. I became concerned for the large amount of cash I had in my wallet. However, I had nothing to fear as the young men threatened me that, "If you say anything bad about Tim, there will be trouble". I wholeheartedly assured them that being critical of Tim was the last thing on my mind. We concluded this confrontation by reassuring one another with a fraternal hug.

Tale Five

I was invited to provide a plenary address to the annual Austrian Child Psychiatry Conference, in Salzburg, Austria, in 2012.

I wondered how to emphasize to such an audience the variable ways of coming to know another – as merely diseased with such misfortune becoming one's identity or as a person whose character is being tested, as Arthur Frank writes (Frank, 2010, p. 29):

> Stories have the capacity to display and test people's character.... A story's characters are those who, in Bruner's words, exert efforts to come to terms with whatever the trouble is. The story tells the success or failure of those efforts, or in a more philosophical tale, the difficulty in exerting success or failure. Stories have a singular capacity to delve into the character of characters who deal with trouble. Stories incite or guide reflection on 'who' these people are and the significance of being that kind of person. Many stories, if not most and possibly all, involve some test of character: at decisive moment at which a character's response declares what kind of person she is, or he is.

I accordingly began my address posing a dilemma to my audience:

> Imagine this if you will. You have lived a very long life – 80 or 90 years or more – during which you have achieved many of your life goals. You know the time that remains to you is very short, although you are not experiencing any pain or suffering. You determine to advise those whom you intend to organize your funeral as to how you wish to be known by those expected to be in attendance- immediate and extended family, close

friends, former colleagues, and so on. Let me put this another way – how can you best represent the life you have purposefully lived? You know there are distinct genres or modes of representation. Do you prefer that those whom you request to remember do so according to your moral character and your moral values? Or do you prefer a post-mortem psychiatric assessment that will be read aloud as a representation of your life? If you are like me, you will find this an easy choice. You will want to be represented in terms of your moral character, your moral virtues.

Much of a professional person's time is spent representing the people who consult us in a particular and specific genre of representation. This trend has markedly expanded and grown in influence over the past 50 years or so. Such representations have little or no reference to matters of moral character or moral virtues, the very terms you wish to be known by when your life is characterized in your eulogy and obituary.

Oliver Sacks, known as the poet laureate of medicine, wrote (Sacks, 2017, pp. 193–194):

> If one looks at the charts of patients institutionalized in asylums and state hospitals in the 1920s and 1930s, one finds extremely detailed clinical and phenomenological observations, often embedded in narratives of almost novelistic richness and density…With the institution of rigid diagnostic criteria and manuals (the Diagnostic and Statistical Manual, or DSM) this richness and detail and phenomenological openness have disappeared, and one finds meagre notes that give no real picture of the patient or his world but reduce him and his disease to a list of "major" and "minor" diagnostic criteria…The old case histories and charts, however, will remain "invaluable".

Once again, I welcome you to join Nina and her team as they enter the 'worlds' of the families they meet and the families who are welcomed in their 'world'. I hope you will agree with me it is a very congenial meeting place.

David Epston

BA, Dip.Comm.Dev.Dist., MA (Applied Social Studies), CQSW (UK), NZAC, D.Litt

References

Frank, A. W. (2010). *Letting stories breathe: A socio-narratology*. University of Chicago Press.

Mauss, M. (2002). *The gift: The form and reason for exchange in archaic societies*. Routledge.

Sacks, O. (2017). *The river of consciousness*. Picador.

Addendum

Overview of a course

Referral phase and visitation

Two therapists share the responsibility of one case, preferably with different backgrounds and education (i.e., nurse, psychologist, psychiatrist, pedagogue, social worker).

Invitational phone call: One therapist calls the family and describes the Family Therapy Team (see Chapter 2 for the standard introduction). The family is invited to share their thoughts about the reasons for the referral and their expectations and hopes for the treatment. A mutually arranged time is set for the first clarifying conversation.

Clarification phase

This phase begins at the clarifying conversation, where the therapists introduce themselves, the Family Therapy Team, and the family therapy course.

Conversations include a wonderfulness-interview (see Chapter 3), exploration of the family's narratives about their problems and their hopes and vision for the treatment.

The family is told that the case will be presented at the next team conference, and they are asked to consider at home whether they want to receive an offer for treatment.

The case is presented and accepted at a clinical conference. A therapist calls the family and offers them a course of treatment and asks if the family wants to accept the offer.

One or more conversations are used to examine the family's expectations and hopes for the treatment. The clarifying phase concludes when a shared understanding of the goals/hopes/visions for the treatment has been achieved and a plan for the treatment course has been written and agreed to by therapists and family. The written treatment plan must be approved by the family before entering the medical records.

These conversations are often held at weekly intervals.

Addendum 223

Working phase

The working phase comprises sequels of five or six conversations, each ending with a taking stock conversation (see Chapter 6), based on the family's visions. This phase begins when the family decides the first dates for five or six conversations with the secretary. The final conversation of each sequel will be the taking stock conversation.

A collaboration with the rest of the network around the family is established, when necessary. Family community meetings can be held when appropriate, often at three to six months intervals.

The taking stock conversation's main focus is co-evaluation of the course. This is accomplished according to the visions/goals/hopes described in the treatment plan. Feedback informed treatment outcome scales (Miller et al., 2016; Tilsen and McNamee, 2015) can be used or another systematic evaluation method, if desired. The family is asked what the therapists can do more of, do less of, or change in the sessions.

Cases are presented at the clinical conference before or after a each taking stock session. Cases can also be presented at supervision when necessary.

The sequence can be repeated for as long as therapists and the family experience the desired progress, and the time spent at the sessions is worthwhile for all participants. The prospect of terminating the course and factors to consider when deciding termination is on the agenda of each taking stock conversation.

These conversations are often held at weekly, every two weeks, or monthly intervals and can change over time.

Final phase

The family therapy course is often concluded by one to three concluding conversations depending on the needs of the family.

These conversations are used to evaluate the course of treatment, examine the family's visions/goals and hopes for the future, and expand the family narratives about their achievements.

The family is asked to provide the team with advice based on their experiences with the family therapy course at the final conversation.

The family's evaluation of the course and their advice is presented at the following clinical conference. The information from the family is documented in the medical record and can be used for manual/guide revisions.

Families can schedule a "booster-session" or become "sleeping members", if this is considered feasible.

Four different agendas for clinical conferences

After the first clarifying conversation

Referral with a genogram.

224   *Addendum*

- The helping map is used to present the paper chart through the eyes of the child and parents, including visions/goals, problems, supports.
- Therapist's own reflections about the problems and supports, and their relationships and effects on family visions.

Questions from the team.

- Reflections from the team, therapists are the last to speak.
- Conclusion and plan on the treatment plan, family conversations, individual sessions, extended family conversations, and family community meetings.
- Remember to document in medical records.

Around taking stock session

Short resume of the case.

- Family vision and evaluation of progress and present status.
- New goals/visions?
- Therapist's own reflections about the problems and supports, and their relationships and effects on family visions.

Questions from the team.

- Reflections from the team, therapists are the last to speak.
- Conclusion and plan on the treatment plan, family conversations, individual sessions, extended family conversations, and family community meetings.
- Remember to document in medical records.

Ad hoc problems

Short resume of the case.

- Presentation of the specific problem.
- Therapist's own reflections about the problems and supports, and their relationships and effects on family visions.

Questions from the team.

- Reflections from the team, therapists are the last to speak.
- Conclusion and plan on referral to other units, changes or adding help, treatment plan, family conversations, individual sessions, extended family conversations, and family community meetings.
- Remember to document in medical records.

After the final session

Short resume of the case.

- The family's initial and final goals/visions, evaluation of progress and status.
- Family achievements.
- Family advice for us.
- Therapist's learnings.
- Team's learnings.
- Bullet points for revision of guide/manual.
- Remember to document in medical records.

Template for invitational letter to a child

Dear Parents (insert name)

This is the short invitational letter that you can read to your child (insert name). Please decide for yourself, whether you think this will be helpful for (insert name) or not. Since we do not know (insert name), we will not be able to know what the best preparation will be for her/him. But imagine that this is to prevent the uncertainty that any child will experience when meeting new people.

Dear (insert name)

We (insert our names) have met your mum/dad/parent. We think they are really nice!

You and your parents will come together at our next conversation/meeting.

When you come, we will sit in (insert name)'s office. We will spend one hour together on

Insert date and time

You can either sit next to or between your parents, on an ordinary chair or in a bean bag.

We have attached a picture of me and (insert name) in the office that we will meet in, so you will know what it looks like. (Remember to attach picture!)

We will ask your parents all about what they really like and appreciate about you, so we can get to know you.

We will also ask you about what you like to do and like about yourself. And we will ask all of you what you like about your family and what you like to do together.

We have paper and crayons, tangles and more on the table for you to use, if you like to do something with your hands while we speak.

If your parents or we say something wrong or forget to say something, please tell us. We will appreciate this a lot.

226 *Addendum*

You can bring a snack or something else to eat, if you like. We have tea, coffee, and hot chocolate in the waiting room, and we will have water on the table, that you can drink if you want to.

We really look forward to meeting you (insert name)!
Many warm regards, (insert our names)

The "Be-sustained-folder"

I store letters and e-mails from past patients and families in a paper folder that is labelled my "Be-sustained-folder".

I revel in these letters received at Christmas and during the summer holidays, when parents describe how their child is, and where they are today. Such letters often arrive unexpectedly during the year too and are invaluable in helping me to maintain hope for other families. Reading stories about gaining freedom from psychiatric problems are a reminder that healing is possible.

When we meet people only during the most terrible crisis of their life, our experience is limited to that period in their life. We don't know what their life was like before the crisis occurred, or the outcome of the crisis and its aftermath. This limited experience means a realistic view of a prognosis is difficult.

But real-life knowledge and stories about people who come through a crisis and proceed to live a good life can supplement our professional knowledge and sustain us. Such stories let us know about the effect of our help and give us strength to carry hope for other families (Rasmussen et al., 2021; Williams, 2016).

Opening the folder during challenging times helps to sustain me. I encourage every health professional to have a "Be-sustained-folder".

References

Miller S.D., B. S., Chow, D., Seidel, J., Maeschalck, C. (2016). Feedback-Informed Treatment (FIT): Improving the outcome of psychotherapy one person at a time. In M. A. O'Donohue W. (Ed.), *Quality improvement in behavioral health*. Springer.

Rasmussen, A. J., Mai, A., Hansen, H. P. (2021). *Narrativ medicin - i uddannelse og praksis*. Gads Forlag.

Tilsen, J., McNamee, S. (2015). Feedback informed treatment: Evidence-based practice meets social construction. *Family Process, 54*(1), 124–137. doi:10.1111/famp.12111

Williams, S. (2016). *Recovering from psychosis. Empirical Evidence and lived experience*. Routledge.

Index

A

addendum 222–6; "be-sustained-folder" 226; clinical conference agendas 223–5; course overview 222–3; template for invitational letter to a child 225–6

ADHD (Attention-Deficit Hyperactivity Disorder) 13, 43, 46–7, 72, 116, 120, 125, 183, 210

ad hoc problems: clinical conferences 224

adverse and favourable effect chart 129–131

advice, taking from families 5, 97, 108, 111, 116, 120, 142, 156–7, 164, 166, 172, 223, 225

after the final session: clinical conferences 225

after the first clarifying conversation: clinical conferences 223–4

after-talk, purpose of 91–92

afterword 214–21

Alexander, June i, 8–9

anorexia viii, xi–xii, 7–8, 26–7, 40–1, 53–6, 80, 85, 90, 97–8, 117–18, 155, 177–80, 193, 204–6

anxiety 5, 26–29, 31–2, 46, 52, 103–7, 109, 111, 129, 132–4, 143–6, 170, 180, 198, 205; making fun of 95–7

appreciative partner, becoming 26–8

art of true helping; *see* dare to care

Attention-Deficit Hyperactivity Disorder (ADHD) 13, 43, 46–7, 72, 116, 120, 125, 183, 210

authors 7–9

autism 20–1, 41–5, 72, 118, 120–6, 131–8, 141, 146, 151, 169–75, 182–4, 210–11; am I autistic? Yes, but does it bother you? 182–4

autism spectrum disorder (ASD) 41, 120, 125, 172, 210; *see also* autism

B

beautiful illustration of my life, not untidy scribbles 62–75; becoming a better "scribbler" 74–5; let's map that problem 67–70; metaphors 72–3; organizing notes on the paper charts 64–7; the others always hide their notes from me 63–4; reach for the stars 73; tracking a story 70–1

becoming the family's appreciative partner 26–8

becoming partners in unmessing a messy family life 18–22

being humble and asking for help 196–7

being met as a person worthy of respect 12–14

being recognized and witnessed as the best version of yourself 103–12

being witnessed as worthy 93–4

"be-sustained-folder" 226

Biting the Hand that Starves You (Epston) 90

blame 4, 14–16, 21–2, 29–30, 56, 59, 82–3, 86, 137, 173–4, 178–9, 184–96, 210–11

boardroom psychology and seating etiquette 167–8

bulimia xii, 8

C

can we join you in your struggles? 33–4

child, template for invitational letter to 225–6

Child and Adolescent Mental Health Services (CAHMS) 1

clarification phase of a course 222

clinical conference agendas 223–5; ad hoc problems 224; after the final session 225; after the first clarifying conversation 223–4; around taking stock session 224

228   *Index*

CMM (Coordinated Management of Meaning) 166–7
co-creating the treatment plan 81–6
co-creating shared wisdom 141–51
co-creating new knowledge by digging into the messy business 170
collaborative e-mail-writing practices 91
Collaborative Family Therapy (CFT) 1, 25–34; becoming the family's appreciative partner 26–8; can we join you in your struggles? 33–4; the Worry Mum or the Mama Bear? 28–33
Collaborative Family Therapy with Psychiatric Multi-stressed Families 5
Collaborative Helping Maps 166; *see also* helping map as a guiding light
collaborative spirit, weaving through all our practices 177–86; the dangerous or the scared dad? 177–80; do I have autism, or am I autistic? Yes, but does it bother you? 182–4; how do we speak about the patients and their families? 181–2; mutual trust and respect in psychiatry, is this possible? 180–1; take on wonderfulness, when blame and shame tries to get in the way 184–6
conferences, clinical 224–5
consulting our consultants 147–51
continuously curious learning team 189–99; being humble and asking for help 196–7; co-therapists as dancing partners 194–6; discourses and their implicit values 189–91; hierarchical languages and conferences cultures 192–4; may we have a lifeline into the hospital? 198–9; we all have unique knowledge and are worthy of being in the room 191–2
conversations 4–6, 16–17, 32, 42, 47, 51, 53, 58–59, 62, 65, 69, 71, 77–81, 87, 101, 109, 118, 122, 125, 135, 139, 142, 147, 150, 157, 160, 162, 164, 166, 169, 177, 182–4, 193, 197, 206, 216, 218, 222–4
Coordinated Management of Meaning (CMM) 166–7
co-research 88, 141, 147, 151, 186, 218–9
co-therapists as dancing partners 194–6
counterbalancing problems 98–9
course, overview of 222–3; clarification phase 222; final phase 223; referral phase and visitation 222; working phase 223
creating e-mail-writing practices collaboratively 91

creating and revising our guide collaboratively with the families 141–3
creating a unified story about our family 80–1
curiosity 14, 17, 21–2, 32–3, 54, 62, 66, 82, 92, 101, 118–19, 141, 143, 156, 158, 169, 175, 179, 182, 189–99, 204, 209

D

dangerous or scared dad? 177–80
dancing partners, co-therapists as 194–6
dare to care 202–12; daring to be in the not-knowing position 209–12; if I don't like the parents, there's something I don't understand 204–6; literate means to therapeutic ends 206–9
deconstructing 47, 164, 183, 186
depression 4–5, 70, 97, 128, 194
developing and co-creating shared wisdom 141–51; consulting our consultants 147–51; creating and revising our guide collaboratively, with the families 141–3; how might we understand our child's problems? 143–7
diagnoses: the doctor's externalization of the problem 116–17; how might a diagnosis be best for me? 116–26; struggling with understanding 117–18; when to use and why to use 125–6
dialogic communications and the production of knowledge 171–5
digging into the messy business, let's co-create new knowledge by 170
disclaimer, role of 92–3
discourses 2, 15, 47, 67, 79, 103, 108, 114, 128, 154–5, 172–3, 181–4, 186, 192, 198–9, 211; and their implicit values 189–91
dreams 1, 4, 30, 37, 39–40, 46, 50, 53, 56–7, 67–70, 74, 78–79, 83, 93, 120–1, 156, 170, 184–5, 199, 202, 205

E

eating disorders i, 8–9, 28, 41, 56, 80–6, 177, 206; *see also* anorexia; bulimia
e-mail-writing practices collaboratively 91
empowering the entire family 154–64; don't forget the siblings! 157–8; naming Seytan and working collaboratively 155–7; next-of-kin involvement 158–64
empowerment and recovery movement 6, 50, 141, 181

Epston, David i, vii, xviii, 5, 8, 37, 67, 88, 90, 147, 271
externalization of the problem 116–7

F

families: becoming the family's appreciative partner 26–8; can we join you in your struggles? 33–4; joining forces with 16–18; when one person suffers, everyone in the family suffers 14–16
family community meetings that matter 166–75; boardroom psychology and seating etiquette 167–8; dialogic communications and the production of knowledge 171–5; let's co-create new knowledge by digging into the messy business 170; meet me by understanding and respecting my handicap 170–1; parents at the head of the table 168–9
family wisdom 3, 154, 199
family therapy, collaborative 25–34; becoming the family's appreciative partner 26–8; can we join you in your struggles? 33–4; the Worry Mum or the Mama Bear? 28–33
family therapy, empowering the entire family 154–64; don't forget the siblings! 157–8; naming Seytan and working collaboratively 155–7; next-of-kin involvement 158–64
final phase of a course 223

G

guide 5–6, 25, 43–44, 53, 66, 69, 78, 88, 91, 100, 116, 120, 141–2, 191, 204, 220, 223, 225

H

having each other's back
hierarchical language 4, 192–4
hierarchical relationships 29, 66
hierarchy 30, 50, 59, 87, 168, 174–5
helping map as a guiding light 77–88, 166; co-creating the treatment plan 81–6; creating a unified story about our family 80–1; ideas/plans 83–6; obstacles 83; supports 83; taking-stock session 86–8; vision/hopes/dreams 83; visions 81–3
hope 3–5, 8, 11, 13, 16–18, 25, 29, 33, 37, 50, 52, 60, 63, 65, 67–70, 72, 74, 78–9, 81–3, 91, 93, 103, 106, 111, 114, 119–121, 147, 151, 156, 164, 168, 170,

178, 193, 195, 199, 202, 204, 222–23, 226
how do we speak about patients and their families? 181–2
how might a diagnosis be best for me? 116–26
how might we understand our child's problems?
how to read this book 7

I

I am not the problem! We are the heroes! 37–48; the wonderful children, parents, and autisms 42–5; wonderful family post-it notes 45–8; the wonderfulness interview 37–40; the wonderful stick girl 40–2
ideas 3, 5–7, 16, 21–22, 33, 46, 55, 57–9, 74, 78–79, 82–6, 87, 92, 133, 150, 161, 167, 169, 172–5, 177, 189, 192–3, 195–6, 217, 219
if I don't like the parents, there's something I don't understand 204–6
insider knowledge, using 138–9
International Classification of Diseases (ICD) 116
interview, wonderfulness 37–40
introduction 1–9; about language, words, and naming 3–5; about the authors 7–9; bringing a guide or manual to life 5–6; how to read the book 7; multi-storied clinical work and research 6; a psychiatry of two minds 2–3; vision for the book 7
invitational letter to a child, template for 225–6

J

joining forces with families 16–8
joining in struggles 33–34
Jorring, Nina Tejs i, 7–8

K

Kierkegaard 202–3, 206
knowledge 1–3, 6, 15–16, 20–22, 25–26, 29–31, 34, 40–41, 43, 47, 50, 55–6, 59, 72–3, 77, 81, 85–8, 90, 92, 99, 106, 112, 118–119, 122, 128–9, 137–9, 141, 144, 147, 150, 156, 159–160, 162–4, 167–71, 174–5, 183, 190–192, 198–9, 203, 210, 217, 219, 226
Kuhn, Thomas vii

230   *Index*

L

language, words, and naming 3–5
letter-writing 90–101; being witnessed as worthy 93–4; counterbalancing those problems 98–9; creating e-mail-writing practices collaboratively 91; having each other's back 93; making fun of anxiety 95–7; making the project of writing un-daunting 93; purpose of the "after-talk" 91–2; role of the disclaimer 92–3; therapeutic letters are inestimable! 99–101; using letters as templates 94–5; you are welcome to use the letters 97–8
lifeline into the hospital 198–9
literate means to therapeutic ends 206–9
Løgstrup, K.E. 203–4

M

manual, bringing to life 5–6, 142
Mama Bear or Worry Mum? 28–33
mapping a problem 67–70
mattering is at the heart of the matter 50–60; being genuine or putting on a facade of seriousness? 53–6; everyone matters in a mattering team 58–60; holding onto our values 56–8; It's the mattering, that matters. But how we matter, matters a lot 50–2; there was no ultimatum with you 52–3
may we have a lifeline into the hospital? 198–9
medicine, my diagnosis, and me 128–39, 158, 181–183; how does your medicine work? 128–9; let's create both the adverse and the favourable effect chart 129–31; making sense of me, my diagnosis, and my medicine 137–8; using insider knowledge 138–9; what's that medicine good for? 131–7
medical science 2–3, 139, 192
meet me by understanding and respecting my handicap 170–1
mental health services 1–5, 25, 141, 164, 177, 180–1, 190, 211; Child and Adolescent Mental Health Services (CAHMS) 1
metaphors 6, 19, 21, 45, 47, 66–7, 70, 72–3, 75, 79, 82, 84, 91–2, 95, 99, 103, 116, 129–130, 137, 161, 164, 182, 186, 194–6, 198, 202, 204, 206, 212
multi-storied clinical work and research 6

mutual trust and respect in psychiatry, is this possible? 180–1

N

naming 3–5, 51, 87
naming? How might a diagnosis be best for me? 116–26; diagnoses are the doctor's externalization of the problem 116–17; Seytan or OCD? 118–20; struggling with understanding diagnoses 117–18; what makes sense, how is it helpful? 120–5; when to use, and why use, a diagnosis 125–6
naming Seytan and working collaboratively 155–7
narrative, alternative 164
narrative, preferred 51, 86–7
narrative ethics 19, 164
narrative family psychiatrists 12–22; becoming partners in un-messing a messy family life 18–22; being met as a person worthy of respect 12–14; joining forces with families 16–18; when one person suffers, everyone in the family suffers 14–16
Narrative Means to Therapeutic Ends (Epston and White) 90
narrative technique of witnessing 196
next-of-kin involvement 158–64
notes 13, 26, 45–6, 62–7, 70, 75, 90, 94, 100, 147, 168, 173, 193, 221
not-knowing position, daring to be in 209–12
not untidy scribbles but a beautiful illustration of my life 62–75; becoming a better "scribbler" 74–5; let's map that problem 67–70; metaphors 72–3; organizing notes on the paper charts 64–7; the others always hide their notes from me 63–4; reach for the stars 73; tracking a story 70–1
Nylund, David 100

O

Obsessive–Compulsive Disorder (OCD) 56–7, 118–25, 129, 155–7
obstacles 56, 78–83, 125, 163, 169–71, 173
Open Dialogue 166
organization 8, 64–7, 88, 177, 181, 186, 190–1
overview of a course 222–3; clarification phase 222; final phase 223; referral phase and visitation 222; working phase 223

P

paper charts 64–7
parents at the head of the table 168–9
partners 18–22, 194–6
Playful Approaches to Serious Problems (Freeman) 90
Poetic Means to Anti-anorexic Ends (Nylund) 90
post-it notes 45–8
psychiatry of two minds 2–3
psychosis 80, 98, 128, 134, 182
psychotic symptoms 84, 97, 120, 131–2, 134, 136, 166

Q

questions 5, 14, 18–9, 22, 30, 40–41, 43, 52, 55–6, 58–60, 65–7, 70–1, 73, 78–9, 81–2, 84, 87–8, 91–5, 97, 99, 109, 111, 121, 132, 134, 139, 142–4, 146, 155–6, 159, 169, 171–3, 175, 179, 182–3, 186, 190–1, 193–6, 204–5, 224; star questions 73; wonderfulness-questions 37, 45–47

R

reach for the stars 73
reactive attachment disorder (RAD) 171–2
recovery and empowerment movement 6, 50, 141, 181
referral phase and visitation (of a course) 222
respect 2–4, 8, 12–16, 18, 25, 28–9, 37, 41–2, 50, 52, 55, 57, 60, 62, 87, 90, 99, 101, 104, 112, 118–20, 128, 138, 143, 147, 150–1, 156–7, 166–7, 169–72, 175, 177–8, 180–2, 192–6, 202, 204–5, 207, 209, 212, 216–17, 219
respecting my handicap, meet me by understanding and 170–1
revising (and creating) our guide collaboratively with the families 141–3

S

schizophrenia 16, 33, 72, 182–3, 210–11
self-blame 22, 30, 56, 211
Seytan 118–20, 155–7
shame and blame 184–6
shared wisdom, developing and co-creating 141–51; consulting our consultants 147–51; creating and revising our guide collaboratively, with the families 141–3; how might we understand our child's problems? 143–7

siblings, don't forget 157–8
star questions 73
stars, reaching for 73
stick girl, wonderful 40–2
stories that make sense and inspire 103–14; being recognized and witnessed as the best version of yourself 103–12; visual narratives help to express and endure the incomprehensible 112–14
story, alternative 21
story, preferred 79
story, tracking 70–71
struggles, can we join you? 33–4
struggling with understanding diagnoses 117–18
supports 79, 83–85, 137, 193, 224–5

T

taking stock session 86–88; in clinical conferences 224
Tale One viii–xiii
Tale Two xiii–xvi
Tale Three 214–16
Tale Four 216–20
Tale Five 220–1
therapy session 4, 93–4, 101
therapeutic letter-writing *see* letter-writing
tracking a story 70–1
trust 3, 8, 14, 25, 29–30, 37, 52, 60, 93, 106, 111, 119, 139, 151, 184, 194–5, 202–4; mutual trust in psychiatry 180–1

U

understand our child's problems 143–7
understanding and respecting my handicap 170–1
unique knowledge and worthy of being in the room 190–2

V

values 2–4, 6–7, 19, 22, 26, 29, 37, 39–40, 46–47, 50, 52–3, 59, 67, 69–72, 78–79, 82–3, 85, 94, 108, 147, 150, 154, 156–7, 178, 181, 186, 189, 192–3, 202, 204–5, 212, 221; holding onto 56–8
violence: dangerous or scared dad? 177–80; risk of 204
vision for this book 7
visions 81–3
visual narratives help to express and endure the incomprehensible 112–14
volcanos 116

232 *Index*

W

we all have unique knowledge and are worthy of being in the room 191–2qu

White, Michael i, viii, xvi, 67, 90

wisdom 1–3, 5, 15, 22, 47, 50, 56, 60, 62, 71, 114, 125, 141–151, 154, 159, 163, 190, 199, 206

witnessing 45, 54, 82, 84, 92, 103, 156–7, 185, 196, 204, 212, 219; being witnessed as best version of yourself 103–12; being witnessed as worthy 93–94

wonderfulness 37–48; wonderful children, parents, and autisms 42–5; wonderful family post-it notes 45–8; wonderfulness interview 37–40; wonderfulness questions 37, 45–7; wonderful stick girl 40–2

words, language, and naming 3–5

working phase of a course 223

Worry Mum or the Mama Bear? 28–33

worthy, being met as worthy of respect 12–14

worthy, being witnessed as 93–4

Printed in the United States
by Baker & Taylor Publisher Services